BITTERSWEET

Moor or Less

A Collection of 100 of Bill Moor's Best Columns

by Bill Moor

Diamond Communications, Inc.
South Bend, Indiana

Moor or Less
A Collection of 100 of Bill Moor's Best Columns
Copyright © 2001 by Bill Moor

10 9 8 7 6 5 4 3 2 1

Manufactured in the United States of America

Diamond Communications, Inc.
Post Office Box 88
South Bend, Indiana 46624-0088
Editorial: (219) 299-9278
Fax: (219) 299-9296
Orders Only: 800-480-3717
Website: www.diamondbooks.com

Library of Congress Cataloging-in-Publication Data

Moor, Bill.
    Moor or less : a collection of 100 of Bill Moor's best
columns / by Bill Moor.
        p. cm.
    Columns originally appearing in the South Bend Tribune.
    ISBN 1-888698-48-9
    1. South Bend (Ind.)–Social life and customs–Anecdotes.
2. South Bend (Ind.)–Social conditions–Anecdotes. 3.
South Bend
(Ind.)–Biography–Anecdotes.   I. Title.
    F534.S7 M66 2001
    977.2'89–dc21

                                        2001042252

Table of Contents

To Mag, who loves me anyway.

Introduction

The best journalism is local journalism, and local journalism doesn't get any better than in the columns of Bill Moor.

Sometime, if you live here long enough, you will probably meet him on street, or hear him speak to an organization you're a member of, or even become the subject of one of his columns.

When that happens, you will see a man who exudes modesty, who is intense and kind, who endeavors to see others as human beings rather than pieces of news stories.

Everyone who works with Bill Moor can cite some favorite columns or stories that show off his uniqueness as a writer. The one I quote most often was a news article Bill wrote about a police negotiator who climbed to the top of a silo and talked a suicidal young man into climbing down with him. Bill wrote that piece while he was doing a stint on the police beat a couple of years ago; in the hands of another journalist, it might have been a routine brief.

But Bill told it through the eyes of the officer, conveying the fear and tension he felt 75 feet above the ground as he tried to persuade the boy to keep on living. The story didn't end, though, as he and the boy reached the bottom of the ladder that night.

We learned that afterwards, the officer was too keyed up to sleep right away. So he did a crossword puzzle. This was not what you usually expect in a police news report. But to Bill, an important part of the story was how an officer who does a life-or-death job has to unwind afterwards. The police-reporter's guidebook might say otherwise, but I suspect readers would agree.

The pessimists among us fear for the future of newspapers. Is journalism as we know it going to survive the instant-gratification, personalized information systems that loom around the bend? If the world is wired for moment-to-moment communication, customized to your tastes, will the craft of journalistic reporting for general audiences become obsolete?

Bill Moor is one of the reasons that this will never happen. If you have followed his column, you already know that what he offers, no Microsoft-style instant update service will ever replace.

For Bill Moor practices the best, and oldest kind of journalism. He is a storyteller. The stories he tells are about your community. Your friends and acquaintances. Your schoolteachers. Your police officers and firefighters. Your neighbor down the block.

But they're written not for the city editor or the journalism contests or the instant-message Internet system. They're written for you.

Part of the pleasure of reading a Bill Moor column is knowing that thousands of others in north central Indiana and southwestern Michigan are reading it, too. He is a tradition here, like football games and January snowfalls and muggy summer nights. And what he writes is not just a report on our community, the columns themselves are a part of the community.

At their best, newspapers give readers that kind of shared vision of themselves.

Ask a journalist what he or she dreams of doing, and you're likely to get two answers: Writing a book, or writing a column about whatever strikes one's fancy.

Bill Moor is one of those rare writers who gets to live that dream. The South Bend Tribune has given him a license to pursue interesting stories about people, whether the stories are happy or heartbreaking, cautionary or inspiring. Probably, if you have this book in your hands, you already understand why. If not, you soon will.

Tim Harmon
Managing Editor
South Bend Tribune

CHARACTERS

April 10, 1990
DIFFERENT HEROES

It's not easy being a role model these days.

It's even tougher being a hero.

So many pitfalls. So many people watching and wondering.

But people, especially young people, need heroes.

Two Indiana teen-agers—both 18 years old—stepped forward in recent times and, in their own wonderful ways, provided these roles.

One lived out his fairy-tale athletic career and captured the hearts of those who watched how his countless hours of work make him the best. The other died gallantly while battling an opponent far stronger and far more unfair than any young person should ever have to face.

One was Damon Bailey; one was Ryan White. Both are inspirations for people of all ages.

Bailey, of course, is the young man who led Bedford North Lawrence to the state basketball championship last month while scoring more points than any other Indiana schoolboy ever had.

Years after he retires from the game he loves to play—and played close to perfection in high school—he still will be an Indiana folk hero.

Bailey's popularity goes beyond his uncanny athletic ability and awareness. An honor student and a member of the school choir, he remained the ever polite, ever-focused young man even when the odds were against his team in the biggest game of his life.

Eighteen years old and baby-faced, he has a quiet confidence and dignity that spells role model and hero.

All this and a twinkle in his eye, too.

Ryan White, also 18 years old, had that twinkle, too.

A hemophiliac who contacted AIDS more than six years ago through a blood-clotting agent, Ryan White looked like a frail youth who would have been the last one picked in a choose-up backyard basketball game.

Yet he showed an inner strength that was truly amazing as he battled a deteriorating disease that finally claimed his life in an Indianapolis hospital two days ago.

He died a young hero, educating the nation about the tragedy

1

of AIDS and emerging as the national spokesman for children suffering from this virus that destroys the body's immune system.

White's physician, Dr. Martin B. Kleiman, may have described his patient the best when he said: "He was the boy next door who first showed to a stunned nation that no one is safe from the risk of AIDS. He had no bitterness. With an honest simplicity, his voice was the first that many, if not most heard—even though his was not the first voice."

His voice, soft as it sounded, nevertheless, was a confident and courageous voice.

Like Bailey, White seemed mature beyond his years, blotting out others' emotionalism with his own sensibility.

Unlike Bailey, White was battling terrible odds and terrible consequences with his only victory being the opportunity to serve as a glowing example of the dignity and courage the human spirit could bring forth.

That's a lot to expect from an 18-year-old who should only have to worry if he's going to make the varsity or whom to ask to the school prom. But even when close to his deathbed, Ryan White delivered his message with no catch in his voice.

The whole world listened. From the White House to Hollywood. Celebrities walked by his side much of his last year of life.

Yet as Dr. Kleiman aptly labeled him, the boy-next-door behavior never left White. Even at age 18, even while dying, he successfully juggled his nationwide influence with the human touch.

He touched us all.

Like all athletes, Damon Bailey will learn someday that fame is fleeting. Ryan White taught us that, too.

At 18, Damon Bailey stands on the threshold of great things, many of which will go beyond the basketball court. At 18, Ryan White died.

As years go by and Bailey continues to entertain us with his vast talents, I hope from time to time I think of another young man who would have been the same age.

When I look at Bailey, I hope I see a little of Ryan White, too.

Both of them were heroes at 18. One of them won't be with us at 19.

April 24, 1990
TAKING A STAND

On the morning before Earth Day, Jim Creech may have felt like he was up against the world.

The self-employed South Bend businessman had decided to take a stand. And some folks decided they didn't like where he was standing.

It all started when Creech took a stroll around Irish Park—an area of soccer fields across Edison Road from the Notre Dame campus. He was there to watch his son Jason play in a Michiana Soccer Association game.

As Creech cut across one of the soccer fields, a bird called a killdeer suddenly flew away. A man interested in wildlife, Creech knew what he was going to find if he took a closer look.

And sure enough in the grass about 30 yards out from the northeast corner of the field's goal was the killdeer's nest. In it were four eggs—black-spotted and buff-colored.

"It was a typical place for a killdeer's nest," Creech later said. "Their nests are well-camouflaged but usually just out in an open field."

For those not familiar with the killdeer, it is a member of the plover family with long legs, a brown back, white belly and two black breast bands. It eats insects, is protected by law from hunters and has a knack of feigning a broken wing when trying to lead a potential enemy away from its eggs.

Creech knew all this. He also knew the eggs had little chance if any games were played on that field.

"The teams were warming up and getting ready to go and so I went over and told the refs about the eggs and said that I didn't think a soccer game ought to be played on that field," he said.

The refs listened but said there was little they could do. They said the games would have to go on.

Then Creech said if that was the case, there would be an extra man on the field—himself. He had decided to stand in front of the eggs to protect them from getting run over by a boy or ball.

"We can't let you do that," said one of the refs.

"Then you better call the police because I'm not moving on my own," Creech replied.

So the referees huddled and decided they were dealing with a committed man. Some onlookers thought he ought to be committed.

"There obviously were some upset parents," said Creech, whose son was playing on another field at the same time. "But I wasn't going to leave those eggs."

And he didn't. He stood his ground—and the soccer players played around him as if he was some sort of ground-rule oddity.

He ended up getting kicked a couple of times but the play went on. "I think the eggs would have had it on at least one of those kicks," he admitted.

The players, in the 12-to-14 age group, didn't seem to let his presence bother them, but some parents weren't so happy. "I heard one of them calling me, 'The Egg Man.' And when I was kicked, someone said, 'Kick it a little harder next time.'"

But the general mood may have changed at halftime. Along with the players, Creech went over to the sidelines. A few minutes later, the killdeer came back and sat on her eggs.

At that point, more people understood. Maybe what Creech was doing was what Earth Day was all about.

When halftime was over, Creech took over for the bird again. In a 2-1 victory, the team of "Mr. T Pierogies" survived, and so did the killdeer's four eggs.

When Creech came off the field again, many people came up to him and said they admired what he had done. Obviously, some had changed their minds.

By that time, a couple of Notre Dame security officers had shown up and they, along with MSA officials, were able to move the rest of the games scheduled for that field to another site. The security officials then brought out barricades to put around the nest and keep people from getting too close.

Later that morning with Creech and a few others looking on, the killdeer came back to its nest. All seemed well with this little part of the world.

Unfortunately, this story doesn't have a happy ending. Sometime in the late afternoon after Creech had gone home, the eggs were smashed. With the barricades up, Creech thought it had to be on purpose.

"It seems so absurd why someone would do that," he said. "The birds weren't costing anyone anything and they're not harmful.

"God—not man—put this world in balance for a reason, and there's a lesson here to teach our children. We must learn to co-exist with those that inhabit the Earth with us."

When he viewed the cracked eggs, he may have thought his efforts were all for naught.

But years from now, the youngsters who participated on that field won't remember the score of that game, or if they even won or lost.

They may remember "The Egg Man," and Earth Day—and that some things are far more important than a game.

April 21, 1991
WARSHIP REUNION

Robert L. Miller, Sr., and Joe Klebosits had passed each other in hallways for several years.

Friendly nods, a few words maybe.

"I'm a Democrat, though," said Klebosits, a tireless party worker who held various political posts in the county. "And there's just very few Republicans I can support. I just won't change on that."

"That sounds like Joe, all right," laughed Miller, a former Superior Court judge and a staunch Republican who unsuccessfully ran for the U.S. Congress against John Brademas in 1964.

Both served their respective parties well. Both did their part in making local government a little better. And both knew what side of the fence the other one was on.

But back in 1982, they suddenly discovered that they had once been on the same side—practically side-by-side. It was a time when the issues at hand weren't how one viewed the finer points of democracy, but how best to defend it.

During World War II, both Klebosits and Miller had served on the same aircraft carrier, the USS Essex, in the Pacific theater.

Both from South Bend, their paths apparently never crossed on the ship. They never knew each other even existed.

"I was an aerial gunner on the starboard side of the ship and Bob was a gunnery officer on the port side," Klebosits recalled.

Klebosits still can remember the kamikaze plane that crashed in the water right below his 20-millimeter gun mount. "I could have hit it with a fishing pole," he said.

"I remember that plane coming in so vividly that I could paint a picture of it even today—that is if I could paint. For some reason, I looked over the side just as it crashed and got wetter than a dog."

Miller wasn't as lucky on the other side of the Essex. A kamikaze plane hit below his 40-millimeter gun and threw him across the deck. He suffered a concussion among other injuries. Although he received a Purple Heart for the incident, he didn't seek medical attention until he got his gun crew firing manually again.

Both Miller and Klebosits sailed triumphantly into Tokyo Bay on top of the Essex. Both took great pride in serving on a ship that withstood 357 Japanese air attacks and set a naval milestone by spending 79 consecutive days in combat. Both put some holes in kamikaze planes themselves.

Yet when they started their lives anew back in South Bend, neither really wanted to talk about his battle experiences.

"I knew my kids were interested, but it just wasn't something I really felt comfortable about discussing," said Miller.

"My time in the war was the most significant time of my life," said Klebosits. "But I kept it inside me for several years. Even today, I still get nightmares. I'll wake up and my wife will ask me what's wrong. 'Just another suicide plane flew by,' I'll say."

So when the reunion group called the USS Essex Inc. was founded to perpetuate the old aircraft carrier's name shortly after it was scrapped in 1969, Klebosits joined with enthusiasm. "It's been great to get together with old shipmates and talk about things nobody else can understand," he said.

"They were there; they know."

Klebosits, who later served as the group's chairman of the board and is its current treasurer, was instrumental in getting the Essex reunion group to South Bend for its annual meeting in 1982.

That's the first time that Miller had heard about the group. That's also when he found out that Klebosits and he had served on the USS Essex at the same time.

All those years ago, all those shared feelings—and never knowing.

"It was a surprise when I found out Joe was on the Essex, too," Miller admitted.

Now, the old Republican and the old Democrat chat comfortably from time to time—usually about the Essex, sometimes about the emotions they still feel.

"Actually, Joe was the one who sort of got me out of my shell about talking about the war," Miller said.

It's good therapy, they both say.

There are other shipmates around as well. In South Bend alone are Richard Glass, Frank Nemeth, Clem Sobieralski and Charles Lenyo. All share a common bond.

Just a month ago, the Essex group met again. The meeting took place at the shipyard in Pascagoula, Miss., where the christening of a new USS Essex took place.

A multipurpose amphibious assault ship, the new Essex is 844 feet long, only a little shorter than its namesake. Its primary mission is transporting and landing 2,000 troops and all the vehicles and supplies necessary to support them. It also has the option of operating helicopters and Harrier jets from its deck.

Both Miller and Klebosits were there, snapping pictures and slapping backs.

"It's quite a ship," said Miller.

"It gave me goose pimples just seeing it," said Klebosits.

But the best part of this new ship, of course, is its name—the USS Essex.

That name has a lot of history. Both Klebosits and Miller are part of it.

It means a lot to them—even more than politics.

September 12, 1993
LIFE'S CHALLENGES

Our friend Ron got out of bed one morning last week and decided right then that was going to be the day he would do it.

He was going to buy—or at least put on layaway—a new stereo system.

His last stereo had blown up some weeks ago, and he was getting tired of listening to music on his little wake-up radio.

For Ron, music—especially rock 'n' roll—is one of life's enjoyments. And partly because he is in his early 20s, the louder the music the better.

Ron would have preferred to purchase a new stereo right away but there was a question of money. Ron works part-time as a custodian and lives like so many of us do—from paycheck to paycheck.

But there is another reason Ron put off the trip to the appliance store. He wanted to do this on his own, and he doesn't drive. He also is just now learning to read.

Ron is handicapped—both physically and mentally. He also can get frustrated when people don't immediately understand what he is saying. And he wishes he could get around better than he does.

Yet at the same time, he can be so perceptive, so sharp. He misses very little.

But to get to the store for his new stereo, Ron had to take two different bus rides, cross a busy road on feet that don't work as well as yours and mine, deal with a salesperson and write out a check with a hand that has a hard time grasping a pen.

Going shopping isn't an entertaining assignment for a lot of people. It could be considered out-and-out courageous for Ron to undertake it on his own.

Because Ron doesn't walk very well, he admitted the scariest part of the trip was crossing the busy street where there was no light.

But you also can bet that Ron had butterflies in his stomach when he stepped in the front door of the store.

Apparently, all went well, though, as Ron was shown different stereos by a helpful salesperson and eventually put some money down on a unit he liked. He left with a sales slip and a pretty good feeling inside.

That all changed, though, when he got home and studied the sales slip a little closer. He discovered that the service agreement on his purchase was almost as much as the cost of his new stereo.

Ron may have some learning disabilities, but he is nobody's fool.

Even so, he felt helpless—which is a terrible feeling for a young man who has worked so hard to be self-sufficient. In fact, just in the last year Ron has been able to move out of a Logan group home and into an apartment he shares with one other person.

So Ron got on the phone—an object he is not overly fond of—and asked a friend for a ride back to the store.

Ron's friend picked him up the next day. After listening to Ron's story, the friend checked the sales slip himself and saw that there was a $200 services agreement on a $250 stereo.

Hmmm, the friend thought.

Ron had more than that to say as he choked back a little emotion. "They probably think I am stupid, but I am not."

No, he isn't.

And although this time in the store he let his friend do the talking, he listened closely to every word.

To her credit, the customer service person in the store was very apologetic, immediately admitting that the service agreement should have been $20 for Ron's stereo, not the $200.

She blamed the mistake on the inexperience of a new salesperson just learning the ropes.

Another person behind the counter couldn't help but blurt out, "They know this wasn't done on purpose, don't they?"

Ron just smiled. He made it easy for them. He even joked about it a little.

In fact, he even felt comfortable enough to put another $20 down on his stereo before he headed home with his amended sales slip.

Ron's friend thought he might say something to the counter person as Ron headed out the door, but then changed his mind. Honest mistakes can be made by anyone—and to anyone.

On the way home, Ron looked like he had lost a ton of worries—and gained back, oh, about $180.

Ron's friend mentioned that the people in the store had been quick to set things right.

"I think they were a little embarrassed," Ron said. "I feel better."

His friend perceived that Ron was feeling better about a lot of things—his stereo, the store and maybe people in general.

"Mistakes happen," Ron said. "I can live with that."

Ron was very forgiving. He gave others the benefit of the doubt.

The hope is that Ron and other people with special needs always get that same benefit of the doubt, too.

July 3, 1994
MUSIC TO THEIR EARS

Steve Mullin, the pastor at South Bend's Memorial Presbyterian Church, knew his words weren't going to be music to the ears of his congregation.

Anything but.

Nevertheless, he had to announce before the Father's Day service that there would be no accompanying music. The church's search for a new organist was still coming up empty and a substitute performer had suddenly fallen sick.

"I'm about as tone deaf as you can get," Mullin admitted, "but I do know how important—and how enjoyable—that organ music is with a service, especially when there are three hymns and five other musical arrangements to play.

"I'm not exaggerating when I say that I was about as down as I've ever been going into a service," he said.

"Reverend Mullin was hiding his feelings pretty well that morning," said Bill Ferguson, one of the church's deacons. "But I knew that he was as low as a snake's belly."

After all, music can clear voices and lift spirits.

And having no organ music at a Memorial Presbyterian Church service was almost unprecedented.

So Mullin slowly stepped to the pulpit and said that unless some volunteer stepped forward to play, Memorial's sopranos, altos and monotones were on their own. "If someone can fit the bill, please let me know immediately or we'll just go along the best we can," the pastor said.

He didn't even bother to scan the 70-some people in the congregation that morning. He knew his members well and— God bless them—he also knew none of them could play the organ any better than his 8-year-old son Patrick could play it with his toes.

But had Mullin looked at the back of the sanctuary on the right side, he might have seen a hand hesitantly go up as he told his sad story. A little man, with a bald head and an unfamiliar face, had tried to get the reverend's attention. Then he appeared to change his mind before jumping up and heading down the middle aisle.

Ferguson had been sitting right behind this man. "When he jumped up and started for the pastor, I didn't know what to think. I'd never even seen this guy before. I was wondering if I should run him down and tackle him."

Fortunately, Ferguson stayed put.

Just as lay leader Louie Batiz was finishing "the call to worship" and launching into "the prayer of confession," Mullin suddenly found this man by his side saying he could play the organ.

"It was like he dropped out of nowhere," Mullin said. "I hadn't even seen him coming. He said his name was Jim Alward and that he played the organ back in his home in Hawthorne, Calif. I didn't know what to think, but he seemed sincere and confident in his abilities, so I said OK.

"I didn't have much to lose, did I?"

Jim Alward not only played the organ, but he played it beautifully. He glided through the hymns, the Doxology, the Gloria Patri and other musical arrangements without a hitch.

He might as well have been Beethoven or Bach or, for that matter, an angel from above, as far as Mullin was concerned.

"It almost seemed like a miracle the way he suddenly appeared," the pastor said.

After the service, Alward was almost mobbed by the congregation. And then ironically, some of the older members of Memorial Presbyterian Church learned that this wasn't the first time they had heard him play.

"Jim just happened to be in town for his 40th class reunion at Adams High School and decided he would go back to the church where he had played the organ as a teenager," Mullin said.

Alward was the first organist Memorial Presbyterian Church ever had when it was built back in the mid-1950s to replace the old Hungarian Presbyterian Church. He had played at the original church, too.

Louie Batiz, a church elder, listened to Alward's story. "You know, I remember a skinny kid who used to play the organ way back when."

"That was me," Alward said.

Who would have guessed. The one time that a church is in dire need of an organist and the church's first one from 40 years ago just happens to be in town for his class reunion and decides to worship at his old church that very day.

"What are the odds of that happening?" Mullin said in amazement.

A complete stranger walks down the aisle and takes over the organ he grew up playing.

"I think it was Divine Providence," Ferguson said.

"All I know is that it was one of the most pleasant surprises I've ever had as a pastor," Mullin said.

When Alward was leaving that morning, Mullin did kiddingly ask him if he wanted a job.

"Already got one," Alward replied with a smile.

But when his 50th high school reunion comes around . . .

August 25, 1996
WHAT'S IN A NAME?

Suzanne Wiwi (pronounced wee-wee) has a sense of humor.

The principal at St. Joseph Grade School in South Bend tells her students when they leave for summer vacation that none of them better grow taller than her while they're gone.

It's one of her standing jokes. She stands 5-foot-1.

"I may have to ease up on that one, though," she said. "I had one fifth-grader who came back convinced that he was going to get after-school detention for growing too tall."

Mrs. Wiwi got a tee-hee out of that.

"I'm from a family that laughed a lot," said the South Bend native who attended St. Joe Grade School herself. "Having a sense of humor was almost essential for me when I was growing up."

Of course, it is not all fun and games under Mrs. Wiwi. A whistle always around her neck, she directs the traffic and lines up the kids in the morning and is back doing the same in the afternoon. In between, she is all over the place—reading to the little kids, counseling the older ones and sometimes even finding time to do some work in her office (where she never had to go as a student, of course).

Both her enthusiasm and dedication earned her the Light of Learning Award last spring as an outstanding Catholic school principal in the Diocese of Fort Wayne-South Bend.

They even hung a sign by the back door of St. Joe that reads: "Home of the Principal of the Year."

"It's on the wall that I allow the kids to bounce their balls up against," Mrs. Wiwi said. "But I told the first- and second-graders when we were going over the rules that they would hurt my feelings if they hit my sign."

There's that sense of humor again.

But then, it's probably just as well she has one, considering the pronunciation of her last name and the fact that she is around kids all day.

"Actually, it's never the kids who say anything," she said. "Oh, I'm sure my name is great supper table conversation at the beginning of the school year. And I think the junior high kids ... OK, I know they do ... sometimes get a little silly about it. I never hear it from them, though."

But parents? "I can see it throws some of them off the first time they hear it," Mrs. Wiwi said with a smile. "The first reaction by some is a laugh, while the ones trying to be tactful might ask, 'Is that French?'"

Good guess, but nope. It's not "oui, oui."

She admits she laughed the

first time she heard it, too. After all, her name was Suzanne Lazzara when she was a young teacher in the Union-North School System and first met Mark Wiwi.

"We hit it off," she said. "So of course, when you think you someday want to get married, you might try out the sound of a name."

And she laughed again when she said Suzanne Wiwi to herself for the first time.

It didn't keep her from saying "I do" more than 20 years ago.

She enjoys her name now and her husband never has seemed to mind it. "He grew up in Liberty, Ind., across the state line from Oxford, Ohio, and north of Cincinnati," Mrs. Wiwi said. "There are a lot of Wiwis in that area and all the way over to Hamilton, Ohio.

"It's German, actually."

"A couple of staff members and I were down at Indianapolis for a convention a few years ago when a man got on the elevator with us," she said. "We all were wearing nametags and he gave mine a good stare before he let out a little laugh. Then he said, 'What kind of name is Wiwi?'"

With her best "rolling r," Mrs. Wiwi sang out a magnificent, "It's Frrrrrrrrench," as she made her grand exit from the elevator.

She is not so quick to entertain a salesman who bothers her on the phone. "If one of them snickers at my name, I tell him he ob-viously must have the wrong number and I hang up. So it proves to be convenient at times, too."

Monday will be a busy day for Mrs. Wiwi. The St. Joe kindergartners come for the first time. "I think I'll stand out there with a box of Kleenex for the mothers," she said, "and then send them on their way."

She's kidding again, of course. She welcomes them like family. She couldn't stand the thought of any of them going "wi-wi-wi" all the way home.

September 15, 1996
FADING MEMORIES

Ralph Rosenberg, somewhere in his 70s and living alone, knows his memory is failing.

But he can remember the past easier than the present and he thinks that's the better option.

After all, Ralph Rosenberg has more than 40 years of memories from what he thought was the greatest job in the world. "I got to work in show business," he proudly states.

It was in 1941 when Ralph got the opportunity to take off his apron behind the soda counter and exchange it for a smart-looking usher's uniform in the old Palace Theater.

Those were the days. He still can smell the buttered popcorn ... hear the buzz in the lobby ... and feel his heart skip a beat as the giant curtains were slowly but surely pulled open.

"I remember when my Aunt Alice took me to the old Granada when I was little," he said. "I put my hands together and then slowly moved them apart as the curtain opened," he said. "It was as if I were opening them.

"I loved going to the movies."

He loved the old theaters of South Bend, too. He worked at the Palace, the Granada, the State and the Colfax—majestic places then and all jointly-owned.

He climbed the ladder of his profession—from usher, to head usher, to chief of services, to manager. Later, when the downtown movies houses were closed, he moved out to the Scottsdale Mall theater until he retired sometime around 1989.

"There was just something special about working in show business," he said. "I can remember when there were 2,500 people inside the Palace and just as many people in the lobby and out on the sidewalk waiting for the next show."

But then he also remembers spelling the cashier in the Palace's box office one day and looking across the street to see the Granada being torn down. He almost cried. The Colfax later got hit by the wrecking ball, too. The State closed down. The Palace now is Morris Civic Auditorium.

Something seemed to die inside of Ralph when all that happened.

"Really, I don't go to the movies anymore," he said. "I've never driven anyway and there aren't any actors now I like very much. And those prices ..."

Ralph remembers when it cost a dime to go to the movies. He knows it is far more expensive than that now.

He can't even remember the last movie he saw. "Must not have been very good because it has slipped my mind."

So have other things, he admits. Somewhere in his small but

tidy South Bend apartment—his home since his mother died 22 years ago—he has scrapbooks full of movie ads and pictures of the big stars.

Tucked away in some drawer or cubbyhole is Bette Davis' autograph. "Most stars who came to the Palace left by the stage door," he said. "She went out the front and I followed her outside in my usher's uniform. She was a great star but more than happy to give me her autograph."

He knows it is somewhere.

Those kind of mementos make his memories even more precious. "I don't throw much out," Ralph said. "I've got magazines here about some stars. I'm not sure when I bought them. But I'll pick them up and read them from time to time."

Retirement has been lonely for Ralph, a lifelong bachelor. He admits he is sometimes depressed.

Church helps. He goes almost every day. "The synagogue is only a few blocks away but it's up the hill. But you know, somebody always seems to be there to offer me a ride home."

He also eats at Barnaby's most nights and sometimes strikes up a conversation with other patrons. "Almost evey night, at least a few people talk to me. They soon find out I have the gift of gab. It means a lot when people take the time to talk."

Occasionally, someone will even remember him from his days in show business. "I don't know how they do," he said. "I look in the mirror and hardly recognize myself."

If his life were a movie, he knows there would be a happy ending for him. He doesn't live on a Hollywood set, though, but in a basement apartment near downtown South Bend.

"When I was growing up during the Depression, people used to say, 'We're making ends meet.' I like to say that now. I'm doing the same."

What makes it a special day for Ralph is when he is given a helping hand or a friendly word. "I know my memory is going," he said. "But I do think I remember people who are kind for a longer time—even if I don't know their names."

Real life doesn't roll the credits at the end of the day. Real life has its stars, though, and Ralph Rosenberg still can pick them out.

October 20, 1996
MILES TO GO

His alarm clock sets off the sound at 4:38 AM, but Brian Regan usually has a tune already dancing in his head.

"Maybe four times a year does the alarm wake me up," said the 56-year-old Regan. "My own body clock usually has me stirring a few minutes earlier."

He jumps out of bed, reels off his 52 push-ups and 52 sit-ups, pulls on his Marine Corps T-shirt and sets out on the best part of his day—his six-mile run.

"Gosh, I love it," he said. "It helps me begin each day with my hair on fire."

He is out his door across from the Notre Dame golf course at 5:11 AM—give or take a minute— a smile on his face, the sleep rubbed out of his eyes. He runs around St. Joseph's High School, through the Saint Mary's College campus and up into Roseland. Then he circles home at his 7:40-a-mile pace.

"It is just a glorious time," he said. "During part of the year, I can watch the sun coming up through the trees, the mist rising off the golf course. Other times, I feel the snow hitting me in the face. What a great feeling."

Back at home, he adds the mileage to his log. In the almost 37 years he has been running, he has trained and trotted through more than 80,000 miles. Or to be precise, 80,496 miles, as of Friday.

If that isn't incredible enough, take into account that he has missed only 58 days of running during that span—less than two days a year.

"Some would call it a compulsion, but for me it's a habit," the 5-foot-7, 136-pound Regan said.

He started out as a swimmer while growing up in Joliet, Ill. Ranked No. 2 in the country in the 100-meter backstroke, he failed to make the Olympic team in 1956.

Putting that disappointment aside, he replaced swimming with running while attending Notre Dame. "I was going to a prom and wanted to lose some weight so I'd look good," he said. "So I started running around the lakes in my Sears and Roebuck high-top shoes."

Now, he gets free running shoes from Reebok as a consultant. After all, how many opinions can a shoe company get from people who have run the equivalent of three and a half times around the world?

Brian Regan is the executive vice-president of Goodwill Industries . . . a retired colonel in the U.S. Marine Corps Reserves . . . a former administrator at both Notre Dame and St. Mary's . . . a community volunteer extraordinaire . . .

. . . but a man all alone with his thoughts early in the morning.

15

"While I run, I concentrate on what's ahead of me," he said. "I try to fully prepare myself for my day. Then during the last mile, I pray—the first seven minutes in thanksgiving and the last minute in asking."

He never asks God why He suddenly took away his wife of 33 years on August 23.

"Nothing is going to bring Sharon back," he said. "I must accept that. I'm going to continue to be excited about the future."

Sharon Regan, a mother of three, also was a pillar of the community . . . a co-founder of Shamrock Nursery School . . . a past president of the Ladies of Notre Dame and Saint Mary's . . . a kind, gentle person whose funeral overflowed Sacred Heart.

Brian Regan comforted those who mourned his wife's death on that emotional day. He had made up his mind to be strong on his run that morning.

He continued to run through his loss. It helped him keep his sanity, his composure, his Marine Corps sense of mission.

"Actually, the morning of Sharon's funeral was one of the nicest runs of my life," he said. "My son Douglas and I stopped at the Cedar Grove Cemetary where Sharon was to be buried, then at the Grotto where we lit a candle.

"You have choices in life," he continued. "I can choose between a green suit and a blue suit in the morning. I also can choose to mope or not to. I choose not to."

He takes on the trials of living alone. "Many people have given me helpful hints. One woman reminded me to check the dryer's lint trap, so I do. Another friend told me to get a microwave cookbook.

"I've learned to clean the house the way I like it," he added. "But my granddaughter Abby was over and it was nice to get some cookie crumbs on the floor."

He eventually picked them up. He hasn't had to pick up the pieces of his life. He hasn't allowed himself to fall apart.

"I'm not going to read books on grieving," he said. "I'm not going to let society dictate the standards by which I grieve."

He continues to run straight at the challenges that face him. He starts out by running six miles a day.

"Sharon thought I was nuts about running," he laughed. He was just plain nuts about her. Someday, he may be put to rest in the plot beside her.

"My ultimate goal," he said, "is to be the healthiest and happiest person in the graveyard."

But there are miles to go before he rests. Thousands and thousands of them.

March 23, 1997
ON HIS KNEES

Mussa Muhammad, the owner and operator of J & L Try Twice Exterminating Service in South Bend, wears kneepads to work.

"You can't be any good at the extermination of pests if you're in an upright position," he said. "Cockroaches don't stand up and look you in the eye when you're after them. You've got to get on your knees to find them—and I find them."

He finds more than crawly critters while on his knees. He is a Muslim and also finds his own peace five times a day as he prays in his kneeling position.

During those parts of the day, the pests give way to prayer, but the kneepads still come in handy.

After all, the diminutive Muhammad is 71 years old, often works 16-hour days and rarely takes one off.

"God lets me make a good living," he said. "And I would rather die in a crawl space someday while doing my work than lying in a hospital bed that is draining away the money I've made for my wife and my cause."

His cause is to warn people of the evils of drugs, alcohol, nicotine, guns and errant lifestyles. He only wishes he had a pesticide in his canisters that could eradicate these kind of problems from the world.

A cockroach could look cuddly in comparison.

"This is a confused, complex and corrupt world," he said. "I'm about change—for the family's sake. Long ago, I used to drink, smoke a little reefer . . . but never felt good about it. I would wake up the next morning feeling guilty."

He changed—30 years ago.

And now in his own quiet way, he works for a change in others.

He uses signs—big wooden signs in his front yard on Western Avenue, billboards on his vehicles and messages, which are signs of the times, on the shirts and hats he gives away for free.

"When you're shackin', something's lackin'," is one of the many messages standing sturdy in his yard.

"Don't submit to dope, submit to hope" is written on the side of one of his station wagons that he calls the Truthmobile.

"Crack is the undertaker" jumps off the front of the baseball hat he wears to work.

"My signs are a good way of talking," Muhammad said. "People can't spit in the face of a sign. And signs work for you 24 hours a day."

He knows when his signs have really made an impression. "I will either be given the finger or a thumbs up," he said. "I had one woman say she didn't even want to cross the street in front of my house because a certain message out there scared her."

17

On the weekends, he often takes his Truthmobile out into the neighborhoods, playing music with messages over his outside speakers. "I play all kinds of songs but rap; that's degrading music," he said. "I don't stop, but drive slowly so people can hear the music and read my signs without me causing a disturbance."

Although they can be found in several other places, he doesn't wear his messages on his sleeve. He waits until people approach him before he shares his views.

Especially during work hours. "I don't start conversations in another man's house. And I don't go beyond the questions he might have."

He gives his time and his money to promote his religion and the good in people. He has more than 50 copies of the Koran in his basement's prayer room and gives them away freely. He buys the hats and shirts he passes out and designs the messages on them. He even has been known to do some of his extermination work for free when he thinks it is the right thing to do.

"You can't be a good Muslim and not work in the community," he said. "One of my main purposes right now is to promote womanhood. I think everyone should remember that it's your mama who first whispers in your ear when you come into this world."

His wife's name is Lois, but he calls her Clay Baby. Between them, they have 15 children. "She takes good care of me," he said.

Sometimes, she worries about him, especially because of Mohammad's condemnation of drugs. He understands. "When you take on crack [cocaine], there's a chance you might not get home at night," he said.

"But I have no fear."

Of either creatures in crawl spaces or creeps in the other dark corners of our world.

Mussa Muhammad has his jobs to do—spraying pests and spreading peace.

July 27, 1997
ALWAYS A COMPETITOR

Gordon Barclay can almost work the temperamental clasps on his briefcase now. Not quite yet, but he is working on it.

It is an important task for him to regain. After all, the tan briefcase contains his essays . . . his thoughts . . . his heart and soul on typewritten pages.

With the help of a visitor, he refers to the pages that pertain to education. He is worried that our society is not concerned enough with the schooling of our youth. The former teacher and coach says he has worried about this a long time—the yellowed, dog-eared pages of some of his educational essays serving as vouchers.

Gordon Barclay, now 65, has other concerns these days. One of them is that he can no longer write down his thoughts.

On Sept. 12 of last year, Barclay suffered a severe asthma attack that led to respiratory arrest. He was able to call 911 and open the front door of his Mishawaka home before he passed out from lack of oxygen.

He fell into a coma before the paramedics arrived. He almost died. His doctors expected that he would. "We almost had to give up on him," Dr. Tae Gee Kiehm says.

Somehow, he lived on. But the brain damage he suffered left him without the use of his limbs or the ability to speak. It also affected his vision.

During his youth in South Bend, Barclay had been a national champion in table tennis. He later became a pretty fair fast-pitch softball catcher and tennis player. He played golf just a few days before his attack. And even in his 60s, he still could whip just about anyone in table tennis.

"The fact that he had been a fine athlete may have helped save him," Dr. Kiehm admits.

But life never will be the same for Barclay. Through therapy and medication and sheer willpower, he is doing the best he can. He knows he is sometimes hard to understand during a conversation, but he can now speak. He also lifted himself out of his wheelchair three weeks ago to take his first shaky steps in 10 months. He even has been able to return home, though a nurse and a home care helper visit regularly.

His progress has been nothing short of miraculous. Only time will tell whether there will be any more significant improvement.

Barclay, however, seems more interested in other improvements—like the educational system and more support for teachers.

"I know I must sound like I am standing on a soap box," he says.

If only he could.

"I'm making it," he adds.

He has no family. He does have

old friends and teammates who stop by to help him pass the time. "There are many good people in this community," he says. "I feel very fortunate."

He watches more TV now, including baseball. "Poor Cubs," he says with a smile. "When I watch them, I don't know whether to laugh or cry."

He turns serious for a moment. "I cry sometimes now and I never did that before. I laugh sometimes, too, and I never did that much before, either."

Then he smiles again at the irony of that. "Maybe I should keep the way I am right now."

He will keep battling to make as full a recovery as possible. He understands he won't return to some everyday activities he once took for granted.

"I sold my car," he says. "I don't want to be a Mr. Magoo."

He wants to stay in the home in which he has lived for almost 30 years. Some of his caretakers would prefer him to be closer to their services.

Barclay wears a medical "lifeline" around his neck that has a button he can push to alert the hospital. It could save his life; it can't help him open his brief case.

Although he struggles with the spoken word, the words inside that briefcase flow with feeling and conviction.

He is humble about his writing talents, and information about his five national titles in table tennis has to be pried out of him.

"I will brag one time," he finally says as he motions to several trophies on a coffee table. He points to an ancient, tarnished trophy near the front. It is from the 1944 table tennis national championships where he was a runnerup as a 12-year-old.

Then he points out another— a newer, bigger, shinier one behind the lamp on the table. It is from a local tournament in which he won the two-man team championship with his partner. Its date is 1995.

"Fifty-one years apart," he says.

His point is clear: He always has been a competitor.

He can hardly grasp a paddle now. He has no problem grasping the enormity of the odds that face him. Every day.

"I am improving," Gordon Barclay says. "That's all I can do."

July 29, 1997
PART OF HER PAST

Lee Korzan thought he had just run over something the way his wife, Mary, let out a shriek from her passenger seat.

He hadn't. She had.

Mary Korzan had just run smack-dab into a part of her past.

While reading from the best-selling book *Chicken Soup for the Soul*—a Mother Day's present from her husband and three kids—she came across a poem that was very familiar.

"At first, I thought Lee must have used the computer to somehow add the poem to the book," she said.

After all, it was HER poem, written 17 years ago when she was about to graduate from Bowling Green University. "When You Thought I Wasn't Looking" was written by Mary as a tribute to her mother, Blanche Schilke.

Not long after that, Mary read it at her wedding reception. When several people asked for copies, she sent them out in her "thank you" notes.

"When You Thought I Wasn't Looking" is a beautiful poem that tells how a little girl learned to love life by watching the way her mother lived hers.

"I couldn't believe it when I saw it in print," Mary said.

Especially when it carried an "Author Unknown" tag.

Even though some minor changes had been made, it definitely was her poem . . . and her title . . . and her feelings for her mother.

If Mary was in a daze, Lee remembers the exact moment of the discovery as they drove from their South Bend home to the Columbus, Ohio area for two graduations and a baby shower. "We were on I-75 just north of Findlay when Mary let out a scream. We had to pull over for a few moments."

What a surprise. And what a gift within a gift.

Of course, Mary wanted to find out how her poem had been published without her knowledge—and without her name.

"Since high school, I've probably written 150 poems," she said. "I often write them as gifts for people on their special occasions, but I never have had any of them published before."

Her wonderful words have been spread across the United States, though. Lee Korzan was a Marine officer for 13 years before setting up a law practice in South Bend four years ago. Mary taught school at a couple of their stops, including at Corpus Christi when Lee attended law school at Notre Dame while still in the Marines.

She always shared her poetry with people. And now, to her utter surprise, *Chicken Soup* was sharing her favorite poem with millions more in its fourth installment, "A Fourth Course Of . . ."

How did they get it? According to Nancy Mitchell, the director of publishing for *Chicken Soup*, they gleaned it from the book *Stories for the Heart*, compiled by Alice Gray. According to Gray, she first came across the poem in a book called *Learning to Love when Love Isn't Easy*, by Dr. David Walls, a minister in Elyria, Ohio.

Click.

Elyria is the hometown of both Mary and Lee Korzan . . . and where they were married . . . and where "When You Thought I Wasn't Looking" first circulated. But the copy that Walls received some years ago apparently didn't have Mary's name on it. Thus it was tagged Author Unknown.

Fortunately, Mary copyrighted her poems in 1989, although everyone has been more than accommodating in an effort to set the record straight. "The next printing of *Chicken Soup* will have my name with the poem," she said. "And I've also received checks of $500 and $400 from the publishers."

The money, of course, is not important.

The love for her mother is. "I have a wonderful mother," she said. "She makes every occasion special."

The publishing of the poem couldn't have come at a better time for Blanche Schilke, either. Her husband—Mary's father—left their marriage just before their 40th wedding anniversary, turning her life upside down the last couple of years. "She prayed and worked hand-in-hand with God to put her life back together again," said Mary, one of six children.

Her daughter's poem always had been an inspiration to Blanche Schilke. It meant even more to her recently.

"It was one of the easiest poems I ever wrote," Mary said. "I believe God helped me write it."

Neither He nor she got credit.

That will change.

Mary, meanwhile, will continue to write poetry and might have more of her work published. *Chicken Soup* editors asked for more of her poems.

"It's kind of exciting," Mary said.

And very heartwarming, too.

WHEN YOU THOUGHT I WASN'T LOOKING

When you thought I wasn't looking
You hung my first painting on the refrigerator
And I wanted to paint another.
When you thought I wasn't looking
You fed a stray cat
And I thought it was good to be kind to animals.
When you thought I wasn't looking

You baked a birthday cake just for me
And I knew that little things were special things.
When you thought I wasn't looking
You said a prayer
And I believed there was a God that I could always talk to.
When you thought I wasn't looking
You kissed me good-night
And I felt loved.
When you thought I wasn't looking
I saw tears come from your eyes.
And I learned that sometimes things hurt —
But that it's all right to cry.
When you thought I wasn't looking
You smiled
And it made me want to look that pretty too.
When you thought I wasn't looking
You cared
And I wanted to be everything I could be.
When you thought I wasn't looking
I looked .....
And wanted to say thanks
For all the things you did
When you thought I wasn't looking.

March 8, 1998
HUMMING THROUGH LIFE

Sister Ida Shinkel still would flutter around like a hummingbird if she could. But as she approaches her 88th birthday, her legs are failing her.

Sometimes her memory is too. But not her enthusiasm . . . or her cheerfulness . . . or her love of nature—especially her love for those cute, little hummingbirds.

"Oh, they should be coming back soon," says Sister Ida of her favorite flyers.

She already is on the lookout for their return from her favorite viewing point—the southeast corner of the library in Our Lady of the Angels Convent off Dragoon Trail. Out those windows are where her feeders will hang and her morning glories will bloom.

For the last 19 years, she has been the dutiful librarian here. "You say it and we have it," she says.

Especially if your interest is hummingbirds.

She has all kinds of books, videos and charts on these smallest of birds. She also has hummingbird music boxes, hummingbird jewelry and hummingbirds on cups and cards and calendars. She even has little hummingbird feathers after one got caught in a screen and had to be helped back to its freedom.

But even more impressive are her nine little notebooks chock-full of statistics of the humming-birds that have sipped her red sugar water. She flips one open and reads, "On May 22, 1990, Hummingbird No. 2 took 22 sips at 10:30 AM."

These little birds with the needle-like beak and the non-stop wings are her passion, her special spark.

"She used to be able to give you every fact and figure on hummingbirds," says Sister Julitta Biegel, the Superior of the convent and a member of the Sisters of Saint Francis of Perpetual Adoration. "How fast they fly, how much they eat, where they go in the winter."

She still knows plenty about her ruby-throated friends. "How fast do hummingbirds move their wings, Sister Ida?" Sister Julitta asks.

"Seventy . . . seventy . . . seventy-something [a second]," she answers. "And their eggs are the size of a penny."

Even the encyclopedia won't argue.

"I sit and watch the hummingbirds [out the library window] and people ask what I am doing," Sister Ida says. "I tell them I am taking my vacation."

This is her domain, although she must have people talk un-librarian-like loud for her to hear them now. "Some of the sisters who want to read the papers in here do it in the morning before

Sister Ida takes over," Sister Julitta says with a smile.

She is a wonderful, little woman, so full of God's love. Earlier in her life, she worked with Indian children on a reservation and now makes bookmarks out of old paper and stickers for little children who visit the convent.

"She is like a pack rat," says Sister Julitta. "People throw things out and she makes useful things out of them."

Her "Twelve Days of Christmas" display is legendary with all of its little animals and miniature props—down to the toothpaste caps for the "eight maids a-milking's" buckets.

"Sister Ida has been so creative, so energetic over the years," Sister Julitta says.

Because Sister Ida has trouble getting around, she relies on others to help fill her feeders. Besides the hummingbirds, she takes care of the deer and squirrels and raccoons, too.

"There was one raccoon that got in her flower bed and she looked at it as her enemy," Sister Julitta recalls. "But then it walked by the window one day showing off her eight babies and Sister Ida was so touched. After that, she started feeding them too."

She has broken a hip on three different occasions and uses a wheelchair much of the time. But talk of hummingbirds—and anything else that interests her—will bring her to her feet.

Once, she fell backwards and down a flight of steps while in her wheelchair. "Ten steps," she says. "It wasn't that bad. I counted the steps as I went."

After breaking a hip one time, she was at the hospital and suddenly told the technician: "I was awful sick last night, I nearly almost died. I ate animal crackers that my mother brought to me from town. I ate dogs and pussy cats. Bears and lions, too. And elephants with curly trunks like any girl would do. After I had eaten almost a pound, some things seemed to run and jump inside . . ."

There is more to the rhyme and the technician listened to all of it. And then smiling, he asked her to repeat it for the doctor when he came into the room. And she did, word for word.

"When we have a program and we ask if anyone has anything to add, she will grab the microphone and repeat it there too," Sister Julitta says.

Sister Ida is full of life and happy thoughts. "The hummingbirds will be coming back soon," she repeats.

"They come in May, right?" Sister Julitta asks.

"No, not yet," Sister Ida answers.

"But this is only March," Sister Julitta reminds her.

Sister Ida smiles.

"Oh, those hummingbirds like red ribbons," she says. "Once they were using one of the ribbons as a hammock."

Hummingbirds obviously know where they have it good.

April 26, 1998
CASTING STONES

Nate Bradford may be a pastor but he isn't shy about casting stones.

Tons and tons of them.

Right down the back of his dump truck.

He works for Kuert Concrete eight hours a day and for the Lord all the rest.

"Actually, I have my Bible right on my dashboard so while I'm waiting to get loaded up, I open it up and read it," says the pastor of New Covenant Baptist Church on Prairie Avenue. "I sometimes tease my congregation when they say I preached a good sermon that it came right out of the cab of my truck."

He loves both of his callings—delivering rocks, sand and gravel during the week and God's word on Sunday.

"My bosses here (at Kuert Concrete) are very understanding of my work as a preacher," says Nate who carries a portable phone with him. "They will rearrange things for me if I have to be at a funeral or have other important church business."

"We think Nate's worth it," says Cordell "Woody" Woodiwiss, the products manager at Kuert Concrete. "He has a tremendous work ethic and manages his time so well that his church work doesn't cause a conflict. And he's absolutely great with our customers, with all people."

He's great with trucks too. Nate used to drive a concrete mixer—"I loved to pour that concrete"—but he switched over four years ago to the dump truck because the hours are more consistent.

"Driving big trucks was one of my childhood dreams," the 41-year-old South Bend native admits.

Nate may have had his dreams back then, but he was a nightmare of a kid for others.

"I was so bad that I got kicked out of four high schools—Riley, Washington, Adams and Central," he admits while counting off the schools on his fingers. "Although I never used it, I carried around a hatchet and was called 'the Head Hunter.' I just think it was a case of wanting attention. I wanted to hear people say, 'Don't mess with that Nate Bradford. He's crazy.' "

Maybe he was just lonely. His parents moved to Buffalo, New York when Nate was 15 and he stayed behind, living in the family house and fending for himself. "They sent me money for rent and food, but I was pretty much on my own. A lot of crazy things went on in my house and I was popular with some older guys, but I missed having the regular teen-age years."

He got into fights, he dabbled in drugs and drink and he

wasted his potential. "I could have gotten A's in school, but I was rebellious. I blamed my problems on my parents, on the schools, on the white man, on this person or that person. I was the kind of guy who might try to pull someone out of his car if I thought he looked at me funny."

He could have been a great athlete in track, baseball and football. He says he once even broke 10 seconds in the 100-yard dash while half-drunk. He also missed an interview with a baseball scout, just because of his immaturity. "I was my own worst enemy," he says.

Deep down, Nate Bradford knew that he probably was on his way either to jail or to an early grave. But three powerful influences eventually came into his life—and saved him. "The Army, my wife and God," he says.

The Army got to him first when he was 17. "I went AWOL three times and it looked like I was going to Fort Leavenworth (military prison)," he says. "Instead, they sent me to Fort Sill and put me with some guys meaner than me, including my squad leader. I learned to be a good soldier. I started to be a man."

He also got to drive trucks in the Army. He came back to South Bend and worked as a private contractor, delivering the U.S. mail around northern Indiana. After a first marriage ended in divorce, he married his second wife, Cindy. "She's Hispanic and Swedish," he says. "And she's a great influence on me. I had met my match."

They have been married 18 years and have a daughter Shontel, a senior at Grace Baptist School. Nate also has two daughters, Candace and Crystal, from his previous marriage and a 1-year-old grandson, Theron.

Life had taken a nice turn for Nate, he thought, even though his sister-in-law and brother-in-law, John and Star Ryan, kept bugging him and Cindy about going to their church. "We would be out late on a Saturday night and they would be on the phone early Sunday morning asking us if we wanted to go to church with them," Nate recalls. "Finally, I said, 'Let's put an end to this and go one time so they'll get off our backs.'"

So they went to a service at Faith Baptist Church where Rev. George Joseph was preaching. "I had this perception of black churches being all this shouting and falling over," Nate admits.

He almost fell over himself when Joseph's sermon seemed to be aimed right at him. "It was from Chapter 9 of the Book of Acts about the conversion of Saul," Nate recalls. "But I thought he was talking about me. I gave my wife a look and grumbled under my breath, 'Who told this pastor about me? Did you?'"

Cindy just shook her head.

"What was actually happening

was that God was filling my heart," Nate says.

He and his wife became Christians. "Whenever the church doors were open, we were through them," he says.

Nate worked with the youth ministry at the church while attending Faith Baptist Bible Institute. "I started helping problem kids while always reminding myself that if God could save me, he could save them too."

Then five years ago when New Covenant Baptist Church was looking for a new minister while meeting at the YMCA, Nate was asked to fill in for a few weeks. "I was just trying it out," he says. "I didn't think I was ready to have my own church. But after my second service, I guess the congregation decided they had found their pastor."

About the same time, his congregation moved to its current location on Prairie Avenue, and the work really began—both on the physical church and the spiritual growth of its members.

"We've gone from just a handful of people to about 85 members," Nate says. "Our problem— a good problem—is that we're almost outgrowing our situation here. We're trying to buy a lot next to us for better parking and we can end up with as many as 18 children per one teacher some Sundays."

"Nate is a tremendous guy," says church member Richard Williams, who also drives for Kuert Concrete. "He's very approachable, very easy to talk to and has been a comfort to me and others during some tragedies in our lives."

Nate loves to spread God's message and light up people's faces.

And to think what he was like as a teen-ager . . ."I remember leading a prayer at another church (that he was visiting) and seeing one of my old teachers. I could just see her face when she realized I was the same Nate Bradford. Afterwards, I told her how sorry I was for all the trouble I caused when I was younger. I wish I could personally say that to all my teachers. I think she was impressed that God could change me."

Now, even after he dumps a load of gravel on someone's driveway, he always ends his lively conversations with a "God Bless You."

Nothing is better for Nate Bradford these days than a truckful of rocks and a heartful of love for God and his fellow man.

"I've been blessed," he says. "I used to be called Head Hunter and now they call me Pastor."

August 2, 1998
UNDER HER WING

A mallard duckling with a tiny cast on its leg lolls around in Diane Kuhl's lap while she gently cuddles a baby wood duck she is feeding with a syringe.

Diane is in her sun room, where she also is watching a young Canada goose race down the hill in the back yard, its wings spreading and its lanky body almost airborne before it slows to a walk to keep from plopping into the little moss-covered pond.

"He's almost got it," Diane says. "Another day or two and he'll be flying."

Diane Kuhl, the Duck Lady of Hudson Lake, may not fly herself . . . may not have wings . . . but she definitely is an angel for these fallen and forgotten waterfowl.

She cares for the injured and orphaned, often housing as many as 300 birds during the summer months at her Hudson Lake home in LaPorte County. She and her husband, Michael, live on a four-acre wooded lot about 100 yards off the lake.

For the last 14 years, this nurturing and nursing have been her full-time labor of love. She has baby ducks in a brooder box in her house . . . little ducklings waddling through the straw in her walk-out basement . . . and almost-adult ducks in a pen outside in her yard, waiting for Mother Nature to tell them it's time to fly away.

On this day, she also has a mature Canada goose with a broken foot and a couple of bigger mallards—one whose throat was gashed by an animal and another that swallowed a fishing hook.

"I take all kinds of ducks and geese and the occasional loon and heron—any birds that hang around the water," she says.

In the summer months, they wake her up with their quacking around sunrise and it's often past sunset before she and her husband sit down to dinner.

"I quit a good-paying job [as a trucking company branch manager] for this," she says. "My husband's job (as a salesman) allows me to do this. It's all volunteer and it costs me about $2,200 annually for the material, so you know I must like what I do."

The Duck Lady . . . shall we say . . . never ducks this commitment she has made to the animal kingdom.

"But I am not these birds' mother," Diane stresses. "They don't belong to me. They belong to nature. I'm here to give them a second chance. I don't hand out little names and I don't make cooing sounds. I'm their caretaker."

Mama Mallard she may not be, but most of these ducks wouldn't have a chance without her. Little wood ducks need several feedings a day through a syringe during their first five or six days and she can have as many as 20 under her care at one time.

There are different seasons to her work. This is the busiest—the time when the baby ducklings show up on her doorstep. "A mother duck crosses the road and is either killed or a car scatters her and four of her babies one way and six the other way. Some concerned passer-by stops and scoops these cute little ducklings up and then says, 'What am I going to do now?' "

If they call the Department of Natural Resources, the Wildlife Alliance, the Humane Society, Animal Control, Fernwood Nature Center, various veterinarians or pet stores, they will usually be told to call the Duck Lady.

These organizations know she will take them under her wing—figuratively speaking, of course.

"After the babies grow up, then it becomes hit-by-a-car season," she says. "Then it's migration season when I can see all different kinds of birds. After that, it's hunting season with birds coming in with gunshot wounds. In January and February, things finally slow down because everybody who is going to migrate has migrated and everybody who's going to get shot has been shot."

Diane first started caring for water birds when she found an injured grebe—a loon-type bird—limping through her yard. She made countless calls before she found out that the wildlife

center at Rum Village would take it. "When I got there, I said, 'This is great. Can I help?' "

She did—for several years as a wide-eyed volunteer.

The wildlife center has since closed, but Diane continues caring for birds as a member of the Wildlife Alliance. She is now the expert—attending seminars, consulting with vets and reading anything she can get her hands on. She sometimes even performs necropsies to see why some of the birds didn't make it.

It can be grueling work. But even when feeding baby ducks becomes her almost overwhelming duty during some summer weeks, she still listens to books on cassette. She is also learning Portuguese that way.

"I don't want you to think I'm sitting in here, feeding these ducks and turning into a vegetable," she says with a laugh.

When the baby season is over, she finds time to take to the water, too—in her sailboat or kayak.

But most of her time and energy goes into caring for little creatures with wings and webbed feet. She admits her passion is made much easier by a couple of area veterinarians who donate their time when needed.

She also has a handful of volunteers who help her. Just recently, the Calvert Rod & Gun Club took about 30 of her young ducks for their pond. "I have to give them a pat of the back," she says. "They wanted to get involved and foster some ducks. Hey, conservation clubs ought to do more than just sell beer and play bingo."

Diane, her husband and a couple of volunteers transported the ducks in cages to the Calvert Club's location southwest of South Bend. Usually, she is picking up injured or orphaned birds, not dropping them off. Sometimes, she will make a 100-mile round trip to take home a duck in need.

When she does get new boarders, they are not always so happy to see her, especially the adult birds. She has been beaten by wings until her arms have turned black and blue and she gets nipped and pecked almost every hour of the day. "That's just part of the job," Diane says. "You always have to remember that they are doing it only out of self-defense."

She has to know what she's doing, though. "A blue heron with its long beak could put your eye out if you didn't handle it the right way."

One might think her ducks could be in peril, too, with Diane's five cats roaming around. She also has four dogs, a goat and a chicken that apparently has convinced itself that it's a duck.

"They all know the meaning of 'No,' " she says. "I don't have all summer to teach my dogs and cats to leave the little ducklings alone."

Diane, of course, can't say no to any waterfowl.

Occasionally, she will get a Pekin duck—the white ones from the pet stores. She will do what she can for them. "I know how they are so cute when they're little and how the kids can't resist little Peepers. But eventually, they grow big and people need to realize this. A lot of people don't show much responsibility when they dump these ducks."

But even the Duck Lady can't fret about the ducks when they leave her home. "I'm not in charge after they leave," she admits. "People hunt this lake, too, but I can't worry about that. I've given them their second chance.

"The payback for me is the satisfaction of bettering the environment in some way," she says. "That's enough for me."

She gives life and sees her share of death, too. "Sure, it affects me when some don't make it," she says. "When it ends up not mattering, it's time to find something else to do."

She doesn't expect that to happen soon. "Too many people know me as the Duck Lady. I'd have to change my name and number."

Besides, she has learned to love spending her day with a bunch of quacks.

February 1, 1999
BURIED TREASURE

When John Zmudzinski scurried onto Omaha Beach during the Normandy invasion, he was hauling a bazooka, an M-1 rifle, a gas mask, an ammunition belt, a light field pack, an inflatable life jacket and a small brown paper bag just in case he got sick on the landing craft.

"But besides that equipment, I tried to travel pretty light during the war," says the Olive Township native and longtime South Bend postal worker. "Not a lot of personal stuff. I can't even tell you what else I had. You were more worried about getting back in one piece."

He didn't even know if he was wearing his GI dog tags that fateful day almost 55 years ago.

"I've been meaning to tell my youngest daughter Jane, who is the jokester in our family, that I probably left them hanging on my bedpost the night before."

He didn't. But before he and the rest of the 37th Engineer Combat Battalion left Weymouth, England, for the French coast, someone may have collected several of the men's dog tags.

"I have tried to remember something like that happening, but I just can't," he admits.

Why would he? He was a 19-year-old kid, after all, who was getting ready to take part in an invasion that would determine the course of the war. He saw buddies die beside him and heard bullets zip over his head.

When he revisited Normandy in 1984, on the 40th anniversary of D-Day, tears rolled down his cheeks before he had even cleared the tour bus. "You know in the movie *Saving Private Ryan* when Ryan visits the cemetery where his captain is buried? Well, my captain really is buried there."

He knows that could have very easily been his fate, too. Fortunately, it was only his dog tags that were left behind—buried in the ground.

"I never knew what happened to them. Never gave them much thought when the war was over. I just was happy to come home."

Almost 55 years later, John Zmudzinski's dog tags have come home, too.

While using a metal detector on a Dorchester farm in southern England, a Brit named Ron Howse unearthed dog tags belonging to 28 American soldiers.

That was in November. He assumed that the owners were killed in the war.

Howse contacted Paul Braddock, a collector of military memorabilia who lives in Pittsburgh. With help from the Department of Veterans Affairs, Braddock located Zmudzinski and five other soldiers whose dog tags were found.

Then just last week, Zmudzinski's dog tags from World War II were back in his possession, via priority mail.

"I felt like a little kid who just got a new bike," he says. "The dog tags just weren't that important to me back then, but they are nice to have now."

On them are his name, his Army serial number, an A for his blood type, a C for Catholic, a T43 for when he received his tetanus shot and his mother's name and address as his next of kin.

They are discolored and slightly dented and a little hard to read, but that's fine with Zmudzinski.

"I don't know where I am going to keep them," he says. "I do know that I am very reluctant about taking them out of the house."

He once bought a little display case when he decided to ask the Army to send the four battle star medals he earned but never received. That would have been nice for his dog tags, too. But his request never got a reply. "Someone told me I should write my congressman, but I figured he had enough things to do without having to bother with that."

The memories of the war remain, although they are not as harsh as the ones from 1976 when he lost his wife Jean to breast cancer.

Now 74, Zmudzinski lives alone in his house just west of South Bend. His three daughters and their families live out of town, but they stay in close contact.

"The house and yard are getting a little big for me now," he admits, "but I think I will pass on a condo or apartment and go right off to the loony bin when it's time."

He thought he was going loony when he first heard about his dog tags. "I don't know if they were part of a collection of ones that were lost or that somebody made us take them off because of the next-of-kin information.

"It will probably always be a mystery and I guess that's OK," he says.

The important thing is that he has them back.

"When Jane called, she asked me if Walter Cronkite had called yet," he says with a chuckle. "I told her 'Tomorrow.'"

But with his long lost dog tags resting in his hands, yesterday is more on his mind today.

March 28, 1999
STRIVING FOR HER A'S

She sat in front of me in my high school English class during my junior year, and I had lunch with her last week.

I kissed and hugged her when we greeted, and then I kissed her again when we parted.

My wife didn't mind.

The "other woman" is now 91 years old.

Her name is Mildred Kern. She was my English teacher and my high school newspaper adviser. After I graduated from Kokomo High School in 1967, she retired the following year to travel with her husband, Frank.

To say that I was enchanted with Mrs. Kern's class back then would be an overstatement. In truth, she scared me half to death.

During my first six-week period in her honors English class, I received my first-ever C. But then again, so did more than half the class. A couple girls in the class could not stop sobbing when they found out their grades.

When I told her what book I was going to read for our first book report, she responded with, "When are you going to grow up, Bill?" I quickly found a more suitable book than the silly sports story I had picked out.

And when I was late turning in a newspaper-related assignment, my mom practically had to push me out of the car before I would go up to her door with the story. Fortunately, she wasn't home, and so I slipped it in the mail slot and scurried away as if I had just dodged a bullet aimed at my ego.

Over that school year, I adapted. I actually starting getting some A's from Mrs. Kern, I put my boyish books behind me, and I learned the importance of a deadline.

Maybe I even started liking Mrs. Kern a little, too.

I do know that some of the most beautiful girls in the school were in that class, but I never took my eyes off the woman directly in front of us. She had my full attention and was one of the reasons I started using an anti-perspirant for the first time.

Mrs. Kern made me a better writer by demanding more out of me. She made me think on my feet and overcome some of my shyness. And she, maybe more than anyone else, influenced my decision to pursue journalism as a profession.

She also instilled in me a love for reading. I still remember the enthusiasm with which she taught Dickens' *A Tale of Two Cities* and how I embraced that book and other classics like it.

She could share in a laugh, too, but not at the expense of classroom decorum. When we were learning about Shakespeare or reading *The Rime of the Ancient*

Mariner, we were in her laboratory of learning. Nobody ever dozed.

When she did hand out praise, it meant something. In fact, it made me feel like a million bucks.

Many people have had a positive impact on my life. Some of them stand out. Mrs. Kern is one of those individuals.

Even now, I occasionally think of her when a phrase in one of my stories doesn't seem to work or my grammar appears suspect. I take the time and try to make it right. I guess I am still striving for her A's.

I recently started corresponding with Mrs. Kern when my mom sent me an article about her from the *Kokomo Tribune.* Her husband had owned a travel agency and when he died some years ago, she continued to serve as a tour guide. Even at 91, she loads people on the bus or in a plane and leads them all over.

After spending time with her last week, I am guessing she will live to be 100.

She had brought a travel group, most of them senior citizens, to South Bend to see the sights. In between their stops, they lunched at Tippecanoe Place and she invited me to join them.

I saw my old scoutmaster, the parents of one of my old schoolmates and the one and only Mildred Kern. I had not seen her since a chance meeting in a department store when I was still in college.

That was almost 30 years ago. But I still would have been able to pick her out of a million people.

We sat together and relived those old Kokomo High School days. When the rest of the group went on a tour of Tippecanoe Place, we stayed behind and talked some more. She said she was proud of me. Then I got the chance to tell her how much she had meant to me when I was a skinny, self-conscious 16-year-old—even if I had not known it at the time.

When it was time for us to go, she took my arm and we walked slowly up the stairs together.

As we hit the landing, she turned to me and said, "I don't get around like I once did."

In my writing, she always is around.

April 25, 1999
ALWAYS A SMILE

Jo Anne Gardner liked to go to Smith's Cafeteria in downtown South Bend for lunch. Unfortunately, the direct route from her work took her through the intersection of Michigan Street and Jefferson Boulevard.

That's where South Bend police officer George Tezich worked in 1950, directing traffic and giving everyone a smile. In fact, he was even called the Smiling Policeman by many of the downtowners.

"I thought he was too sickly friendly, though," Jo Anne now says. "In fact, I started avoiding him by walking a block down to cross the street and then a block back. That's how much he annoyed me."

"Oh, but I had my eye on her," George admits.

After all, Jo Anne was quite a looker. So George arranged a meeting through one of her friends. "She said this guy was going to meet us when we got off the bus that morning, and I said OK," Jo Anne recalls. "But when we got to our stop, all I saw was that silly, smiling cop."

George Tezich wore that same smile when they were married nine months later.

"That's always been my nature," he says.

Not even World War II wounds or two unsuccessful runs in South Bend's mayoral races or a rash of serious health problems a few years ago could wipe that smile off for long.

"I've always been a smiler—even as a kid."

About the only thing that can keep a smile off his face these days is all the killing in Yugoslavia. That was his parents' homeland before they immigrated here as teens. His father was Serbian and his mother was Croatian.

"If I were 20 years younger, I would go over there and kick (Yugoslav President Slobodan) Milosevic's butt myself," says George, now 77.

He might have.

He already fought once in Europe—with Patton's Third Army during World War II. He came home with two Bronze Stars and two Purple Hearts after being hit by shrapnel and a bullet that almost cost him his left arm.

"It was 1940 when I enlisted, right after I graduated from Central High School," George recalls. "I was 17 at the time, and so I had to get my dad's signature. When he wouldn't sign, I got the dishwasher from George's Cafe to go down with me and pretend to be my dad. He signed."

He loved the Army, rising quickly through the ranks and making it to first sergeant when he was still 18. When war broke out, he was in charge of the 5th

Training Regiment at Fort McClellan, Ala., helping get soldiers combat-ready.

"I could have stayed there, but I applied for overseas," he says. "I wanted to be in 'the big bang.'"

He got his wish and was among the third wave into Normandy. That's when the war lost any romantic notions for him. "I had to walk over, and by, thousands of bodies," he still recalls with a catch in his throat. "I don't think you can describe that scene. I do know my stomach was so upset by the stench of death that I couldn't eat for 10 days."

He saw his own action as part of a reconnaissance unit. "Our job was to get as close to the Germans as we could and get as much information as possible without being killed," George says.

His duty included two river crossings—one of them the Seine—in a rubber raft in the dead of night. Both missions couldn't avoid hand-to-hand combat.

Although he was wounded earlier and returned to battle, the bullet he took in his left arm at Metz, France, knocked him out of the war and into a hospital for 41/2 months. "At one point, they thought they might have to amputate my arm," he says.

But he came back to South Bend with his smile—and his arm—intact. He also took off one uniform to put on another.

"Oh, I loved being a policeman," he says. "Everything but the pay."

After seven years on the force and Jo Anne expecting their first of four children, he went into sales and stayed until he was 75. The last 33 years were with Huntington Industries.

All that time, he has played handball at the YMCA. "Three times a week even now," he says. "I got my first YMCA membership when I was eight by washing windows there. I love that place."

"Heaven forbid that I ever went into labor when George had a handball game scheduled," Jo Anne laughs.

George Jr., Gregory, Ruth and Robert were kind enough not to come at those awkward times. Gregory, in fact, has embraced handball as much as his dad, even teaming up with George in the past to win some local tourneys.

"I've been playing for almost 60 years," George says. "My left arm gives me a little trouble but, hey, I'm just glad to be able to play."

He really likes the camaraderie of his playing mates—Art Pine, Joe Hoffler and "anyone else we can drag into the court." He likes to win, too.

In 1959, he tried to win the Democratic nomination for mayor. "A bunch of guys decided I ought to be mayor, and Keith Klopfenstein [the former county commissioner] talked me into running," George says. "I was enough of a renegade to do it."

There was a bond between those two men, who knew each

other back in their South Bend high school days. They also had a chance meeting in France during World War II when George stopped a medical evacuation unit that was getting too close to the front lines.

"I looked at one of the captains and said, 'You're Keith Klopfenstein from Riley High School,' And he looked at me and said, 'You're George Tezich.'"

While Klopfenstein's unit camped on one side of the road that night, he stayed with George on the other. Tragically, an enemy airstrike hit the other side and killed many in Klopfenstein's unit. "He figured I saved his life," George says.

But George didn't become a savior in politics, finishing far behind Edward "Babe" Voorde, the incumbent mayor, in the Democratic primary. "I enjoyed the challenge, though," George says. "And I used to give roses to the ladies during my campaign."

He even had a big picture of his smiling face plastered on a billboard on top of the Coney Island restaurant downtown. "No words on it," George recalls. "But then, with a few months to go, they added 'For Mayor,' and I guess the other candidates just about went nuts."

He also ran in 1963 but mainly to take away votes from some of the others running against Gene Pajakowski, who narrowly lost the primary to Paul Krueper.

"I didn't mind the first time he ran but not the second," Jo Anne admits. "I voted for George, but I also kept my fingers crossed that he wouldn't win."

After that, George concentrated on his sales job, on raising his family (that now stands at four children, 10 grandchildren and one great-grandchild), on rooting for his Fighting Irish and on playing handball.

Since retirement, he has added a 5-mile morning walk to his regimen. "I have always tried to stay in good physical shape," he says.

Just as well. Everything caught up with him in 1993. He had to have a cancerous kidney removed and underwent open-heart surgery along with gall bladder and hernia operations. "All in the same year," he says. "I'll tell you, if I hadn't stayed in good shape over the course of my life, I wouldn't be here now."

He smiles when he says that. A big smile.

But then what else would you expect?

June 1, 1999
LOSING A FRIEND

Some years ago, Craig Gregor and Ron Miller happened to walk into Pat's Barber Shop in Roseland at the same time.

Ron was up first in the chair while Craig leafed through a magazine. They didn't know each other from Adam. But in between Pat Catanzarite's corny jokes, Craig and Ron found out that they had a mutual love—Notre Dame football.

"After that discovery, I had a hard time getting a word in," Pat admits.

They went up and down the Irish roster that day. They analyzed the schedule. They gently second-guessed the coach.

"They had a lot of fun," Pat recalls.

Ron hung around while Craig took his turn in the chair. When they got ready to leave, Craig turned to Ron and said, "Why don't we get appointments together again?"

And so they did—a tradition they continued for more than five years.

Back-to-back in the barber's chair.

"We developed a neat friendship," Ron says. "We never socialized outside Pat's shop, but we looked forward to seeing each other every time we got a haircut."

"Craig would ask Ron when he wanted their next appointments and Ron would always say, 'You

choose a date, Craig,'" Pat says. "And so he would."

During their April 7 appointments, it was the same as usual.

Little did Ron or Pat know then that Craig had cancer. And even Craig would not find out until five days later that it had taken over his body.

A Vietnam vet, a highly respected computer systems analyst and a loving father and husband, 52-year-old Craig Gregor faced his next month of horrible pain with quiet dignity. His main concern was preparing his wife Sharon, his two children, Sara and Ian, and his mother, Nora, for his passing.

"We had no idea," Ron says. "You think you both walk out together in good health and then ..."

It's hard to make sense of it all.

Before he died, Craig wanted to get a last haircut. Sharon told Pat about Craig's illness and then Pat called Ron to forewarn him.

Ron was in the chair when Craig struggled in with his wife. Both Ron and Pat had to fight back their emotions when they saw how the cancer had ravaged their friend's body so quickly, so mercilessly. Always the gentleman, Craig tried to make everyone comfortable by trying to carry on a regular conversation.

"It was obvious he was in a lot of pain," Pat says.

When Ron got out of the chair,

he lingered for a little while, mentioned a Notre Dame basketball recruit and then bid his friend goodbye. He fought back tears in his car. "I just didn't know what to say to him," he admits.

That was Thursday, May 12.

On Sunday, May 16, Craig Gregor died—everything neatly in order for his family down to the hair on his head.

Many people mourned his passing. Sharon said that once you were Craig's friend, you were his friend for life.

She also said her husband loved studying the stars in the sky . . . and telling a good joke . . . and analyzing a new movie or book . . . and watching Jack Nicklaus play golf . . . and nursing a Colorado blue spruce back to health.

Maybe his friend, Ron Miller, knew all this and maybe he didn't. He did know, though, that nobody was more enjoyable than Craig Gregor when it came to debating Notre Dame football.

"I will miss him," Ron says.

He never would have thought that making his own haircut appointment would be so tough.

June 21, 1999
LAST-CHANCE ROMANCE

Cyrus Nifong always had a powerful voice, but he could barely get any words out this time. He asked his girl, Grace Baker, to marry him.

"I was so much in love with her," Cyrus says.

"And I was very fond of him," Grace admits.

But at 21 years of age, she wasn't ready to say yes. Cyrus was a young farmer on the outskirts of Plymouth; Grace wanted to go off to South Bend Business College, and the world of the Great Depression was an uncertain place.

"Right after that, we went roller skating," Cyrus recalls. "I must have said something I shouldn't have. The next thing I knew, Grace was gone. I skated over to the window that overlooked the sidewalk and there she went.

"She went her way and I went mine. That was the last time I saw her."

For 64 years, anyway.

Grace did indeed go off to business college in 1935. She stayed in South Bend, married Rolland Matz, adopted a son and worked at Associates and the First Methodist Church.

Cyrus married Loretta Harley, raised four boys and became a successful farmer. He also drove a school bus for 35 years, served as a county commissioner and sang in his church's choir.

"I never quite forgot Grace, though," Cyrus admits. "I lived a wonderful life with my wife, Loretta, and we leaned on each other heavily. I never had an ill thought or any illusions. We loved each other dearly."

It was like a stab to his heart when Loretta, his wife of 62 years, unexpectedly passed away last November. "I was so lonely without her," he admits.

So when the snows hit in early January and a hip operation limited Cyrus' movement, his sons insisted he not drive anywhere. That meant he was stranded in his farmhouse west of Plymouth, often with only memories for company.

"That's when I started wondering whatever happened to Grace," he says.

While thumbing through some pictures, he found one of her that he had saved all those years. He also found a picture that Grace had taken of him, a good-looking farm boy balancing himself on a fence post and the top strand of barbed wire.

He started thinking back to when he used to croon to her in his 1925 Maxwell coupe. Long, long ago, they had made such sweet music together.

"I knew her older brother Orville had been a barber up in South Bend so I located his number and gave him a call," Cyrus says. "It did take a while to explain who I was, but I finally got myself identified."

Ninety-year-old Orville Baker told Cyrus that Grace had suffered a stroke two years earlier and was living at St. Paul's Retirement Community. She also had become a widow for a second time when her second husband, Harold Fisher, had recently died.

"So I called her up and told her right then that she may as well be congenial because I had already gotten permission from her brother to take her to lunch," Cyrus recalls.

Grace was flabbergasted. "I had all but forgotten about Cyrus," she says. "That seemed like another life ago."

They were both 21 then. "I am not going to tell you my age now, but I am as old as Cyrus and he may tell you how old he is," Grace says.

"We are both 85," Cyrus volunteers.

They were nervous as teenagers when they first met in 1934—both of them a couple of years out of high school. They may have been even more nervous 64 years later.

"I think Grace had recollections of me with dark hair and here I show up with white hair and a cane," Cyrus says.

Grace was still a little hobbled by her stroke. "I couldn't walk or talk very well," she admits.

"I think the way Father Time had dealt with us was quite a surprise," Cyrus says. "But after the dust settled, we started to enjoy each other's company and remembering the good times of long ago."

Twice a week, Cyrus began driving up to South Bend to take Grace out to dinner. "It's exactly 26 miles from my garage to the back door of St. Paul's," he says.

"I did remember him as the nicest boy I ever dated," she says. "I never thought he would come after me, though."

That spark of love that Cyrus had carried for Grace all those years spread into her heart. "I fell in love with him this time, the same kind of love that he felt for me," Grace says.

When Cyrus proposed to her in the spring, well . . . "I didn't have any problems convincing her this time," he says.

They married on June 12 with 80 people in attendance at Union Church of the Brethren outside of Plymouth. Cyrus had to use a walker after another hip operation a month earlier, while Grace refused her cane when she walked down the aisle on the arm of her brother Orville.

"It was a wonderful ceremony," Grace says.

"We probably would have waited longer to marry if we were younger," Cyrus says. "But at our age, we want to make the most of the time we have left."

Their families have been supportive. "We signed a prenuptial agreement and our funeral arrangements are already made and paid for," Cyrus adds. "We don't want each other's money."

They just want each other. They are living in the same farmhouse that Cyrus has called home for the last 62 years. Three of his sons are within hollering distance if needed.

And how is their marriage working so far? "Cyrus is not as good a cook as I thought he would be," Grace says with a smile.

Cyrus blushes. They then grab each other's hands like young couples do.

At times, they must feel 21 again.

They have the picture of Grace as a young beauty. They have the picture of Cyrus in his Abe Lincoln pose on that fence post. Most of all, they have each other.

After 64 years.

"He rescued me," Grace says.

"She was my first love," Cyrus answers.

June 27, 1999
COURAGE TO SPARE

Perry Gordon didn't hesitate. He looked back at the burning house. He heard the cries of little children. He ran inside.

"A man with any kind of courage would have done the same," he says.

Yet Perry, all of 13, wasn't nearly a man. He just acted like one—a very brave one.

He had been helping JoAnn Scott, one of his older sisters, and her husband paint their home. Gasoline that had been used to clean off their brushes somehow spilled and drifted to the pilot light of the gas stove. A fire erupted and quickly spread throughout the two-story house.

His hair and clothes smoking, Perry rushed out of the house to tell a neighbor to call the fire department.

Then he returned and heard his young nephews and niece crying out for help. He rushed into the burning house and scooped up his 3-year-old niece, Debbie. While saving her, he suffered severe burns to his face, arms and chest.

"Sometime it seems as if it just happened yesterday," he says.

The tragic fire actually occurred more than 26 years ago—Jan. 15, 1973, on Falcon Street in South Bend.

Perry's brother-in-law, Harry Scott, jumped out a window while holding his 1-year-old son, Tyrone. Amid the smoke and flames, South Bend firefighter Dale Soos pulled 3-year-old Jerome out from under a bed.

Over the next few weeks, Harry Scott and two of his children, Debbie and Tyrone, died from their burns.

Perry never found out about Debbie until six months later. That was when he was finally released from the Michigan Burn Center in Ann Arbor.

He had almost died himself on three separate occasions, emergency personnel reviving him all three times. "You know how they tell you about that bright light before you die? Well, I saw it and then my life flashed before me. I was ready to see the Lord."

Maybe so, but his time had not come. He only wished it had when he looked into a mirror and saw how horribly he had been burned. "I just wanted to die," he admits. "But there was an electrician in the next bed who had lost an arm and a leg in an accident and he said, 'What are you moaning about? At least you got your limbs.'"

That was when Perry took an accounting of both his limbs and his blessings. "I decided I had to grow up fast," he says. "I had to be a man."

He had no other choice.

Because his mother was still busy raising many of her 14

other children, Perry had to take the bus by himself to Ann Arbor for skin graft operations. He had to handle both the mental and physical pain. He had to deal with the inevitable stares.

"I wouldn't wish that on anybody," he admits. "But I came to the conclusion that nobody is perfect in this world, that life is up and down for everybody and that I was going to make the best of it."

He went on to LaSalle High School and Ivy Tech. "Then I worked as a welder, a painter and a jack-of-all-trades and a master of one—life," Perry says with a smile. "A lot of people wondered why I would weld after being burned like I had. It was my way of facing up to my fears."

He eventually started working full time at Logan after he had washed dishes there as a teenager. He has now been there for 16 years, mostly as a maintenance worker. In 1993, he was honored as Logan's Employee of the Year.

"Perry is one of those people who helps create that feeling of family here," says Ann Lagomarcino, Logan's director of marketing. "He has that quality of bringing people together, and Perry also works very hard at his job."

The Logan clients—most of them developmentally disabled—flood him with affection, wanting to hug him and shake his hand as he goes about his work.

"I feel like a caregiver here," he says. "And I also get the opportu-nity to treat people like I want to be treated. You do that, and it will carry you a long way. Quite frankly, we have a lot of beautiful people here."

Many of the clients at Logan think Perry is a beautiful guy, too, even though he knows that others in the community may stare at his scars for a moment. "Occasionally a little kid will blurt out, 'Wow, what happened to him?'" he says. "If I have the time, I explain to them what happened and why I am different."

Because of all the numerous skin graft operations he already withstood as a teen-ager and the cost of plastic surgery, Perry has accepted his physical appearance. "Besides, I am not in any pain," he adds.

Overall, he thinks he has a pretty good life. He owns a home, holds a steady job, has good friends and a beautiful little 8-year-old daughter named Desiree. Although his daughter now lives in Portage with her mother, Perry tries to see her as much as possible.

To her, he is just Dad, a big, huggable guy.

A guy who had to grow up quickly.

Sometimes, when there is a lull in his day or a night of unrest, Perry Gordon will think back to that day more than 26 years ago.

He answers the inevitable question before it is asked. "I would do it again."

He nods his head. "Without a second thought."

September 26, 1999
A FIGURE OF FAITH

Snow was on the ground, but the sun was shining brightly. So Cheryl Matthew happened to catch a glimpse of the little sparkle on the pavement next to her parking space.

She reached down to scoop up whatever it was. "I have a habit of finding things," the 44-year-old South Bend woman says. "And this little object seemed to be staring up at me."

It turned out to be Jesus.

The little figurine—hardly a half-inch in length—had apparently been part of a crucifix. "But it obviously had been broken," Cheryl recalls. "The only thing left was the body of Jesus, and he was missing his right arm."

She put the figurine in her purse and pretty much forgot about it.

That was in early 1997—a year that would forever change Cheryl Matthew's life.

In July of that year while at the Venetian Festival in St. Joseph, she was coaxed onto a jet ski by an acquaintance. "Because Lake Michigan was so rough, we stayed on the river," she says.

Although she knew her way around boats, it was her first ride on a jet ski.

It will be her last.

For reasons still unknown to her, a motorboat and the jet ski almost collided and both she and the driver of the jet ski were thrown into the water. The boat struck her and she instinctively stuck up her right arm to protect her head from the motor's propeller.

"Everything went white," she recalls. "Then I remember pulling my arm out of the water. It looked like spaghetti."

What followed was a nightmare of pain and anguish and, finally, unconsciousness. She almost bled to death before she could be pulled to shore. Then after doctors made a valiant effort to save her arm, it was determined that her wounds had sustained too much infection from the river.

Her right arm was amputated above the elbow.

Cheryl spent three weeks in three different hospitals. A single mother of three, she didn't spend it alone. Friends and family flocked to her side. "When I was transferred from Henry Ford Hospital in Detroit to Memorial [Hospital of South Bend], the receptionist said she felt like an air traffic controller the way people came in to see me."

It was a wonderful feeling to have that kind of support. But she also knew that there were going to be battles she would have to fight alone.

Well, maybe not alone spiritually ...

A few weeks later, her boyfriend, Bob Nowicki, was helping her change over to a more manageable purse. "He dumped the contents onto the table and the little figurine of Jesus clanged across the table," she says. "I had forgotten all about it."

Her mouth opened. Her mind raced.

Her Jesus was missing the same arm at the same place she was.

"I have to think there is a reason for everything," she says. "I have always been a believer. But after that, my faith deepened and I feel I have gotten my strength through God."

Cheryl had the figurine of Jesus made into a crucifix, and she has worn it on a necklace ever since. "I look at it every day and think that I have been a pretty lucky girl," she says. "I could have very easily been killed."

That's not to say she doesn't have her sad moments. "Oh, I still have my days," she says. "It isn't easy when you were right-handed and you have to learn everything over again. I need help with my hair, I can't take a casserole out of the oven, but I can do a pretty mean job of parallel parking with my steering ball."

She also still carries some bitterness toward insurance companies "who seemed to control my situation more than my doctors did," and to a judicial system that found no one legally responsible for her injury.

"I also know it has been hard on my kids (22-year-old John, 19-year-old Megan and 15-year-

old Lauren)," she says. "They have gone through their own angry stages, but they have been great help for me."

Seven weeks after her accident, Cheryl returned to work at Rink Riverside Printing as a commercial salesperson. She has a prosthesis but prefers not to wear it now, partly because she still faces another surgery.

Cheryl does keep her sense of humor. "One of my friends will say, 'You need a hand?' And I will reply, 'Sure, if I can keep it.' "

The nightmares no longer hit her, but she still sometimes dreams about having an arm. "Those are the times when I wake up and wish I could go back to sleep and dream a little more," she admits.

Yet she gets up each morning ready to take on the day. "I try not to dwell on what I can't do, but what I can accomplish."

She also looks down at her Jesus. "Then I say a little prayer— and count all my blessings."

May 17, 2000
THE MAIL AND MORE

They measure mail with a ruler now—figuring out how long it should take a letter carrier to make his or her appointed rounds.

It's down to a science.

"And if they determine that you have a light load, a printout tells you where you should go to help out after your own route—and also how long it should take you," says John Bullard, a Mishawaka mail carrier for the last 37 years.

That's modern-day business. That's time management.

Tick, tick, tick.

Bullard, now 62, doesn't mind so much. He does his delivering from a truck these days anyway, driving from one mailbox to the next.

He still enjoys his job but he misses the days when he would march through the Mishawaka neighborhoods on foot, delivering both the good news and the bad news with a friendly smile.

"If it wasn't a particularly busy day, you could do a little chit-chatting back then," the father of five and grandfather of 16 says. "I almost felt that was part of the job."

Not a mauling by a dog . . . nor diabetes . . . nor bypass surgery could slow him down for long. "In a lot of ways people on my route were like family," he said.

And mail carriers like him . . . well, they could be a comforting constant in life's sometimes hashy-bashy pace.

Just listen to the rhythm of his routes:

• "There was Mrs. Fisher on State Street who would be waiting for me at her door every day. She always wanted to talk about those Chicago Cubs."

•"Spud Zimmerman on my route called me when his wife passed away. He said he didn't know who else to call. When someone on my route lost a loved one, I always felt like I should go to the funeral."

•"The Stebbins family on East Fourth Street told me they were going out of town the next day and wondered if I could let out their dog when I delivered their mail and then let him back in when I circled back. I said sure."

•"I went to one house and the lady—who I won't mention by name—came running to the door without a top on. She said she just had to get a letter out that day and couldn't find her blouse. She said that she figured if I had seen one—well, you know what—then I had seen them all."

•"Kenneth Armel on Wenger always had a Pepsi for me. So many of the people on my route had nice, cold drinks for me in the summertime. Maybe that's how I got diabetes."

•"Mrs. Campbell on State

Street was wintering in Texas one year and I noticed a couple of young guys driving slowly by her house in an old, beat-up Chevy. I knocked on the door of Bret Bernoff, a police officer, over on Prescott and told him. They caught those guys in the back yard with Mrs. Campbell's TV and some furniture."

• "Gene Dykstra, the old Mishawaka High football coach, would circle the neighborhoods in his Cadillac to find me so we could have coffee together when it was time for my break. Charlie Culp and Dean Benjamin, a couple of cops, used to join us. So would Jim Troyer, who started walking with me a lot of days after his heart problems."

• "An older woman on Wenger, who I hate to say was a bit of a grouch, told me I delivered a neighbor's gas bill to her and she paid it before she realized it wasn't hers. I told her I would drop off my bill the next time."

• "Old Joe near the high school would never leave his house. He asked me once if I could pick up his lunch at Hardee's. I used to do that quite a bit for him."

• "Mr. Warner over on Capital looked really down one day when I brought his mail. I asked him what was wrong. He said he just found out his boy had been killed in Vietnam. What kind of words can you say?"

• "There was a brief time that I started giving biscuits to dogs. But there was one over on Smalley Avenue that would get one and then run over to the next street to get another. And then the next street, too."

• "Mrs. Brenneman's son was a POW and so when I was sorting the mail at the post office, I saw she had a letter from him. I called her up and she came racing over, so excited to get it."

• "Mrs. Parker on Homewood was having trouble with a gang of kids and the police couldn't do much about it. So my wife, Jackie, and I had her over for dinner and gave her our number in case she ever needed me. She always appreciated that."

• "O.J. Curry on Fourth Street turned 90 on the same day I turned 30. We talked every morning when I delivered his mail. One of his daughters finally persuaded him to move in with her and her family in Hershey, Pa., when he was 98. But he came back here to celebrate his 100th birthday. When they asked him who he wanted to invite, he said, 'John Bullard, my old mailman.'"

High praise for a good mail carrier—and an even better friend.

August 20, 2000
BROTHERLY LOVE

For a guy who always tries to live life in the present, Fran McCann admits that his summer has been a season of reflection.

He turned 60 after all, and also married off his and wife Cathy's oldest daughter, Stephanie.

"An interesting summer," admits the Notre Dame physical education instructor and the university's former head wrestling coach.

It also has been a time when he has thought a lot about his brothers.

This year marks the 40th anniversary of his older brother Terry's wrestling gold medal at the Rome Olympics . . . and the 25th anniversary of the end of the Vietnam War, which claimed the life of his kid brother, Jim.

One brother waving an American flag. Another buried with one.

"Hardly a day goes by when I don't think about them," Fran says.

Fran, who also has two sisters, fell right in the middle of his brothers. Terry is six years older and Jim was six years younger.

"Terry was always a great role model for me—still is for that matter—and I tried to be the same for Jimmy," Fran says.

They grew up on the northwest side of Chicago and attended Schurz High School, where all the McCann boys excelled in wrestling. "It was a working class neighborhood with the playground being where everything happened."

Fran liked to tag along with Terry. Later, when Terry was at the University of Iowa and winning two NCAA titles, Jim tagged along with Fran. "Terry was always checking up on us—the ultimate big brother."

Fran tried hard to follow in Terry's footsteps and was a runner-up in the NCAA tournament for Iowa. "I would be lying if I said there wasn't a lot of pressure coming behind Terry," Fran admits. "It was very tough at times—always being known as Terry McCann's younger brother."

But in 1960, it was Fran who did the most in preparing Terry for the Olympics. He served as his older brother's training partner, and they went at it tooth and nail. "I got to the point that I could anticipate Terry's moves and really frustrate him. Sometimes he would even give me a punch, and I would punch him right back."

It was about the only time Fran didn't look at his older brother with awe.

Terry, who now lives in California and is executive director of Toastmasters International, went on to win his gold medal in the 125.5-pound class—an assist to his brother.

"One of the proudest days for all of us in the family," Fran says.

Four years later at the Olympic Trials, Fran lost to Elliott Simons, the same rival who had denied him an NCAA title.

"It hurt at the time that I hadn't been an Olympian like Terry, but I was young enough I could have tried again in '68," he says. "I had already decided I really wanted to coach, though."

Jim McCann went another direction. A state champion wrestler in high school who earned a scholarship to the University of Oklahoma, he opted for the U.S. Marines after his freshman season. "I don't know, maybe the pressures of trying to follow his brothers made him decide to go his own way," Fran says.

Fran knows his kid brother was more of a hero in Vietnam than he ever would have been on a wrestling mat. "He was the one who always took the point when a patrol needed a volunteer. He saw a lot of action and we were starting to count down the days he was to be home."

But a mortar attack near Khe Sanh claimed the life of Jim McCann, only 20 years old. "I can remember the day we got the news as if it was yesterday," Fran says.

"Rick Meis, one of Jim's boyhood friends who married our sister Sheila, wanted the flag on Jim's casket," Fran recalls. "Rick is a four-star naval admiral and still has the flag. Just last month at Stephanie's wedding, he, Terry and I talked a lot about Jim."

They also can't help remembering the day he was buried. "Terry's brother-in-law was a Chicago police officer and suggested that they watch our house—just in case."

With the McCanns at the funeral, two officers listened to the phone ring a few times and then noticed a car driving slowly by. Not too long after, there was a rattle at the front door. Then they heard the back door swing inside.

"At that point, the officers identified themselves and the guy lowered his gun at them," Fran says. "They had to shoot and kill him right there in our kitchen."

By the time the family returned, everything was back in order except for a bullet hole in the back door. "I think we were so numb by Jim's funeral that we hardly even had any emotions to react."

Forty years ago, Fran McCann's older brother had his name forever etched among Olympic champions. Several years later, his kid brother's name was added to the Vietnam Veterans Memorial Wall.

"I am very proud of both of them."

A SECOND CHANCE
September 24, 2000

Holly Tapley, a young physician who grew up in South Bend, wasn't sure how the patient had lived.

She read over the medical reports of the 32-year-old female bicyclist who was hit by a car: A bruise in front of the brain . . . two breaks of the right lower leg that required some bone removal and a rod inserted . . . three breaks in the back . . . five breaks in the jaw . . . loss of five front teeth and the bone holding them in . . . left lung partially deflated . . . a bruise around the right kidney . . .

"The police say the SUV was probably traveling 40 miles an hour at impact," Holly says.

She will take their word for it. She never knew what hit her on that day three months ago when this doctor suddenly became the patient. "I do know I am lucky to be alive," she says. "So very lucky."

* * *

Holly was riding her bike early on the morning of June 28. A family practice physician in Bridgman, she was in Wheaton, Ill., that week, training to be a missionary.

Her dream for the last few years has been to dedicate her life to helping the people of Nepal with her medical talents and spiritual calling.

Despite her busy schedule, she works hard at staying in shape and has competed in triathlons and running events. So about 5:45 AM, she was already whisking down a bicycle path that crossed a road. She apparently thought she had the right of way on this unfamiliar course.

A young male driver didn't even have a chance to hit the brakes when Holly came out of nowhere. "After hitting off his windshield, I was thrown about 60 feet and then slid another 60 feet," she says.

For all practical purposes, she should have been dead. "The one nice thing about the reports filled out by the emergency people on the scene was that I was listed as a 17-to-22-year-old Jane Doe," the 32-year-old says with a smile. "I'll take that as a compliment."

* * *

Time was crucial. "I thought about that later," she admits. "Had I been in a place like Nepal or even in a rural area around here, I wouldn't have made it."

Because the people at the college did not know she was missing, she spent most of the morning unidentified as a team of doctors hovered over her. It was touch and go.

A room key from the college dorm where she was staying finally helped confirm who she was, and the call went out to her parents back in South Bend. "It was one of the longest trips you could ever make," admits Barbara Tapley of their frantic drive to Wheaton, just outside of Chicago.

Dwight Tapley, a family physician himself, drove while his wife, Barbara, read verses from the Bible.

Word of Holly's accident was spread by her four younger siblings and many friends. Prayer vigils were started at her churches—Woodfield Shores Baptist Church in Bridgman, Trinity Evangelical Free Church in South Bend and Agape Fellowship in Williamsport, Pa., where she had done her residency. "I am convinced that good luck and all those prayers are the reasons I am alive," Holly now says. "Everything went right."

* * *

It took Holly almost a week to fully regain consciousness and a month to leave the hospital. Doctors considered hers an amazing recovery.

"In fact, when they took Holly off the respirator, one of the ICU nurses gave a 'thumbs up' signal to me and said, 'This is so cool!'" Barbara Tapley recalls.

Holly quit using her crutches a few weeks ago and may be able to get rid of her neck brace in a couple of weeks. On Oct. 12, she will get her new teeth, too.

She even bought another bike and hooked it up to a trainer, riding it in the basement of her parents' home in southwestern St. Joseph County. "I might as well have had two heads when I limped into the bike shop with my crutches and neck brace and told them I wanted to buy a bike," she laughs.

She puts in the miles and puts on the smiles.

"There is a little pain still, but how can I whine about anything when nothing has gone wrong during my recovery," she says. "I really don't feel traumatized, partly because I have so much to be thankful for."

She seems to worry more about the state of mind of the young man who hit her than her own.

* * *

Ever since Holly went to high school at Niles First Assembly of God, she knew she wanted to help people. She earned her nursing degree at IUSB, worked a year as an ICU nurse at Saint Joseph's Regional Medical Center and then decided to follow in her father's footsteps and get her medical degree at Indiana University.

She already has done two different rotations in Nepal—one while still in medical school and the other as a resident doctor in Pennsylvania. "Such a beautiful country and such poverty," she says. "They need doctors so badly."

She still plans on being one of them—dedicating her life to the people of Nepal both as a physician and a missionary. Bibles and bandages.

"I was supposed to go over there in about a year," she says. "Now, it may be more like a year and a half."

In the meantime, she concentrates on making her full recovery and then returning to her position at Southwestern Medical Clinic in Bridgman at the beginning of the year.

"I really think what happened to me and keeping on top of what I went through might make me a better doctor."

* * *

While in Nepal, Holly hopes someday to climb Mount Everest and be high up in the clouds. Yet she feels she has already been closer to heaven than that just three months ago.

"It wasn't my time," she says.

She gets a second chance at life. With her help, so will others.

NO MUSIC MAN
February 27, 2001

Chickens—two fuzzy, little chicks to be exact—led Cyril Cole to Madison School, a P-H-M outpost amidst the farms and fertile land of southeastern St. Joseph County.

He is in his 28th year as principal of this school with its bucolic setting and very own nature trail. Although you might sometimes catch a whiff of hogs down the road, there seems to be a smell of sweet success inside.

But back to the chicks. "I started teaching a school district outside Detroit after I graduated from Bethel College," Cole recalls. "We had hatched chicks in my room for a science project and I brought them home one weekend to show our first son, Matthew."

He was out in their apartment's lawn with the chicks when the landlord marched over and said they were evicted for having animals. "I said to myself, 'You know something? We are out of here totally.'"

So he picked up the phone and called Fern Hunsberger, principal of Moran School in the P-H-M district. "I had done my student teaching there and so I asked Fern if she had any teaching openings. She said, 'You're hired.'"

He spent three years at Moran and then moved on to Madison as its principal. That was in 1973. He has been there ever since.

"I am a bit of a dinosaur," admits the 54-year-old Cole, who knows the trend is for administrators to move around. "Critics may point out my feet are in cement, but I think there is something to say about continuity. Consistency is a welcome thing to most teachers and I feel that part of my job is protecting my staff from changes that aren't going to be sustained.

"And yes, I have had opportunities to move within the school system and to move outside," he adds. "There have been times I have thought about it, but I never have thought about it long and hard."

The truth is he loves where he is.

And the students . . . the staff . . . and the community seem to love him, too. "He is the greatest," says Patty Boner, the office assistant whose two children attended Madison. "I don't know what we would do without him."

Cole has assured that Madison is a place of pride, as 20 volunteer parents help turn the hallways into a showcase for students' creations, along with countless snapshots of the kids enjoying various school activities.

"I take the pictures at our different events and make doubles for the kids," Cole says.

He has captured their smiling

faces at the PTA-sponsored family swims and family skates and family read-ins . . . and at a recent ski trip that attracted 75 of the 225 Madison students . . . . and at the pancake and sausage breakfast the fifth graders throw for the staff after making their own maple syrup . . . and as the kids practice exiting windows while volunteer firefighters supervise.

Great pictures. Great learning experiences.

If he looks at them for long, Cole admits he gets a lump in his throat.

"Cyril not only is concerned about the kids being good students but also good citizens," says school secretary Elaine Truex, whose four children all went through Madison. "Everyone thinks so much of him."

Part of that is because he has taken the time to understand the Madison Township community and get the lay of the land. "When we send a note home that little Johnny hasn't been very good, we don't get many excuses back," Cole says. "Our parents are very supportive and they will always support you as long as you make sense.

"But I'll tell you, the 'Music Man' wouldn't stand a chance out here," he says with a smile. "You are not going to sell a bill of goods out in Madison Township."

That's what some of the folks thought they might get when P-H-M officials decided to basically tear down the old school in 1986 and build a new one. "Some families thought they were going to get short-changed," Cole recalls.

"There is an awful lot of pride out here."

Cole helped soothe some feelings while Penn superintendent Dean Speicher made good on his word of a top-notch facility. The only part of the old school that is left is the gym that looks right out of the movie *Hoosiers*.

Cole remembers walking into that gym and marveling at it way back when he was a baseball player for Mishawaka High School coach George Wilson. He grew up a city boy who earned his money for college as a meat cutter. "I guess it still comes in handy when we buy a bunch of chicken for 99 cents a pound," he says.

He and his wife Judi, the principal at St. Jude's School in South Bend, live in Granger. Although the Madison Township Lions Club thought enough of him to make him an honorary member, he is not a neighbor.

"I enjoy a little distance when my work day is done," says Cole, the father of two grown sons. "I want to be able to mow my yard in my raggedly clothes if I want. And, really, I like my half hour drive to school in the morning. It allows me to get some of my thinking done."

That drive comes very, very early—so early in fact that Cole isn't comfortable letting people know what time he does get to school. But suffice it to say that if he leaves at 5 PM, he has been there for 13 hours. One of the reasons is because he also is Madison's physical education teacher. That is a three-day work week in itself.

"I was both the principal and p.e. teacher for several years until the school grew a little and they decided to make me just a principal," he says. "But then a few years ago, we were going to lose a teacher due to a cutback. I volunteered to go back into the gym so that didn't have to happen."

Although the gym duties greatly add to his work week, he likes the opportunity to put on his tennis shoes and exercise with the students. "I can blow off some steam and have a chance to connect with the kids a little more. When a parent questions if little Freddie has really been that much of a problem for a teacher, I can say that Freddie hasn't always been the best for me, either."

Exercise is important to Cole. He has lost two sisters to cancer and a brother had a stroke when he was 26. "I always think you should practice what you preach," he says. "In my case, it is crucial."

Just last week, the Madison gym was a maze of playground equipment and toys—set up to demonstrate how blood flows through the heart. Cole helped his students through the course as they both learned and laughed on their "heart-felt" trip.

He tries to make sure their trip through Madison—from kindergarten through fifth grade—is just as smooth.

Madison kids don't forget their grade school principal. Nor does he forget them. "When I read that one of our former students has done well and made the paper, I try to send him or her the clipping, just so they know they may be gone but not forgotten."

On one of the last days of school, Cole puts on a slide show set to music. Pictures taken throughout the year are shown. "It gets to you a little when you see a couple of kids arm-in-arm. and enjoying themselves."

It is dark in the gym as he clicks from picture to picture. It is a time of reflection and of marking another passage.

Cyril Cole smiles. "I usually have enough time to wipe away the tears before the lights come back on."

ALWAYS ON CALL
March 25, 2001

When South Bend physician Hansel Foley recently won $173,000 on *Hoosier Millionaire*, it was a pretty good bet he wouldn't be using any of that money for some fancy vacation.

"The last time my wife, Peggy, and I went on a vacation, the youngest of our four boys was 3," the 70-year-old Foley says. "He is 27 now."

He smiles. "If you want to know the truth, I have never even been west of Chicago in my life."

The reason? "I just love my work and don't want to be away from it," Foley admits. "Heck, I don't even like long weekends. When I went down to Indianapolis for the *Hoosier Millionaire* show, I had to take my pager off my shirt and stick it in my pocket. I am always on call."

He has been working that way in his own family medicine practice for 44 years—since coming to South Bend via the Indiana University Medical School in 1957. For the last 40 years, he also has served as the physician of St. Joseph County, meaning regular trips to the jail and Portage Manor. He also is assistant director of Memorial Hospital's medical education program.

"I don't want people to think I am over-extended, though," he says. "I don't belong to a country club, I don't play golf. About the only hobby I have is eating.

Going out and eating and talking. That's my fun. That's why I'm fat."

He does indeed cut a wide path at 300-plus pounds. And he is a jolly sort, too, although he does admit he has had to withstand the line of "Do you have a sister named Gretel?" more than 60,000 times.

"That's what happens when your first name is Hansel," he says. "But the upside is that I don't get other people's mail by mistake."

Foley grew up in the tiny town of Preble, about 20 miles south of Fort Wayne. "My dad was a teacher and my parents ran a little general store," he says. "We lived above it and if I had fallen through my bedroom floor, I would have landed in the meat case. We sold everything from ice cream to gasoline.

"And I learned to play a pretty good game of checkers by being around the store."

He also learned that he liked being around people. "So when I was down at I.U. and majoring in microbiology, I found myself in the lab one Saturday listening to the rest of the campus over at the football game. I asked myself, 'What am I doing here?' I liked people too much."

So he changed over to pre-med and the rest is history—a history that is still turning pages.

"My 94-year-old mother tells me never to retire. She is the reason why I am alive—her good genes. I have always been big. I played football at Decatur High School at 275 pounds. At a class reunion, there is no mistaking who I am."

He is a legend at the jail and Sheriff Rick Seniff is naming the medical facility at the new jail after Foley. "When I examine the prisoners, I try not to know who they are or what they have done," he admits. "If you are prejudiced against them for their crimes, your care may be skewed."

He remembers several years ago when an illiterate, little man from Gary needed a hernia repaired while he was in the St. Joe County Jail. "I arranged so he could have the operation. He later wanted to thank me and he said that it was the first time anyone really acknowledged the pain he had.

"Then he said he would like to give me a present but admitted he only had this one thing to give—probably his prized possession. He handed me his mug shot of John Dillinger. It was almost enough to make my cry."

When Foley gives away his own gifts, they are usually pizzas. "I guess that's my trademark," he says. "I have an account over at Rocco's and I give them out by writing it down on a prescription sheet."

He likes his pizzas, too. He likes people even better.

"I can think of nothing better than being with my patients," he says. "I even schedule appointments on Sundays. I don't believe in signing off. I am on call what they now refer to as 24-7, which I know is unfair to my wife."

He will continue to doctor as long as he can, though. "My knees are worn out and the orthopods are waiting in line to give me some new ones but I still rarely miss a day."

Or a meal.

Or a chance at a lottery ticket. "I plan on putting my winnings in a trust for my three grandkids," he says. "And yes, I'll continue to buy tickets."

Hansel Foley, after all, considers himself a lucky man.

TIME FOR DAD
April 8, 2001

My friend, Paul V. Boehm, cuts his father's sloppy joe sandwich in half, carves the lemon bar into neat, little squares and then resumes with the sports section.

"Your White Sox won yesterday, Dad," he says before reading the first few paragraphs of the story almost at a shout.

Paul has scooted his chair close to his dad so he can lean forward and recreate yesterday's sports highlights loud enough for his father, Paul F. Boehm, to hear.

Mr. Boehm is 90 now with limited hearing and eyesight. He is also relegated to a wheelchair after suffering through a series of strokes four years ago—about the same time his wife, Elinor, died.

"Dad still likes to keep up with the sports news," says the younger Paul while joining his father for lunch at South Bend's Holy Cross Care and Rehabilitation Center.

Many of you will remember Paul F. Boehm. He was South Bend's first recreation director before retiring in 1973 after almost 20 years in that position. Before that, he was a teacher and coach in the public schools for even longer.

He touched so many young people's lives. He was one of those community pillars and a member of the South Bend Hall of Fame. He even has a city park named after him.

A better man you can not find.

And now, he tries to live his life with as much dignity as he can while his body betrays him.

"It's really tough to watch a parent get old like this," says the younger Paul, who is 57 himself.

But every day during the work week, Paul leaves his job with the South Bend park department after 11 so he can have lunch with his dad.

"It has been pretty much our routine for the last four years," he says.

Paul borrows the sports section from the front desk when he walks in to Holy Cross, helps his dad to the bathroom and then pushes him and his wheelchair down to the cafeteria for his 11:20 meal. He cuts up his father's meal and then reads out the sports section to his dad—and to everyone else who wants to listen from the nearby tables.

"The three of us kids just think this is the thing to do," Paul admits. "Dad does know when we miss."

Those misses are rare. Paul's siblings—his older brother, Mike Boehm, and his younger sister, Anne Choinacky—alternate at supper during the week and also for the Sunday meals. The three of them then alternate for the Saturday meals.

That means their dad has company almost every lunch

60

and supper. "You are so blessed," says an elderly woman as the younger Paul pushes his father on a lap around the facility after lunch.

Mr. Boehm can't make out her words but he would agree.

"I have a great family," he later says.

"Actually, we feel like we have been the lucky ones," says Mike Boehm, a financial planner. "I'm sure it can be a lonely existence for Dad after he lost his lifelong partner—our mom—four years ago. So I think all three of us feel it is a small, small gesture on our part to be with him for his meals. It's our way of saying thanks for all that he has done for us and to let him know that we love him."

Anne Choinacky and her husband, Jim, had even thought about building an addition onto their house for her dad, but more healthcare was needed than they could provide.

"So it's the least we can do to spend meals with him," says Anne, an office helper at Holy Cross School.

Although most are now out of the area, Mr. Boehm's nine grandkids also stop and see him when they can and Judy Boehm, his former daughter-in-law, still often celebrates Mass with him on Sundays.

On his walls in his room are countless pictures of his family. Although he can no longer see them very well, he knows they are there—keeping him company.

Just like his kids do at mealtime.

"I think we have gotten a lot closer after what we see in each other while we try to help Dad," Mike says. "Who knows, maybe Dad would like a break from us, but we won't give it to him."

Their dad wouldn't wish away any of their visits for the world.

On this day, Paul has brought his father a new headset for his room's television. "Dad used to turn up the TV so he could hear it, which meant that the rest of northern Indiana could here it too."

Paul F. Boehm's hearing may be poor but his kids' message comes through loud and clear every day.

He knows they love him very much.

"See you tomorrow, Dad," his son Paul says as he heads back to work.

"Tomorrow, son," Mr. Boehm replies.

A promise always kept.

PLAYERS

February 9, 1992
WANTING A CHANCE

It has become his habit.

When Notre Dame's basketball team goes through its pregame warm-ups at home, Monty Williams suits up for his own game.

When his former Irish teammates are introduced, he usually is walking over to the Rockne Memorial gym, basketball under his arm, ready to do battle with his own invisible foes.

Monty Williams takes the pass from Bennett and takes three quick dribbles...

Williams' old teammates—LaPhonso Ellis, Elmer Bennett, Keith Tower and Daimon Sweet—play no harder than he does during the next few hours. He shoots and dribbles and runs until he is gasping for breath.

But while the Irish play in front of thousands at the Joyce ACC, the crowd noise for Williams is only in his mind.

His gym is nearly empty. So, sometimes, is the feeling he has when he walks back to his dorm room before turning on the television to see if the Irish won or lost.

"Sometimes I feel like crying, even though I don't believe in crying," he said. "There isn't a day when I don't think what it would be like playing basketball for Notre Dame again."

In all likelihood, he never will. After a respectable freshman season in which in started 18 games and averaged almost eight points a game, he was diagnosed as having hypertrophic cardiomyopathy, a condition that involves a thickened muscle between chambers of the heart.

After consulting experts in the field, Notre Dame doctors, administrators and coach Digger Phelps decided it was in the best interests of Williams and the university that he not play.

A year and a half later and midway through Williams' junior year, they still feel that way.

"It was a very tough call," said Dr. Stephen Simons, one of the Notre Dame staff physicians. "I know Monty feels normal and still thinks he should play. But the painful reality is that his heart measurements are outside the normal range."

Minimally, admitted Simons, but still outside the normal range.

"We don't know what his

chances of dying are if he plays basketball," Simons continued. "We do know that his chances are increased if he does play."

But he does play.

Almost everyday.

...he fakes a pass to the Phonz...

"From time to time, I even play with some of my old teammates," Williams said. "They didn't have practice the other day, so Elmer [Bennett] came over and played five-on-five with us. I guarded him because I was the only one who could check him."

Simons wishes he could check Williams—at least some of his activities. "I know it must be frustrating for Monty. We've had numerous discussions about his situation and we don't feel it is necessary for him to stop exercising entirely."

But full-court basketball isn't one of the exercises he endorses.

That doesn't stop Williams, though. "I love the game so much that if I die, a basketball court seems the best place."

If that ever happens, it apparently won't be at the Joyce ACC. Notre Dame officials don't want Williams to put himself in that position in an Irish uniform. They remember how Loyola Marymount shouldered the blame when Hank Gathers collapsed during a game two years ago and died.

"I was told once that if Hank Gathers hadn't died, I'd probably still be playing," said Williams. Simons disputes that. "He has

been told, though, that we don't want anything happening to him like it did to Hank Gathers."

Williams said Gathers had a different kind of heart condition.

Simons agrees, but added, "70 percent of the cases that are diagnosed are during autopsies."

Even so, Williams won't be swayed from the court—holding onto the slim hope that his condition will go away or that an NBA team will take a chance on him. "I've had other schools contact me about transferring but right now, my plan is to stay at Notre Dame and graduate next year," he said.

A telecommunications major with a 2.8 grade-point average, he still has his athletic scholarship and is grateful for that. "I don't have any bad feelings toward anybody at Notre Dame because they have given me a chance to get an education and that's important."

Playing basketball seems more important to him, though. Since his freshman year, he has grown more than two inches to 6-foot-8½-inches and weighs 218 pounds. "When I see that Notre Dame has been beaten by two points to a team like Detroit, I can't help but think that I could have made the difference."

...head-fakes Grant Hill of Duke...

As a sophomore last season, he sat on the bench and helped out during practices. When Phelps retired and John MacLeod came in, Williams thought it was a good time to break off his contact with the team.

"John MacLeod is a nice man, so it doesn't have anything to do with him," he said. "I think he was told though, to avoid any discussion with me about playing."

Joyce Williams, his mother back in Forest Heights, Md., worries about her son and talks to him often. She has given up trying to talk him out of basketball. She concentrates now on making sure he works hard for his degree.

"I know it's tough for Monty to understand because he's had a basketball in his hands since he was five," she said. "He comes home and because he's so tall, people ask him if he plays basketball. I see what his face looks like then. It's hard for him to talk about it."

"I just feel that God is testing me, giving me a lesson," said her son. "In some ways, it has helped me put some things in perspective. And God willing, I'll play again."

. . . and glides to the basket for the score. Two more for Monty Williams.

Monty Williams keeps dreaming.

Dreams sometimes come true. And sometimes, he knows, nightmares do too.

Note: Monty Williams was able to pass more refined testing the following summer and led the Irish in scoring the next two seasons.

November 22, 1992
HIGH SCHOOL HERO

Bo Hundt, a football cradled in one arm and his little sister tucked under the other, walked slowly away from Bremen's Don Bunge Field.

He had just played in his last high school football game.

The helmet he still wore hid a lot of things, including youthful tears over the big game lost.

One of the best prep football players in the state, one of the better all-around athletes in the nation, he and his Bremen teammates had fallen one game short of their goal for a state championship appearance.

On Friday night, visiting Sheridan's hard-nosed defense highlighted a 14-6 victory by surrounding Bo like a war party anytime there was even a hint that he was heading in the ball's direction.

And so Hundt made his slow trip back to the dressing room in his No. 21 jersey for the last time.

People stepped aside to let him pass. Some gave him a gentle clap on the back. Most stayed painfully silent, knowing words would do no good.

Part of a disappointed crowd leaving the stadium even waited a few moments on the walkway between the field and the high school as Bo's mom came through them to hug her son.

It was the end of an era.

On this night the high school hero who could do no wrong, could not do enough.

His high school career is one for the history books. He rushed for almost 6,000 yards and scored 118 touchdowns while rarely coming off the field as Bremen's tailback, free safety, kicker, punter and returner.

If that isn't enough, he has been a solid basketball player for Bremen and just may be better at baseball than football.

"He's by far the best athlete we've had here in my 30 years in the school system," Bremen athletic director Frank DeSantis said. "And one of the most modest too, never trying to draw attention to himself."

"He will be missed greatly," Bremen football coach Marty Huber added.

Everybody in town calls him Bo—a tidy, little name that packs such a punch.

Unfortunately for Bremen, Sheridan knew all too well who Bo is, too.

"We usually had a couple of people assigned to just him," Sheridan coach Bud Wright said. "We knew what he could do if we gave him the chance."

But on Friday night, he was held to just 20 yards on 15 carries—unheard of numbers during his star-studded career. He was bottled up and gang tackled.

"I think maybe the only time I

saw daylight all night was when I got turned backwards on a play," he later admitted, paying tribute to the Sheridan defense.

In fact, the only significant gain of the night for Bremen was when Sheridan overplayed Bo on a reverse that went for 20 yards and set up the Lions' lone touchdown.

But as frustrated as he could have been on offense, he was amazing in some of the other facets of the game.

The hardest hits on defense were delivered by Bo.

The best downfield block was delivered by Bo.

When the ball was loose on a Sheridan fumble, it was Bo who came up with it.

When the ball was up in the air on the last play of the first half and Sheridan deep in Bremen territory, it was Bo who brought it down over the out-of-bounds line.

And when a bad snap from punt formation bounced in front of him, he picked it up, split two on-rushing defenders and kicked it on the run. It traveled some 40 yards and went out of bounds on the Sheridan one-foot line.

Amazing stuff.

Bremen fans are used to it from this 17-year-old youngster who has captured their hearts and drawn attention from such college football powers as Michigan and Florida.

"It just doesn't seem like the season should be over," Bo said after the game, humble in defeat. "I don't really know what to say or do."

He said all the right things anyway. "We sure wanted to go to the state again, but I'm real proud of what we've done.

"I got to play for a great coach and with a great team and in front of great fans."

It is over now.

So Bo Hundt will catch his breath and let his wounds heal a little.

But not for too long—not long at all. Basketball practice is Monday.

September 23, 1994
IT WAS A SNAP

Nifty view.

Nasty job.

Or so it would seem.

About the only time a long-snapping football center gets a piece of the spotlight is when he dribbles the ball back to the punter or air-vacs it into the second row of the end-zone seats.

That snap may only be 15 yards, but try marking a punter between your legs while really big people get ready to knock you over. Sometimes, the punter must look like he's standing in another time zone.

The long snap is an art, with the reward for those who master it being anonymity.

Nobody mastered that art better than Ed Sullivan, a longtime Mishawaka resident and a captain and center on the 1957 Notre Dame team.

How good was he at this thankless job? Well, being modest, Sullivan wasn't sure he should tell.

"Oh, OK," he said after some prodding. "I used to ask the punter which eye he wanted it on. He would say right or left and I'd say, 'I'm not talking about your eyes, but the eyes on your pants.' Back then, we would lace up our pants through the eyes and one of them would be my target."

He got a lot of practice hiking the long ball during the 1956 season. The Irish were 2-8 that season, even with Paul Hornung on the team. "Paul did everything," Sullivan said. "He ran, passed, tackled, kicked and, yes, punted, too."

Enough on his mind, Hornung didn't have to worry about getting the center snap. Sullivan saw to that.

Hornung went on to win the Heisman Trophy that year. Sullivan cashed in on his talents several years later at Cedar Point Amusement Park in Sandusky, Ohio.

"My daughters Kelly and Trish, who were probably 13 and nine at the time, wanted me to win them a prize," he said. "So I tried to knock over the milk bottles and shoot the baskets and just about everything else."

Like most of the rest of us, Sullivan came up empty.

"As the day progressed, I was getting desperate and my daughters were losing a little faith in me," he admitted. "But just as it was getting dark and we were getting ready to leave, we came across this football toss where you put the ball through a little hole in the wall."

He blew a couple of bucks on that, too.

"I was ready to admit defeat and was walking away when I got this idea," Sullivan said. "I asked the guy working at the booth if it mattered how I threw the ball.

He said he didn't care. So I walked about 15 yards away and had my two boys—Eddie and Michael—keep people from walking in front of me.

"Then I got down in my center's stance and . . ."

Plunk! He missed his first one.

His girls groaned. His wife, Rose, grimaced.

Passersby stopped and giggled at this intense guy bent down in the middle of the boardwalk.

But then . . .

Zip, zip, zip!

He couldn't miss.

Three went through the hole. Then four, five, six, seven.

The crowd cheered, his girls squealed and the man running the booth handed him two large stuffed elephants while whispering, "That's enough. How about giving me a break and beating it?"

Hornung gets the Heisman.

Sullivan gets two stuffed elephants.

But then a couple of smiles from two pretty little girls came with the elephants and Sullivan wouldn't trade that memory for any award.

So has he made the county-fair circuit, showing off his talents?

"I'll tell you, I haven't snapped a ball in a long time," the 59-year-old Sullivan said. "And to be perfectly honest, I'm not even sure I could bend down that far anymore."

At a certain age, that apparently gets to be an art, too.

November 6, 1994
FOLLOWING HER SISTER

Katie Beeler couldn't find her swim goggles anywhere. Not in her gym bag, not in her closet, not under her bed.

She finally asked for help. "I've lost my goggles, Mom. Do you know where any are?"

Kathy Beeler knew exactly where a pair was. A special pair. A pair that had not been used in almost three years.

They belonged to her daughter, Meghan. She told Katie how she had stored them away with some of Meghan's other swimming equipment after Meghan had died in the Notre Dame bus crash.

Both paused for a second.

Then Katie asked, "Mom, can I use them?"

Her mom nodded.

It felt right that Katie should wear Meghan's goggles. It felt good that Katie could ask. It felt like both Kathy and Katie Beeler had taken another step.

So last week in the Mishawaka swimming sectional, there was 14-year-old Katie Beeler, a freshman at St. Joseph's High, wearing her sister's goggles and swimming some of the best races of her life. She won the 200 individual medley in record time and was just touched out by Clay's Sarah Holke in the 100 butterfly.

"Many people commented this season that Katie looks just like Meg when she swims," Kathy Beeler said.

Maybe that was part of the reason there weren't too many dry eyes around the Beelers during last Saturday's races.

It's been a long battle back for Katie and her family. And swimming, as much as anything, has helped in the healing.

Meghan Beeler, the oldest of Gordon and Kathy Beeler's five children, would have been a senior at Notre Dame this year. She and her teammate, Colleen Hipp, died in the early morning hours of Jan. 24, 1992, when their team bus overturned on a snow-covered Toll Road just a few miles from the South Bend exit.

"We've learned that there are two things you can do when something like this happens to you," Kathy Beeler said. "You can either give up or you can try to turn things around in your life. Every day can be a struggle and the verdict is still out, but what Katie did last week is the kind of positives you strive for."

It wasn't that long ago when Katie and her sister Molly, a high school junior at Bolles Academy in Jacksonville, Fla., thought about giving up swimming. In some ways, they probably already had.

The summer after their sister's death, they both swam poorly. "What made it even worse was that they both obviously felt so miserable about themselves," their mom said.

At that point, Gordon Beeler knew something had to be done. His family was suffering. They needed a change and he had both the finances and the fortitude to make it happen. So before the next school year started, he moved his family to Jacksonville, where his son John already was attending Bolles.

They returned to their South Bend home during the summer of 1993 and it was obvious that some scars weren't healed. "Everytime I saw a 'United Limo' bus . . ." Kathy Beeler started.

Katie couldn't even force herself to practice at the Notre Dame pool with her Michiana Marlins teammates. Molly tried, but one morning, Marlins coach Kandis (Perry) Durocher had to call Kathy to pick up Molly. "She was trembling and just very upset," Kathy Beeler said.

So the Beelers returned to Jacksonville for the 1993-94 school year and picked up the pieces once again. They planned on staying there. The kids were doing well in school and the swimming—maybe the best measuring stick for how the girls were coping—had improved tremendously.

Katie, the most gifted of the Beelers in the pool, was starting to swim like her old self. Earlier in her career, she had been featured in *Sports Illustrated*'s "Faces in the Crowd," for her five state championships in the 10-and-under competition. That was

when Meghan had taken one look at the magazine and said, "Wooo, we have a celebrity in the house now." Everybody laughed, including Katie.

Katie's big sister knew how to keep things in perspective.

It was Katie, really, who broached the subject about returning to South Bend for her freshman year in high school. "I think Katie missed South Bend the most," Kathy Beeler said. "She wanted to follow in Meghan's footsteps and go to St. Joe."

They talked as a family this past summer and made the decision to return to their hometown. "Really, Katie's desire to swim at St. Joe was one of the main reasons," Gordon Beeler said.

All of the Beeler kids handled the move in their own way.

Molly tried St. Joe for a week and decided she would be happier back at Bolles Academy in Jacksonville. And so she returned to Florida for her junior year.

John is a freshman at Notre Dame, where he always wanted to go, but he has passed on swimming for the Irish, even though he was good enough to have scholarship offers at other Division I schools.

Little 9-year-old Colleen is at Corpus Christi School. During a school assignment, her class was asked, "If there was anything that you could do for a day, what would it be?" She said she would like to spend that day with her sister Meg.

And then there is Katie, swimming well enough to be breaking sectional and pool records and now seeing it all happen through her sister's goggles. "When something like that happens, it can give you goose bumps," Gordon Beeler said.

And a hope that good things will continue to happen.

Later this month, Mishawaka athletic director John Danaher will be updating the swimming records on the wall in the pool area. Katie Beeler's name and her time in the 200 individual medley will be added to the list.

"I can't wait to see that," Kathy Beeler said.

There is more than one reason. Her daughter Katie's name and new mark will go just above the name of the pool and sectional record-holder in the 50 free.

That name is Meghan Beeler.

December 4, 1994
ARA KEEPS BATTLING

Ara Parseghian has put back on his game face.

The Notre Dame legend says he feels like a newly-hired coach poised to take over a program.

And although he has been slowed by four hip replacement operations and a knee that needs the same, there still is a purpose in his stride.

At 71 years old, Ara Parseghian is facing his toughest challenge.

He is trying to save his grandkids.

In September of this year, seven-year-old Michael, six-year-old Marcia and three-year-old Christa—the children of Ara and Katie Parseghian's son Mike—were diagnosed with Niemann Pick Disease Type C.

NPC usually affects children of school age. The long-term prognosis for the children is not promising unless the pace of medical research is rapidly advanced.

"There has been nothing in my life that has hit me so hard as when I found out about this," Ara said.

He grieved. He cried. He wondered why life could be so cruel. "It was just a terrible period," he said. "It lasted for about a month. During that time, I couldn't even talk about it.

"It was my grandkids—little children. I was devastated."

Then Ara did what you would expect from an old warrior. He looked at himself in the mirror and said that it was time to fight back.

"I know competitive athletics gets criticized for a lot of things these days," said the man who posted a 170-58-6 record during his 24 years as a head football coach. "But you certainly can learn some of life's lessons from competition—like not giving up and like meeting the challenge."

So, of course, Ara wiped away the tears and rolled up his sleeves.

With the help of his son Mike, an orthopedic surgeon in Tucson, Ariz., he has researched the disease and contacted people in the field of genetics. Then he started the Ara Parseghian Medical Research Foundation, getting several prominent researchers to be on its advisory board.

His commitment has given strength and name recognition to the cause. He tries to educate others about the disease that he couldn't even bear to mention just two months ago.

From his winter home in Marco Island, Fla., he'll soon be flying to Chicago to do a public service spot about NPC. He'll be off to Washington, D.C., to talk to legislators about funding. But his most important trip will be when he and Katie fly to Arizona, spending Christmas with son Mike, daughter-in-law Cindy and their four grandchildren. Ten-year-old Ara is not afflicted with NPC.

"Mike and Cindy are two of the greatest parents you'll ever find," Ara said. "Everybody is trying to stay positive. We've got a chance to beat this thing. This is doable."

This is not just false hope on a loving grandfather's part. "The advancement of medical research in cholesterol metabolism and genetics has given us a chance for a cure," Ara said. "We know which chromosome has the defective gene. Researchers are now close to isolating the gene."

Ara still can't hide the emotion in his voice. "Ten years ago, we wouldn't have had a chance. Now, we do. If we can just get enough funding to do the needed research. It was put to me like this: It might take one researcher 10 years to find a cure or 10 researchers one year to find one. That's one of the reasons I've set up the foundation.

"People know about diseases that affect the heart and diseases like cancer, but when they hear something called Niemann Pick Disease—or similar storage diseases—they aren't sure what it means. Right now, it means a grave prognosis."

Ara and his family will take on the odds. He will be tireless.

He works out in the pool 30 to 50 minutes a day so he will be in better shape to meet a grueling schedule.

He is 71. A new battle rages.

"You're going along in life and, suddenly, you find yourself and your family thrust in this kind of situation," Ara said. "All you can do at that point is ask yourself what you are going to do about it."

If you are Ara Parseghian, you fight back with all your might.

God be with him.

July 21, 1995
SWIMMING THE CHANNEL

P.H. Mullen hoisted a pint with some Englishmen Thursday night.

Lord knows he drank enough of their water earlier in the day.

In the 10th fastest time ever recorded, the 26-year-old South Bend native swam the English Channel while battling jellyfish, nausea and the frigid Atlantic waters along the way.

"I had always pictured myself thrusting my hands into the air and jumping for joy when I got to France," Mullen said by telephone last night. "But by the time I got out of the water, I couldn't even lift my arms."

Part of that was from fatigue and part was from the welts left behind by the jellyfish.

It was nonetheless a moment and milestone to savor, a memory that will never need to be embellished.

"I guess I didn't have that spontaneous rush that a defensive back gets when he runs back an interception for a touchdown," Mullen said. "I sort of took a business-as-usual approach. Mission accomplished."

It was quite a day, though, and a tremendous accomplishment—the first channel crossing by any South Bend area swimmer.

Escorted by two English fishermen brothers in their trawler, Mullen couldn't have asked for a better support crew. "These guys have been doing this for 26 years. Even so, I still gave them six pages of instructions—everything from how to work my VCR camera to how to give me CPR if I needed it."

For the first four hours, it was smooth swimming. In fact, his crew told him that he was only 30 meters behind the record pace of seven hours, 17 minutes.

But then about 10 minutes later, he got the jolt—several jolts, for that matter—of his life. He found himself in the middle of a shoal of jellyfish, stretching for some 200 yards.

"It seemed like every part of my body in the water was stung," he said. "It was like a Miami street gang working me over with baseball bats."

Those attacks took their toll. Besides the welts, Mullen suffered an allergic reaction, became light-headed and got the heaves.

"Oh, I was crying—I was a baby," he said of his jellyfish encounter. "I wanted out, I wanted my wife, I wanted my parents."

But he kept on going. "Really, there wasn't any question about that," he admitted. "I had adopted the simple mantra that I wasn't going to stop until I was finished.

"But after the jellyfish, fear also became a motivating factor."

Without knowing it, he swam dangerously close to other shoals of the stingy stuff. His crew kept quiet, figuring what he didn't know wouldn't hurt him.

Minutes felt like hours. Arms felt like anvils.

Finally, the fishermen told him that the French coast was in sight. He didn't want to look. He knew the channel tide could send a swimmer in strange directions.

But after eight hours, 26 minutes, former South Bend Adams swimmer P.H. Mullen touched French soil. He had accomplished his goal in the 10th fastest time ever.

"There were a few people up on shore watching and my crew was pretty excited, but that's about it," he said. "I was in France all of five minutes before I got on the boat and headed back to England."

He had done what he had set out to accomplish. He couldn't help but feel both proud and yet humble, too, as the return trip revealed the enormity of his feat and the good graces granted by Mother Nature.

"I'll probably buy my boatmen a beer," he said Thursday night before walking gingerly out of his Dover hotel.

With his new bride in San Francisco and his family in South Bend, he hopes to be stateside soon.

"The darn airlines messed up my flight," he said. "I'm not sure when I'll be back."

He does know his return won't be by sea.

December 20, 1995
DIGGER MISSES AGAIN

Digger Phelps broke down and cried.

After all, it was 25 years ago when he first started putting his signature on this series.

Close games, great games.

His game.

"This game has been very important to me throughout the years," the former Notre Dame coach said. "I'm just not sure what the future holds. I'd like to stay a part of it if I can."

You think he's talking about the UCLA-Notre Dame series, don't you?

Naaa, that's over after tonight.

What brought more than one tear to Digger's eyes was not the recently announced breakup of that college basketball series but his own matchup with the Special Olympics team at the annual Logan Christmas party's basketball game.

For 25 years, Digger and Co.—former assistants and friends—have taken on Butch Waxman and other Logan Special Olympians.

For 25 years, Digger has never won a game.

For 25 years, Digger somehow always gets the ball stolen by Butch in the late going and that turnover usually leads to the winning basket.

For 25 years, Digger takes the last shot and misses it.

On Sunday, Butch's team rallied from a four-point deficit in the waning moments and watched with glee as Digger's potential game-tying shot before the buzzer bounced high off the rim and over the backboard.

But that miss was not what made Digger cry.

It was later in the afternoon when Logan honored the former Irish coach and the current ESPN analyst for his contributions to Logan—including his 25 years as a participant in the annual basketball game.

"I started to lose it a little when I saw the 'We Love You Digger' sign in the gym, but then when they honored me with a ceremony, I got all choked up."

How important has this game been for Digger?

"I once had to reschedule the UCLA game because it was going to fall on the same day," he said.

That should tell you something. The UCLA series, after all, gave Digger some of his great moments as a coach.

His 1974 team stopped UCLA's 88-game winning streak, his Irish once won four straight games in UCLA's Pauley Pavilion and also broke a 115-game UCLA winning streak against nonconference teams there.

"There's a lot of great memories from the UCLA series," he said. "What I miss the most is

77

going into Pauley and getting booed by the UCLA students. We had a real love-hate relationship and it was great."

But the series is over after tonight.

"That's too bad," Digger said. "But those things happen. Notre Dame probably knows how DePaul felt [when the Blue Demons were dropped from the Irish schedule]. I think everyone understands, though, that these things sometimes have to happen—with no bad feelings."

He planned to watch the game tonight at the home of his oldest daughter, Karen. "Jimmy Harrick [the UCLA coach] actually asked me to sit on the UCLA bench a while back," Digger said with a laugh.

"Yeah, could you imagine how that would go over? We're good friends, but I'm good friends with John [MacLeod], too. It's good that I just stay away."

He's never stayed away from the Logan game, though. On Saturday night, he was working the Cal-Minnesota game for ESPN in Minneapolis and was up at 5 AM Sunday morning so he could catch a flight back to South Bend to be in time for Butch and his gang.

"They're God's little angels," Digger said.

And tougher to beat than UCLA ever was.

November 17, 1996
TWICE A WINNER

Steve Hollar may be the only Indiana prep basketball player to start for two state championship schools.

In 1984, he hit a pair of free throws in the waning seconds for the Warsaw Tigers to clinch a 59-56 final game victory over Vincennes.

Then a few years later in 1951, he helped the Hickory Huskers to their last-second crown.

What?

"Not only did I get a chance to play on my hometown's championship team, but then I also got to celebrate another title some 30 years earlier," Hollar said.

Figured it out yet?

Hollar was one of the actors in *Hoosiers*, the fictional movie about the farm town of Hickory that won it all—in Hollywood fashion, of course.

Starring Gene Hackman as the coach, Barbara Hershey and Dennis Hopper, the story is based loosely on Milan's little-school miracle in the 1954 state tournament.

Hollar and a handful of other former Indiana high school standouts were picked to play the Hickory team members and to make the action scenes look authentic. All of them ended up turning in pretty good acting performances, too.

OK, if you're a true Hoosier, I'm not telling you anything you don't already know. But did you also know that the movie opened in South Bend, Warsaw and other Indiana cities 10 years ago this week?

"Ten years," Hollar repeated. "Well, sometimes it seems that long ago."

Like his dad, Hollar is now a dentist in Warsaw. Life is good back in his hometown with his wife Jennifer expecting their third child.

Yet there aren't many days that go by when he isn't remembered as Rade Butcher, a somewhat rebellious guard on the Hickory Huskers.

Warsaw has produced Rick Fox who plays for the Boston Celtics ... a former Mr. Basketball in Hollar's old running mate Jeff Grose ... and last year's Mr. Basketball, Kevin Ault. Among former Warsaw players, though, Hollar may at least be the most recognizable face.

He had a great time filming *Hoosiers*, which was created by Angelo Pizzo and David Anspaugh. They also gave us *Rudy*.

Hollar also attended a 10-year reunion of the crew and cast of *Hoosiers* last weekend in Indianapolis. "One of the highlights was sitting down with a box of popcorn and watching the movie one more time on the big screen," he said.

He was 19 when the movie was

made and playing basketball at DePauw University. He thought acting might be the way to go at the time.

"I was having a blast," Hollar said. "And I talked to Gene Hackman a number of times. But he tried to discourage us, saying a lot of people who try to make it in Hollywood end up starving."

NCAA officials, meanwhile, stuck their noses into Hollar's participation in *Hoosiers*. They wanted him to pay back all the money he made from the film since they said he had used his basketball ability to secure his part.

"But I wasn't even on an athletic scholarship at DePauw," he said. "I had an academic scholarship."

He ended up giving back a small percentage of his earnings to Orion Pictures—based on the time he was actually playing basketball in the movie. The film company gave it all back to him after his graduation . . . with interest.

Hollar still watches *Hoosiers* from time to time. "But usually it's with friends who just want to poke fun at me."

His favorite part? "When I get to punch out a player from the other team [while he hassles Hackman on the sidelines]. Until that time, my character and I were a lot alike—both sort of rebels who do it their own way. But I would have never gone that far in real life. That's when I felt I had

delved into something new . . . and was really acting."

Ten years ago.

"Since then, a whole new generation of kids have seen the movie," Hollar said. "It's fresh to them. Some of them seem a little star-struck around me."

Not his own son, four-year-old Bennett. "He was over at some friends the other day and they showed him *Hoosiers* for the first time. I was expecting a few accolades from my own boy, but it was no big deal to him. He sees himself all the time on the videos we take and doesn't yet differentiate between a movie and that."

But Steve Hollar can easily differentiate his feelings about Hickory's title and Warsaw's. After all, one was fact and one was fiction.

"It seems more people want to talk about what happened in the movie," he said. "But, really, winning a state title for Warsaw is what means the most to me."

Of course, he won't forget the other championship, either.

He won one for Hollywood and his hometown.

November 24, 1996
LOU'S LAST GAME

Notre Dame coach Lou Holtz's voice broke a little, but he forged ahead anyway like a fullback on fourth-and-short.

"I can look up at Our Lady [on the Dome] or go down to the Grotto and look up to God and say I think I left it [the Notre Dame football program] clean," he said.

As his voice wavered on him again, he repeated it. "I think I left it clean."

Then he quickly exited the interview tent on the north side of the Notre Dame Stadium just before his face melted into a sea of tears.

The Notre Dame coach had held back those tears for so long that when they finally came, they ran like rivulets down his nose.

Lou Holtz crying? Then pigs can certainly fly.

Sometimes a terror . . . often a taskmaster . . . and never one to need a tissue . . . Holtz still couldn't command his own emotions late Saturday afternoon as an extraordinary chapter in his own story—and Notre Dame's, too—came to a close.

He had just coached his last game in Notre Dame Stadium . . . in the House that Rockne Built . . . in his own personal theater for the past 11 falls.

It was his 100th win as the Irish head coach, but the 62-0 thrashing of hapless Rutgers seemed only a warm-up act to the Lou-fest that followed.

In fact, the homage began in earnest at the end of the third quarter when the entire stadium pointed at Holtz and chanted, "Lou! Lou!" while the band played the 1812 Overture.

He pretended not to notice, but his game face was in serious jeopardy.

Soon after, Holtz began mugging for some pictures on the sidelines as the other kind of mugging continued on the field.

And then the hugs and handshakes became almost as intense as the hitting that Rutgers had to take.

Oh, yes, it was a different day for the cagey, old coach who has been known to rant and rave into the final seconds of a massacre.

Lou Holtz had actually let his guard down a little.

"I think today is my favorite memory [of coaching at Notre Dame]," he would later say.

It may be the Notre Dame faithful's favorite memory of Lou Holtz as well.

After the game and in front of the student body, the Notre Dame players lifted their gold helmets in salute. Then they lifted their coach even higher.

He was held head and shoulders above his players as his voice boomed out his appreciation to the student body and Notre Dame family.

Again they chanted "Lou!" And again he successfully fought back the tears.

Maybe old soldiers are supposed to just fade away, but this old coach was exiting to a cheering stadium that looked like it was right out of a Hollywood movie.

"I will miss Notre Dame," he said. "I don't think Notre Dame will miss Lou Holtz, but I will miss Notre Dame."

Make no mistake about it, he will be missed—especially if a national championship doesn't come quickly to the next coach . . . or when a couple of losses come in the same calendar year.

He will be missed when a session begs for a clever quip and he is not there to deliver it.

He will be missed when a crowd needs firing up and the powerful voice that is somehow emitted from his puny frame is being used elsewhere.

He does have at least one, maybe two, more games to coach in the Irish colors, but no more in Notre Dame Stadium.

"I believe I will walk through the tunnel one more time by myself," he said. "I believe I will walk onto the field one more time."

He will have to hurry. Renovation on the stadium gets going full tilt again on Monday.

So when he makes that last trip, he may have a hard hat on his head, but a soft spot in his heart.

And maybe, just maybe, the Notre Dame Fight Song will be on his lips . . . and a few tears in his eyes.

If there are any left.

April 27, 1997
HIS SPIRIT'S UP

A few weeks ago, former Notre Dame fullback Marc Edwards went to see his "little brother," Johnny, in the hospital. Ten years old and Edwards' buddy in the Big Brothers Big Sisters program for the last few years, Johnny was recovering from an appendectomy.

"What's up?" Edwards asked.

Johnny could barely talk, but he had his answer ready anyway. "The sky."

Once again, Marc Edwards felt like Curly of the Three Stooges. "How come he always gets me like that?" he later said. "Without thinking, I always seem to be setting him up for that line . . . even when he's lying there in a hospital bed."

Then Edwards laughed. "When I first became Johnny's Big Brother, he would hardly say a word to me. Now I can't get him to shut up."

What's up?

Well, besides the sky, Johnny was up — and out of bed — just a few days after his appendectomy when Edwards received the Patrick John Niland Memorial Service Award as the Notre Dame Big Brother of the Year.

"He had his surgery on Monday and the banquet was Thursday, but he really wanted to be there with me when I got the award," said last year's hard-nosed captain.

But to Edwards, the real award has been just being able to have Johnny and his family as friends. "I mean come on, it's not like this is a hassle what I do with Johnny," he admitted. "Really, it's a nice switch for me to be able to spend time with him and be a little bit of a kid myself."

After all, Edwards has entered the man's world of pro football when he was drafted in the second round by the San Francisco 49ers last weekend. He's been talking to agents, analysts, assistant coaches and anyone else who wants a piece of his talent and time.

But who did he call when he was changing planes in St. Louis on his way out to San Francisco? A 10-year-old kid named Johnny, of course. "I knew he wanted to share in the good news," Edwards said.

This is how a worthy program like Big Brothers Big Sisters should work. This is how a role model should be. This is what every young boy without a father should be able to experience.

Edwards has been there to cheer on Johnny and his older brother, Joey, in their sporting events and has taken them to play miniature golf, out to the batting cages, to laser tag, to movies, even to Notre Dame.

"I went out to his championship football game last fall and

ended up passing out trophies to about seven teams," Edwards said. "Johnny kind of liked that. I guess the other guys look at [a Notre Dame football player] as sort of a big deal."

Especially when one is as cool and as caring as Mark Edwards.

He even called Johnny when he was on the road for Notre Dame football games, letting his "little brother" share in the feeling of victory or to commiserate with him after a loss.

"But when we are together, we also can get pretty competitive," Edwards said. "I hate to lose to him and he hates to lose to me. We were playing [the board game] Stratego not long ago and Johnny beat me. That was bad enough, but then right after that, Joey beat me, too. I'm still upset about that."

Not really, but Edwards knows it makes the victory sweeter when he rants and raves a little.

"I look at Johnny as an extension of my own family," said Edwards, who has three younger siblings and four cousins younger than 7.

When Johnny's mother recently remarried after raising three kids by herself for several years, it was Edwards who stepped up and helped Johnny with the transition. "I went through the same thing when I was 7 or 8," he said. "Everything seems to be working out great."

For both of them.

"I'll be moving to San Fran-

cisco pretty soon, but I know Johnny and I are going to stay friends," Edwards said. "I know I'm going to stay in touch with him."

He hopes he has made Johnny a better person. He already knows that he's a better person because of Johnny.

Of course, Edwards will continue to ask Johnny, "What's up?"

And Johnny will continue to respond, "The sky."

At least partly because of each other, that sky may end up being the limit for both of them.

March 3, 1998
LIKE HIS FATHER

His sons were young and Carl Evans was eager. He had taken Isaac and Philip to a freestyle wrestling camp when they were little tykes, wanting them to enjoy the same sport that pulled him out of the ghetto and helped make him a man.

Isaac, unfortunately, got roughed up pretty badly during one of the matches. "He rushed over to me and jumped in my arms crying," Carl Evans recalls. "Then he said, 'Daddy, I never want to wrestle again.'"

Carl Evans looked at the hurt in his young son's eyes and decided then and there he would never push his kids onto a wrestling mat . . . into a headlock . . . or away from a hearty home-cooked meal.

"Oh, we played around a little in the basement, but I let them make their own decisions about wrestling."

Then came the 1996-97 season—Carl Evans' 25th as the head wrestling coach at his Washington High alma mater. When he turned to his captains that season, he was facing his sons—Isaac, a senior, and Philip, a junior.

"But when we were home, we didn't talk about why they didn't do this or didn't do that during practice," Carl says. "They didn't need that in addition to me asking them why they didn't carry out the trash or make their beds."

At home, he just wanted to be their dad.

* * *

There is a plaque down in their basement that states that Carl Evans was the 1968 Indiana state wrestling champion at 154 pounds.

Thirty years ago.

"I've looked at it," Philip Evans admits. "But I don't think I ever heard my dad mention [his state title] before."

That's because Carl Evans, a physical education teacher at Navarre Middle School and a member of his church's choir, is a modest man . . . a soft-spoken man . . . a gentleman.

"I never wanted to put any pressure on the kids that they had to try to do what I did," he says.

That's why it took Philip by surprise when his dad, his coach, strolled out onto the mat a few weeks ago and challenged him and Washington teammate John Comeau in a way he never had before.

Like he had in the past, he was going to wrestle with them during practice. But before each one squared off with him, he said, "I'm a state champ. What are you going to do with me?"

Both Comeau and Philip

85

Evans took their turns and wrestled him like they never had before. After all, both were undefeated and both were heading to the state finals a few days later.

"I still can't beat him," says Philip who wrestled at 189 pounds his senior year. "But we really went at it."

"I have to use my weight," says Carl, who still can move pretty well at 214 pounds.

"I went 100 percent that time," Carl says. "I usually don't because I don't want to hurt them."

Does Carl ever get hurt? "A lot," he says.

"He's always moaning and groaning," Philip laughs.

Hey, he's 47 years old. He gets that moaning and groaning out of his system before he gets home, though. "I have to fake it a little around my wife," Carl says. "I don't want her to know I got hurt—again."

* * *

Carl Evans had decided that when his boys were done wrestling, he was going to retire from coaching. He had been in it for 26 years with his first season when he was 22 years old and right out of Ball State.

Isaac, who graduated last year, had been a solid wrestler for Washington while Philip had the chance of winning a state title just like his dad.

"I remember being a little kid and going to the wrestling room with my mom and telling her,

'I'm going to be the star someday,'" Philip says. "And I really wanted to wrestle for my dad."

Then he pauses for a moment. "I wanted to win a state title for my dad."

In some people's mind, he became his dad out on the mat. "I didn't really notice until this year," Carl says. "That's when I saw in Philip many of the same mannerisms that I had. Some of the same techniques and moves."

"People were saying to me all the time, 'Do you know how much you look like your dad out there?' " Philip says. "I knew what they were talking about but I still said, 'No' anyway."

But, yeah, he wanted to be like his dad. Just like him.

* * *

Philip went through his senior year in wrestling like a whirlwind. He was undefeated during the regular season—except during practices when he faced his dad.

Philip was on his way to setting a school career record of 144 wins (against only 17 losses). Not even his dad came close to that. In fact, Philip had 32 pins in his senior year alone. Heading into the state finals, no opponent had even scored a takedown on him.

"I'll be honest with you," Carl says. "I wanted him to win [a state title] even more than I wanted to win my own championship all those years ago."

Unfortunately, history didn't repeat itself. In one of the great battles of the tournament two Saturdays ago, Philip lost in the semifinals to eventual state champion Anton Talamontes of Fort Wayne Dwenger, 2-1.

Beaten by just one point—but a point as sharp as the tip of an arrowhead.

Philip Evans cried and couldn't look his dad, his coach, in the eye when Carl grabbed him and hugged him. Had Philip raised his head, he would have seen that his dad was crying, too.

"I told him I still loved him and I was proud of him," Carl says.

"I just wanted to win so much for him," Philip says. "I wanted to make it like a family tradition."

Carl Evans had lost most of his voice during the match. Words didn't matter for a while anyway.

* * *

The season wasn't over. There was a consolation match for third place and teammate John Comeau, who eventually finished second at 171 pounds, needed to be cheered on.

"We had five rows of friends and family and members of our church [Ardmore-LaSalle Church of Christ] who had come to the meet," Carl Evans says. "Mr. [Dave] Kaser [the Washington principal] and Mr. [Mike] Sacchini [the assistant principal] already had come down to the

floor and given us hugs. I wanted Philip to finish strong for them . . . for everybody . . . for himself."

As hard as it was to return to the mat, Philip knew he had to—and to do his very best. "There were some of the little kids from church there and I wanted to show them how you handle yourself even when things go against you. Besides, I didn't want any of the ladies crying for me again."

They didn't have to. Philip charged onto the mat and pinned his opponent in the first period. Third place wasn't first place but . . .

". . . but maybe my loss will make me a good witness for other people sometime in the future."

* * *

Both Carl and Philip admit that it's been pretty quiet around the house for the last week or so. "We're trying to recover from colds, lost voices, fatigue and some heart pain," Carl admits.

Carl's wife Mary, daughter Joy and oldest son Isaac have shared in the pain—and in the healing.

Carl may have been a state high school champion but he can remember his own bitter blow. As a Ball State senior, he was undefeated in wrestling and had a shot at a NCAA title until he suffered a leg injury in his last regular-season meet.

He soon learned his career was over. His discovered life wasn't.

For more than a quarter of a century, Carl Evans has been a wonderful teacher, coach, church leader, husband and father.

"I want to be a role model like my dad," Philip says.

Carl Evans thinks his son already is. He's been nominated for the National Honor Society and a Kiwanis award. "I've also had teachers at Washington give me good reports on him. That's more important than the wrestling.

"I told Philip that you wrestle for only part of your life," Carl Evans continues, "but that you live as a man the rest of it."

Win or lose.

August 14, 1998
BIG MAN, BIG CAUSE

Entee Shine bit his lip and didn't say a word. One of his Notre Dame teammates was wondering out loud why the basketball team was sleeping on cots lined up on a dance floor in a K. of C. Hall instead of in a nice Louisville hotel.

Entee decided a history lesson wasn't in order. Nor an impassioned speech. Nor even a complaint.

But Entee knew the reason why his teammates' toes were hanging well over the ends of their cots and why the Irish weren't getting room service that particular evening. So did Joe Bertrand, the other black student-athlete on the Notre Dame team.

All they had to do was look down at the color of their skin.

Both were sophomores on that 1951-52 squad, and both were key performers. They also were the first blacks to play sports at Notre Dame.

And they were just 19 years old—carrying a cause and expectations as big as a fieldhouse on their shoulders.

"Moose Krause [the Notre Dame basketball coach and legendary athletic director] had recruited me out of South Bend Central," says Entee, an Indiana All-Star who had led the Bears to the Final Four in 1949. "He said I was going to be the school's version of Jackie Robinson.

"I think Moose and the athletic department were ready for blacks on the team," he continued. "I'm not so sure that the rest of the university, including some of the students, was ready, though."

University of Louisville fans didn't react well to black athletes playing against their Cardinals. In fact, he and Bertrand were given a police escort into the gym before the game as a precautionary measure.

"On one play, I turned and accidentally ran right over one of their players, Chuck Noble, and a foul wasn't called," Entee said. "The fans started throwing all kinds of stuff on the floor. It went on for about five minutes, and [first-year Irish coach John] Jordan felt he had to take me out of the game."

Entee sat on the bench for a while, more upset with his coach for subbing him than with the crowd for its reaction. Yet when Entee re-entered the game and hit a couple of baskets as Notre Dame cut into the Louisville lead, the Armory crowd erupted in anger again.

Entee didn't have to be told why Louisville fans acted that way. He knew that many of them didn't want blacks in the same sports arena as their stars.

He and Bertrand found out later that night that at least a few

89

Notre Dame fans apparently had similar feelings. "After that game [a 65-59 Irish loss], a rich alumnus (in the Louisville area) invited the team over to his house for dinner. Everybody but Joe and me. When you have money, I guess you can have your way. So there we were, 19-year-old kids wandering the streets of Louisville that night."

That happened more than 46 years ago, but Entee Shine, who recently retired from the South Bend Water Works, remembers that night as if it were yesterday.

Frightened, frustrated young men don't forget that kind of humiliation.

Is he bitter after all those years? "Oh, no," the 67-year-old said. "Even though I didn't graduate from Notre Dame, I got a good education there . . . and just being out there was a wonderful experience. I also met some lifelong friends like my old teammate Dick Rosenthal [the former South Bend banker and Notre Dame athletic director].

"And over the years, things have gotten much better for blacks and . . . well, as I've gotten older, I've sort of mellowed out, too."

Divorced for several years, he has three children—Mike, Robin and Anthony—and nine grandchildren.

"Oh, yeah, they all had it better than me when they were growing up," he says. "It was a better time for blacks."

Entee grew up on the near-west side of South Bend and saw his share of racism. He didn't know it had a name back then. It was just a way of life.

"There was a drug store on Washington and Walnut where I could go in and get an ice cream to go, but I couldn't sit at the counter," he said. "I knew that and didn't question it. That's just the way it was."

It was a time when he didn't see black teachers or black police officers or black mail carriers or hardly any blacks holding what he considered meaningful jobs. "I don't think I saw black *Tribune* paperboys back then, either," said Entee, who now works part time as a security guard at the *Tribune*.

He was raised by his mother, Rosetta, who had grown up in Arkansas. Entee and his sister, Callena, came to South Bend with her when he was 2. His father, meanwhile, stayed in the South and raised the couple's three other kids.

"When I was born, I weighed 12 pounds, 9 ounces, and my poor mother was only a 98-pound woman."

He was almost the size of a man before he got out of Linden Elementary School. He also was developing into quite an athlete and caught the eye of a pretty famous neighbor. "I grew up real close to where Goose Tatum [of the Harlem Globetrotters] lived when he wasn't on the road. We

90

lived on Orange, and he lived over on Liston.

"I guess you could say he was a hero. I had a chance to play with him in some exhibitions, but he wouldn't let me. He figured it might make me ineligible for high school sports. I really wanted to play, but he did me a favor—my coaches later told me I would have been ineligible."

Entee was an outstanding football and basketball player while also an honor-roll student at Central. He was popular, too.

"I got asked to join the top social club even though I would have been the only black in it," he said. "I knew why I was being asked. It was because I was a good athlete."

Because of that, he didn't join. But he still mostly enjoyed his Central days.

His size—6-foot-2 and almost 200 pounds in high school—kept him from hearing many racial epithets. "But I do remember being over in Michigan City for a B-team football game and sacking the quarterback a couple of times. I heard him say, 'Who's supposed to be blocking that big nigger?' I remember how he said it so matter-of-factly, and I think that bothered me more than anything. I figured that was reason enough to sack him three or four more times."

Entee said he had some great coaches at Central, including varsity basketball coach Bob Primmer and football coach Bob Jones. "They really looked after me and other kids, too. They wouldn't allow any racism. Coach Jones would take me home sometimes, and I can remember coach Primmer buying me shoes. I'm sure that would be against the rules now."

Entee played well enough his senior year to finish third in the Mr. Basketball voting. Against the Kentucky All-Stars that summer, he had a whale of a game —scoring 15 points, grabbing 12 rebounds and dishing out 16 assists.

Then he was off to college — the Jackie Robinson of Notre Dame, and the kid who Moose Krause said would be the first two-sport All-American since . . . well, Moose Krause himself.

Freshmen weren't eligible for the varsity then, so Entee played on the freshman football team as the first black. It wasn't easy, especially when some of his teammates didn't readily accept him. He decided to concentrate on basketball as a sophomore.

"Several years later, one of the guys on the team told me there had been some players who had been out to get me. When I started thinking back to some of the things that had happened— the late hits I had chalked up to overenthusiasm, the fist I thought was thrown by just a hothead—I figured he might have been right.

"But I do think coach [Frank] Leahy wanted me to succeed and some of the other guys did, too. When I run into a guy like [Heisman Trophy winner] Johnny Lattner even today, he's so friendly it's like we never quit being teammates."

Entee had his share of supporters; he only wished he had known more about them. After running into academic difficulties after his sophomore year, he transferred to Tennessee State. "So many people from the community came up to me after that and told me how they had been pulling for me to succeed at Notre Dame. I didn't know that. I was sort of out in a vacuum on campus and felt alone. If I had known that so many people were concerned about me and rooting for me, maybe I would have tried a little harder. That's my one regret about being there.

"And I'll have to admit that I think Notre Dame overall really tried with me."

He added that going to Tennessee State as a junior was a mistake. "I didn't like it there at all. I knew there was going to be trouble when I got off the train [in Nashville] and they had one waiting room for whites and one for coloreds, and they were anything but equal. I left after a semester."

A month later, he was drafted into the Army, where he played sports for various military posts and served as a stock records clerk. "I remember playing for Fort Carson against the Dallas Texans and the coach telling me and the other three blacks on the team we couldn't stay at the regular hotel in Dallas. He gave us some money and told us we had to find a hotel in the colored section. Then when we came back for the pre-game meal, we had to eat in the kitchen."

He liked the Army, but the uniform didn't shield him from racism. He was married at the time, and his wife was light enough in skin color that she could sometimes pass for white. "So she got us a nice apartment out at Colorado Springs when I was at [Fort] Carson. But then things changed when I showed up with her the next day. We got the, 'We're sorry, we made a mistake. That apartment already has been rented.' Yeah, right."

After his military service and a tryout with the Los Angeles Rams, Entee returned to his hometown of South Bend. Jobs weren't easy to find, but he did manage to catch on with Studebaker before it folded and later with Oliver Corp. before its foundry was closed.

"When I was working at Studebaker, I do remember a guy coming over and talking to Jack Morrical. Jack was my old Central teammate and a good friend. The guy offered Jack a job as a loan officer. Jack turned it down, but I said, 'I would be interested.'

"The guy just looked at me and said, 'I don't think so.'"

Entee eventually was hired to

work for the city, taking care of the parking meters. When the meters were taken out, he hooked on with the Water Works.

A voracious reader, he retired last October and now works at his part-time security job. He lives in a northwest-side neighborhood that has become more black than white. "I like a nice mix," Entee said. "I even talked one of my white neighbors out of moving a while back. I don't want this to be just a black neighborhood."

He admits that he has some black friends who don't like whites. "But personally, if I don't have any reason not to like somebody, then it doesn't matter what their color is."

Has life gotten better for blacks? "Oh, yeah, but race relations seem to have leveled out some lately. I think people have gotten a little complacent. I look around and I don't see the progress now."

He sits back in his chair in his living room and gives his sad smile. "I'll let other people worry about it now. I'm at the age where I just want to enjoy life."

September 13, 1998
HER IRON WILL

Lisa James—her freckles flashing in the early morning light, her face fixed in a determined stare—sprints barefooted up the carpeting from Barron Lake while wiggling her arms out of her wet suit.

She has some making up to do. But then she always does after the swim segment of the triathlon. "Swimming is not my strong point," the 33-year-old from South Bend later says with a smile.

Oh, but how she can bike and run. During the 70 minutes of pedaling and pounding the pavement, she overtakes all of her female competition and easily wins last weekend's Niles Solo Triath-lon. It's an event composed of a half-mile swim, a 17 1/2-mile bike ride and a five-mile run—and it's all done before breakfast.

As she crosses the finish, she raises her hands, kisses her husband Mark, and then makes plans with her training partner, Steve Smith, for an 80-mile bike ride later that day.

That's what you do when you are training for the Ironman triathlon world championships in Hawaii. That's what you do when you will go back to back to back against a 2.4-mile ocean swim, a 112-mile bike ride through the lava fields and then a 26.2-mile survival run. That's

what you do when you want to be one of the best around.

"You have to put in your miles," Lisa says.

That kind of long-distance training is what is taking her all the way to Hawaii on Oct. 3.

It also is taking her further and further away from the most horrific chapter in her life.

It was on April 3, 1997, while riding her bike on Roosevelt Road, that Lisa James . . . a rookie triathlete . . . a full-time physical therapist . . . and a mother of three . . . was run off the road by a man with a lengthy criminal record, abducted at knifepoint and then brutally beaten and raped.

At one point, her abductor tried to strangle her to death and later began hitting her in the head with rocks. She tried to escape but was repeatedly slammed to the ground. Among her injuries were a skull fracture, broken fingers and thumb and a severe ankle sprain.

She survived, though, partly from fighting off her assailant as best she could and partly from using her wits in conversations with him.

"There was a point when I said to myself, 'I'm going to live through this,'" she says. "I couldn't help but think of my husband and my children and that I wanted to see them again."

Lisa carries less than 110 pounds on her 5-foot-6 frame but her toughness—both mental and physical—may have saved her life that day. When the police finally arrived after a couple of people heard her screams for help, she was covered with blood but still conscious.

Her assailant was later arrested after fleeing the scene and is now serving a lengthy prison term after being found guilty of attempted murder, confinement, rape and two counts of criminal deviate conduct.

"Kevin Whippo, one of the first officers on the scene, gave me his jacket and put his face down very close to mine," she says. "That's when I really knew it was finally over. Kevin works security at the grocery where we shop, and I still love seeing that friendly face of his. It's still a feeling of security."

Other gentle, caring hands took over for Whippo, a St. Joseph County police officer. She went from one terribly evil man to a whole world of caring people—from the police officers . . . to the medical people . . . to the countless number of concerned citizens.

She spent 12 hours in the emergency room and then a nightmarish sleep. But when she woke up the next day, she vowed not to let the man who assaulted her be the winner. "He will not control my mind, my body or spirit," she said to herself in her hospital bed. "I will be strong . . . I will be a good wife, mother, friend . . . I will compete again."

"I just made up my mind I wasn't going to let him dampen my spirit," Lisa now says.

Happy to be alive, she was ready to go on with the rest of her life. "The one thing I didn't think I wanted to do was look at the next day's newspaper," she says. "I didn't want to read that I had done something wrong—I didn't want to read that it was partly my fault for riding alone. I think that's a classic way that victims feel."

The article didn't read that way at all. In fact, St. Joseph County police officer Charles Feirrell even pointed out that Lisa's top physical condition may have kept her alive.

The healing process began at once. Jim Baker, a bicyclist who happened to find her riding shoes the day of the crime, said he would keep her company on rides as soon as she was ready. Bishop Dan Jenky of St. Matthew Cathedral gave her wonderful counsel. Friend Marty Horn wrote her a beautiful letter that she still clutches when times get tough. Friends stayed by her side. Cards and flowers poured in.

"If I have a theme to share with other victims, it would be to not be afraid to reach out and ask for help," Lisa says. "The amount of support that people have given me speaks very well for this community. I received hundreds of letters—many of them sent to the sheriff's office because they didn't know my name."

Until now, only friends and family knew her identity. "But I want to be open about it now in case my words can help another victim. I even bring up what happened in front of some friends now because I know they often don't know what to say. I do it because it has been from the help of other people that I have gotten through this."

Her training has helped, too.

"My metaphor for dealing with this is that if I could get through something like the Ironman, then I could get through anything—including what happened to me," she says. "Through my training, I've gained a lot of strength that transfers over to other aspects of my life. Some people have other ways of doing this, like playing the piano, for instance."

Her way is going out each week and riding 200 to 250 miles, running 35 to 40 miles and swimming 10,000 meters.

She is putting her nightmare and the trial behind her—with mile after mile after mile.

Winner of five of the 11 triathlons she has entered since her brush with death, she qualified for the Ironman on Aug. 2 in an Allentown, Pennsylvania, triathlon (a 1.2-mile swim, 56-mile bike and 13.1-mile run) by placing third in her age group. The Ironman limits its field to 1,500 athletes from all over the world.

"Actually, I hadn't really talked much about the Ironman until right before the Allentown race," Lisa says. "But deep down, I always wanted to do it. It was always there on my mind."

She and her family were going to Wrigley Field for a Chicago Cubs game on a Friday when she turned to her husband and said she wanted to take a shot at qualifying for the Ironman that Sunday at Allentown. "Well, you can imagine the logistics were a little sticky at that point," admits Mark James.

He didn't even wince. Through it all, he has been the one who has held her during her nightmares and hugged her after her races. And he is the one who drove into the night to get her to Allentown in time to register on that Saturday.

He also is the one who follows her in the car when a riding partner isn't available. "I'll never ride alone but, yes, I still do ride down Roosevelt Road," she says. "That's my route and I've always liked it and I'm not going to let that man take that away from me, either."

Sometimes, little things can trigger a memory, but that's when she just puts her head down and swims a little faster, pedals a little stronger, runs a little harder.

"You know, if this had never happened to me, I don't think I would have pursued something like the Ironman," she says.

"Someone once said that life is 5 percent of what happens to you and 95 percent on how you handle it."

Lisa James has a handle on life as if it were her handlebars during a sprint to the front of the pack. She knows, though, that it has taken more than her own two steady hands to see her through the fray.

"So many other people have helped me make a positive out of this," she says.

Hawaii is on her horizon. Healing is almost behind her.

KIDS

January 17, 1989
GETTING THE YANK

The tooth fairy fluttered and then flopped to the floor at our house two nights ago.

Barely breathing. Cut to the quick.

A tooth fairy can take only so much pain. I know. This particular tooth fairy is me.

I was told I am no longer needed. I was told, in a manner of speaking, for the tooth fairy inside me to take a flying leap.

Not only did my daughter opt to pull one of her last remaining baby teeth instead of coming to me, she wanted to keep it.

"I'm keeping all my molars," she said.

Why? "None of your bee's wax."

Devastating news. For years, my job has been first to pull the teeth of my children and then to sneak them from under the pillow, replacing them with money.

That's what tooth fairies do. And I was good at it. I took pride in a job well done.

First of all, pulling teeth is a real art.

It is not for the weak, nor should it be for the wicked. One must be able to handle the sight of blood but not take satisfaction in causing blood-curdling cries.

Lessons in psychology—or the ability to tell white lies without blinking—also are a must. You can't just tell a kid, "Hey, open up your mouth, I'm going to yank that bloody pulp right out of there and leave you with a gaping hole."

Finesse must come before force.

For me, it starts with a soothing voice: "I'm just going to look. Open your mouth. Come on, I'm just looking. Now, I'm just going to touch it. Don't bite me. OK, just a little wiggle and . . ."

"Ouuuuuuuch!"

"Now that didn't hurt, did it?"

"Yes! And you lied to me!"

Minutes later, though, they are flashing their new jack-o'-lantern smiles and thanking old Dad for a job well done.

I should have my doctorate in toothology by now. I even have devised more than one effective method of pulling teeth. For instance:

•The Flick: If the tooth is hanging by a thread and I can sneak a finger and thumb behind it, I can actually flick a tooth out. Sudden and so sweet. It's sort of like being a diamond cutter, though. Precision is essential.

•The Back-and-Foooooorth: That's the wiggle that suddenly turns into a jerk—and turns me into a jerk, but only for a few seconds.

•The Bend-and-Don't-Back-Off: This method is only used in extreme cases. It's when the tooth proves harder to get out than first anticipated, but it must be done. If not, the kid with the timid tusk isn't going to let me near his or her mouth for a month if I don't get it out.

•The Straight-Arm-In-The-Basement: Only used once and only by accident even then. I extracted one of my sister's teeth when I surprised both her—and me—by breaking one of her tackles. Losing her balance, she also lost a tooth when she hit the floor.

For some reason, we never were allowed to play football in the basement after that.

With that one exception, I really have enjoyed taking out teeth.

I probably should have been a dentist—or at least a first-grade teacher like my mom and wife are. Think of all the potential pulls in a classroom full of 6-year-olds.

But even better than pulling teeth out of mouths is pulling them from under pillows.

There is an art to that, too. To find a little baby tooth . . . under the pillow . . . a pillow that has a sleeping head on it ... in a dark bedroom—it takes practice.

And then a tooth fairy gets to keep the teeth in exchange for a couple of quarters. Little teeth for big money.

In our old house, we had a high shelf in our bathroom where I would stick the kid's baby teeth. There those teeth would stay, like a miniature igloo village. I liked to look at them from time to time.

How can you throw out your kids' baby teeth? I never could.

And now my daughter is saying not only that she is going to pull her own teeth, but she is keeping her molars.

This tooth fairy knows the end is near.

"But I still get 50 cents when I lose a tooth, right?" my daughter asks.

The tooth fairy smiles back. It is a mean smile: "Out-of-work tooth fairies don't have any money."

September 10, 1995
RAZOR SHARP

Once again, my shaving cream and razor were among the missing the other morning.

If I were to keep track of these occasional disappearances, I know a definite cycle would surface. I also know this almost always occurs on the days when I am running very late—as opposed to just late.

I have found a sure-fire way of retrieving my razor and shaving cream, however. I simply yell at the top of my lungs, "Whoever has my shaving gear better return it RIGHT NOOOWWWWW or I'm going to start combing my hair with the orange toothbrush!" In no more than 10 seconds, a hand usually comes around the bathroom door, holding my missing objects.

This actually is quite a feat for the owner of the hand, who tries to remain unidentified by keeping the rest of his body on the other side of the door. He usually has had to jump out of bed, rush into the upstairs bathroom where my shaving stuff has been abandoned, dash down the stairs and then deliver the goods to me in my early-morning inner sanctum—which is known to unimaginative Realtors as the "half bath."

Olympic sprinter Carl Lewis would have a hard time covering this route in 10 seconds or less, especially if he didn't have prior knowledge of the school books and shoes that are usually tossed across steps three through six.

The old toothbrush-through-the-hair threat always works. Many adolescent boys believe that male-pattern balding can be "caught" in a variety of ways.

Facial hair is viewed differently, of course. This is a male rite of passage that is usually eagerly anticipated. This is when a mirror becomes a proud part of a young man's life. "Yes, I do believe that is a hair growing on the side of that pimple."

Old men call this new addition whiskers.

Young men call it a beard.

Dads like me usually call it good old peach fuzz.

Maybe that's why my sons have not wanted to share this moment of glory and growth with me.

Peach fuzz.

Gosh, I love that term.

Yeah, I guess that's probably part of the reason my sons never asked me for lessons on how to apply the foam, when to change the blade, how to stop all that bleeding.

I'm one to talk. My first shave? When I was 16 . . . with my dad's electric razor . . . in the family station wagon . . . parked in the garage.

Both of my boys started shaving on the sly, too.

I noticed something was up

when Son No. 1 was in his mid-teens and my razor and shaving cream suddenly came up missing about once a week. Then it got to be twice a week. Then every other day. Then, it seems, somebody must have told him that a family could own more than one razor at at time.

This cycle is beginning again with Son No. 2. Apparently, the cat licking his face no longer was getting the job done. (That's almost as fun as saying peach fuzz.)

What gets me about both these two shaving sheiks, though, is that they figure that my razor and shaving cream—usually filched during the nighttime hours—will somehow find their way back into the downstairs bathroom on their own power. Yet foam still didn't come with extendable legs the last time I checked.

I grew up with Perry Mason. I learned that if you want to keep a secret, you wipe off the evidence and put it back.

My sons don't do that.

There must be some deep-seated reason for this, something that makes their subconscious minds want me to know that they are indeed of shaving age. At least I prefer this theory over laziness or stupidity.

So with Son No. 2 sporting his peach fuzz, it's back to the war cry from the downstairs bathroom in the morning and then the 10-second scamper about two times a week.

It is different with my wife, of course. When she is out of blades, she borrows my razor but always returns it promptly—without ever telling me.

Have you recently shaved with a blade that's been brutalized by a couple of rough (but still shapely) legs? I think I would prefer trusting my beard to a Bowie knife.

Of course, those are the mornings when I pick up the pink toothbrush and use it to comb my hair.

March 10, 1996
A TATTOO OR TUITION?

I am trying to get a handle on tattoos these days.

Back in college, we had an older buddy who was one of the Marines' "few good men" and he had an outstanding tattoo on his right forearm. He was big and hairy and once held a rather annoying guy out a second-floor window by the ankles.

His Marine Corps tattoo just made him seem that much tougher.

I asked him one evening why he had decided to get a tattoo. "I don't think there was any decision involved," he said. "I got a little crazy one night and I woke up the next morning with this on my arm. I think that's how a lot of guys ended up with theirs."

I then asked if he ever regretted having it. "Naaa," he said. "It's occasionally worth a free soda pop if the bartender happens to be an ex-Marine."

So when I think about tattoos, I see his.

Tattoos, in my mind anyway, always have been for big-chested, hard-knuckled guys who have voices like Bluto and no-nonsense demeanors.

Marines . . . dock workers . . . pile-driving men . . .

. . . not power forwards with Clarabelle hair and pin-cushion skin . . . nor vamp-tramp singers who wear their underwear outside their clothes . . . nor even the ever-collegiate Ryan Hoover with the Notre Dame logo tattooed on his back . . .

. . . and especially not a darling daughter who is still a few weeks shy of her 19th birthday.

And yet . . . "What about if I get a tattoo, Dad?" my very own little girl asked me some months back.

One of her friends had just gotten a tattoo on her ankle—a bluish-green Mother Earth that looks more like a Chiquita banana label, if you ask me.

First, I feigned a loss of hearing at my daughter's inquiry. Then I hyperventilated. Finally, I did what all red-blooded, all-American dads have a right to do: I threatened her with her tuition money.

She laughed at me. She thinks I am a funny, old man even when I'm not trying to be.

I tried another tack. "Sometimes in a fit of youthful exuberance, we do things that we might regret later in life," I said in a rather pleasant voice, considering it had been squeezed through clenched teeth.

"Like what?" she asked.

Like having kids, I thought, but only for a second.

Hmmm, I had a lot of stories I could have told, but none I really wanted to share with my daughter.

"Well, hold that thought," she said, "and we'll talk about this later."

Much later, I hoped. Like maybe in 20 years.

She went off to college soon after that and I held my breath every time she came home. But she said nary a word about tattoos . . . until her spring break last week.

"I'm bringing my two friends—Amy and Amy—home with me because they want to get tattoos up in Niles," she said.

"They do, but you don't, right?" I asked with a tremble.

"Right, I'm not getting one with them," she said. "I promise."

So I saved my lecture for the Amys and secretly kept patting myself on the back because they weren't my problems. Not that they weren't nice girls, but . . .

"Now, let's see, you girls go to Purdue so I'm guessing maybe you'll get a tattoo of a cow," I joked.

"I'm getting a frog," said one of the Amys, very matter-of-factly.

The other Amy was opting for a flower.

Right on their hips. Ouch!

I thought of their parents, I thought of myself and then I smiled.

When they returned, the Amys were in a little bit of pain but proud of their new art. My daughter was bounding around and playing the nurse, obviously true to her word.

"So you had no thoughts of getting one yourself up there, right?" I said to her.

"Right," she answered as she pulled down her jeans a little bit to show me a red rose on her hip. "Why should I get another one when I got mine during Thanksgiving break?"

My thoughts immediately ran back to my Marine buddy and how he had held that guy out the window.

But before I could get a grip on myself—or my daughter's ankles—she said, "Now, you aren't going to tell everybody about this, are you, Dad? Pretty please. It's sort of a private thing."

I regained my breath and thought for a minute. I decided right there on the spot that being the good sport I am, I would honor her wishes and not tell anybody at all.

And I haven't—except for you.

August 30, 1998
COLLEGE BOUND

I am not sure what came first: the pained look of expression on his face or my question.

We are traveling down the highway—15 minutes from home—and I ask my youngest kid, "Is there any possible thing you've left behind?"

I can almost hear him gulp. "Yeah, my wallet."

Well, sure, I could see how that could happen. After all, he did remember the couch . . . the refrigerator . . . the television . . . the fan . . . the lava lamp . . . the tons of clothes . . . the sacks of potato chips and popcorn . . . the CD player and collection . . . the desert plant ... the electronic dart board . . . and on and on. A wallet certainly could get lost in that shuffle.

"I just remembered I didn't have it five seconds before you asked me," he says. "I guess we think a little bit alike."

I don't have the heart to inform him that my wallet is in my pants pocket and not lying on the counter back at home. He is a little nervous already as I drive him down to Indiana University Bloomington. He spent his first year of college in town at Holy Cross (a great starter school, I might add), so this is his big push away from mom and pop.

My wife and I also are becoming true "empty nesters"—sniff, sniff—with the other two kids at Purdue. So this is not an easy drive for me, either—especially when I have to back-track.

A half hour later after retrieving the wallet, we are back at the same point in the road where I first posed the question. I reword it a little differently this time. "Is there any possible thing you've left behind—like maybe your head, for instance?"

We are heading toward my alma mater and the longer I drive, the more I think that Purdue wasn't such a bad choice for my other two kids. After all, I can make it to West Lafayette with only one restroom stop, while Bloomington is pushing it even after two.

We are meeting my sister and her two sons from southern Indiana. My nephews will be living on the same dorm floor as my youngest, and I keep muttering, "I'm not carrying that couch up those stairs. In fact, I'm not carrying anything heavy. You guys can do all the heavy lifting. You've got to quit relying on me to get things done for you."

After about the fourth time I say this, my son looks at me and says, "I think you've got your point across, Dad."

I've always been under the assumption that kids going off to college act in an obnoxious manner their last few weeks at home just to ensure that their parents won't miss them too much. And now, I have to wonder if parents can sometimes be the same way with their kids when the final hours start counting down.

When we finally get to campus, we find ourselves in the middle of a mass of people and possessions and parental emotions working overtime. My nephews find us and the oldest almost immediately says, "Don't worry about carrying anything, Uncle Bill. We'll take everything up."

My son stifles a laugh. Of course, I act semi-offended. "You don't think I can carry the end of a couch as easy as you can? How many times you think I've already carted that refrigerator around? You think my muscles have turned into mashed potatoes since the last time I saw you?"

My son pats me on the back and says, "Why don't you find some shade, Dad?"

Instead, I march up to their fifth floor rooms and see if I can be as big of a nuisance as my bossy sister. She seems on the verge of tears as she makes beds and hangs clothes and tells me not to stand in her way. She is getting ready to be an "empty nester" for the first time, too.

Everything eventually gets carried up, put away and made neat for probably the last time in the semester. We go to lunch, we take a little walk and suddenly I am saying good-bye to my youngest child. His only worry seems to be that I don't get too sentimental on him. Before I realize it, I am back on the road, heading home.

Just south of Indianapolis when I stop for gas, I call my son. I'm not sure why. But I do tell him that if he sees anybody on his floor who looks lonely, he should go up and talk to him and make him feel more at home.

He humors me and says that's a good idea. But he probably knows I am thinking about the loneliness that is setting in on me.

As I drive the rest of the way home, I think of the sign I saw earlier in the summer that read, "Life begins when the kids are gone and the old dog dies."

My wife, who stayed behind for her first day of teaching school, is waiting for me when I arrive. So is my old dog, still hanging in there.

So am I—sort of.

May 23, 1999
GRADUATION BLUES

"One down, two to go." I am mumbling to myself as my oldest kid crosses the stage to accept his Purdue University diploma.

Those five little words sound pretty darn good. I repeat them under my breath. My wife nudges me. She apparently thinks I am breaking out into some sort of strange chant.

"What are you thinking about," she whispers.

"Car insurance premiums," I whisper back.

They will go down, after all, when my son soon starts paying his own premiums. He is heading off to his chemical engineering job in Houston next month and will make more money than good, old dad right out of the chute.

But that's not what I am really thinking about as he carries his diploma down the aisle and back to his seat.

I am thinking about how at 2 years old, he was able to unscrew all the wooden patio furniture and how I could never quite get it properly back together.

I am thinking about when he was hit in the mouth with a bad-hop ground ball that cost him three of his baby teeth and me a good night's sleep.

I am thinking about how he and I raced off together to Space Mountain as soon as they opened the Magic Kingdom's gates and then how he had to coax me, an out-of-breath and sweaty-palmed fud-dud, into not taking the chicken-out exit.

I am thinking of the time he got kicked out of middle school for three days for fighting and (as Neanderthal as this might sound to some educators) feeling more than a little bit proud that he had stood up to a bully.

I am thinking about how he made a better Cub Scout pinewood derby car without my help.

I am thinking about how before his high school soccer team's senior appreciation game, neither my wife nor I got to the game in time to walk with him out to the center of the field and how that still bugs me even today.

I am thinking of the time I took him to a World Series game in Cincinnati and how he made me promise that I would do the same when the Chicago Cubs—our Chicago Cubs—got into the Series.

I am thinking of the time he turned to me when he was in seventh grade and said, "I thought you said you were good in math."

I am thinking about when I would carry him into my work when he was a little guy, while he fussed about his constant companions, stuffed animals Butch and Snoopy.

I am thinking about how it

used to drive me nutty that he could buy a complete set of baseball cards as "an investment" and put them on the top shelf of his closet without ever opening them.

I am thinking about his buddies Corey and Kevin, friends since grade school, and how they sort of went their own ways for a while only to renew their friendships even stronger later.

I am thinking about his old room and the thousands of Lego pieces . . . and the Castle of Greyskull . . . and the Millennium Falcon . . . and pictures of Ryne Sandberg . . . and how I probably liked that room better than my own.

I am thinking of the day when he said he was a better water skier than me and then went out and proved it.

I am thinking of the time we drove down to Port Arthur, Texas, after his freshman year in college and how he tried so hard to hide his anxiety when he realized he was going to be on his own for three months while co-oping for an oil company.

I am thinking of the time he carried a new basset hound puppy into our house with Ernie's body hanging well over both of my son's arms.

I am thinking about prom nights . . . and sports banquets . . . and family whiffleball games . . . and driving lessons.

I am thinking about when I carried him out of Bob Evans

Restaurant like a football, his lungs at full blast because we wouldn't let him have his baby sister's apple sauce.

I am thinking back to the time when he actually started liking his younger brother and sister— and maybe realizing, at about the same time, his parents weren't so bad, either.

I am thinking about all these things when the Purdue choir and orchestra break out into "Hail to Old Purdue" at the end of the graduation ceremonies.

Maybe it is because my first kid is graduating from college . . . maybe it is the fact that my dad went to Purdue and that I went to Purdue Nursery School at the same time . . . or maybe it is because I have become a bit of a softie in my old age.

All I know is that while I listen to that Purdue song, as much as I try to fight it, tears are running down the cheeks of this old I.U. grad.

My wife looks at me. My mom looks at me. My other two kids look at me.

I shrug and say, "One down, two to go."

And maybe if I had said only three or four words instead of those five, my voice wouldn't have caught so awkwardly in my throat.

May 25, 1999
KNOWING YOUR PLACE

"That's my seat," I say.

My youngest kid looks up at me as if I have just told him that we are getting ready to eat seaweed salad with bug croutons.

We are at the kitchen table. And he is sitting in my seat.

"What are you talking about?" he says. "There are four chairs around this table and they all look alike."

He is not taking the hint very well.

"Move over nooooowww," I roar, my Darth Vader imitation at its best.

He stares at me coolly for a moment and slowly pulls his body out of my seat and slides over one spot.

"What is the big deal about that seat?" he mutters.

"It's mine," I say.

Yes, I know I am getting a little set in my ways. But I like the seat on the right side of our little, square kitchen table. One of the reasons is because it is closest to the phone so I can reach over and tell the telemarketers who call at suppertime, "We're eating. But if you give me your home phone number, I will get back to you— probably some time after midnight."

This seat also allows me to sit at a right angle to the window so I am able to look out with a slight turn of my head. That way, I can keep an eye on everything going on outside without looking like the snoop I would be if I sat in the seat that faces the window.

I also am closest to the radio in that seat in case the Cubs are playing an early-evening game. I can play it just loud enough so I can hear Ron Santo's voice when the Cubs score a run but not loud enough to be in my wife's annoyance zone.

I do not bother to tell my son all this, however.

"It's my seat," sounds like a good enough explanation to me.

Besides, after being away from college, he needs to start off the summer by knowing his place— sitting in the seat facing the window at the kitchen table.

You give these kids an inch and they take a mile—or at least a few sips out of your favorite glass.

"That's my milk," I say.

"I set the table and that's the glass I set for this place—because I thought it was where you were going to sit," my son says. "Now you tell me that seat is yours but you want to drink the milk at this seat."

Maybe I am getting too particular—or possessive. I like my order, though, and with the kids now gone most of the year, I do get into my little routine.

I decide I will let up on him a little.

"OK, you can clear tonight and I will do the dishes," I say.

"What do you mean, do the dishes?" he counters. "We have a dishwasher."

"Yeah, well, you still have to scour off some of the gunk. You kids have never been very good about that."

He looks at me as if he is sizing up my nose to see if, with a little applied pressure, it can reach the garbage disposal at the bottom of the drain.

"I am starting to wonder if you are happy I'm home, Dad," he says.

I grab him and give him a hug. "Of course I am, son. Do you think your mom would let me talk to her that way?"

September 7, 1999
EMPTY NESTING

An old shoulder injury has flared up during the last few days. I hate to say it but I think I aggravated it while throwing crab apples at my hound dog. He was ... well, "dogging" it on our walk and I was only trying to give him a reason to pick up his gait.

My dog, his nose always to the ground, came out of this little episode unblemished since my aim is as poor as his pace. It was a different story for me and my shoulder.

If the throbbing usually starts about 1 AM, when I have rolled over on it a couple of times while trying to get the rest of me comfortable. I toss this way and then turn that way until my wife violently pulls the sheets back her way and emits a sigh that does all the communicating we need at that time of night.

Like all good husbands, I take the hint and cart my pain and my pillow elsewhere.

I wander through the house in the dark, deciding where to plop.

I have plenty of choices—a couple of couches, my daughter's room, the bunk beds in my boys' room (which were the same bunk beds my brother and I once used) and even a hammock in the backyard that I got for my 50th birthday.

For whatever reasons, the cat usually follows me on my nocturnal meandering. The dog does not. Even though I didn't hit him with one, he might still be pouting about the dozen or so crab apples tossed his way.

It is sort of a sad time negotiating the hallways in my underwear and in the middle of the night.

I don't think there is a time it hits home any harder that the kids are gone than when I peek into their bedrooms and don't see their little sleeping heads on their pillows.

To be honest, there were very few nights over the previous 20-some years that I haven't gotten up and checked in bedrooms at some point—as reassurance that my little ones were safe and sound and then later, as they got older, that the world was safe from them for another evening.

They are all gone right now—one working in Texas, one finishing up school at Purdue and one who graced us with his presence this summer but who now is back at Indiana University.

My shoulder throbs. Maybe my heart does a little, too.

The dead silence in the house almost catches in my throat. I must feel a little like Tom Sawyer and Becky Thatcher did when they thought they were hopelessly lost in the cave and frantically searched for some sunlight.

At 2 in the morning when there are no snores from my boys'

room or the occasional jumbled phrase out of my daughter's mouth during one of her dreams, that is when I know the real meaning of the empty nest.

Empty nest.

It's not as easy as I thought it would be . . . even in the middle of the night . . .especially in the middle of the night.

Darn, old shoulder.

March 4, 2001
GOOD CONNECTIONS

My wife, the trouper that she is, keeps trying.

She recently bought a cell phone with all those free long-distance minutes and it works beautifully just about everywhere but . . .

(And this is a big but) . . . but from our house.

"The sales rep says it's probably the pine trees in our front yard that mess up the signal," my wife says. "But they are going to build a tower out in our area soon and it should vastly improve the reception."

If it is one of those 1000-foot towers, my one hope is that it is built at least 1001 feet from our house.

Wanting to take advantage of her free minutes, my wife still tries to call our kids from our house. Rarely is it a good connection. In fact, she would get much better reception if she called from our car while I drive her around the block.

It has gotten to the point that when our oldest kid's roommate hears a bunch of static on the other line, he hangs up the phone and then says to our son, "Your mom just called."

Our son usually calls back—to our regular phone.

It is expected on Sunday. I call my mom on Sunday, my wife calls her mom on Sunday and our kids call their mom (and me) on Sunday.

I have mentioned in the past that talking to my mom on Sunday nights sort of re-establishes the order in the world for me. As I talk to her, I visualize myself as a kid again—back in our old house, lying lazily on the floor beside my dog Buddy, eating popcorn and apple slices, watching "The Wonderful World of Disney," and savoring the last of the weekend before school the next day.

That Sunday call to mom is a quick connection to my past and a nice reminder of who I am.

Nowadays, our kids do the dialing. I don't know if they feel that same kind of "blast from the past" I feel when talking to my mom. I am not sure if I did at their ages—22, almost 24 and 25—anyway.

Ironically, I do have my own strange connections with them.

•••

My younger son calls not only from the same old frat house where I lived on the I.U. campus but from the exact third floor room I called home as a senior. Thank goodness those walls can't talk.

Son No. 2 apparently feels very little nostalgia in the knowledge that old dad used to pile his dirty clothes in the same place he now does. "Are you the one who tore the top door off my closet?" he asks.

113

I tell him that may have happened some time after I moved out of there 30 years ago.

At least I have a mental picture of where he is when we talk on the phone—and that triggers some fond memories as well.

"And clean up that pit," I often tell him.

"How do you know it needs cleaning?" he answers while munching down his Sunday night pizza.

Oh, I know.

•••

My daughter lives so close to Wrigley Field—home of the Chicago Cubs and my own personal paradise—that if I had any kind of arm, I could throw a ball off her apartment's little balcony and one-hop its turnstiles.

I don't think she moved there just to please dear old dad, but she does know that I could not have found her a lovelier location. While talking to her on the phone on one occasion, I could even hear "Take Me Out to the Ball Game" being sung during the seventh inning stretch.

During one recent gloomy day, I asked her to look out the window and tell me that Wrigley—and its promise of spring—was still there. "Still there," she answered. "Pretty dull-looking right now, though."

She obviously is getting spoiled with her view. But just imagining what my daughter is seeing while we talk on the phone, I can see Wrigley, too. And if I really want to push my imagination, I can also see a "W" on the center-field scoreboard.

•••

My older son lives in Houston. Except for him, I have no personal connections to this city known for its spectacular off-ramps and a domed stadium once called "the eighth wonder of the world" and now deemed unfit for baseball.

But I do get a warm feeling while talking to Son No. 1 on the phone. He knows what one of my first questions this time of year is going to be.

Sometimes, he doesn't even wait for me to ask.

"It's 75 and sunny, Dad," he says. I can almost feel the heat over the phone. I wish I was there.

In the summer, I still ask. "It's 102 and humid, Dad."

I can almost feel the heat over the phone. I am glad I am here.

And I am glad our kids call us every Sunday night.

PETS & PESTS

August 1, 1989
HOUSING HAMSTERS

The kids want a dog.

There are stipulations—many from my wife.

I only have one. "We'll get a dog only if it likes to eat hamsters," I say.

They think I am kidding.

Hamsters are our current house pets—or pests.

They are cute and cuddly and colossal pains.

Have you ever had a hamster in your house? If you have, then you know exactly what I mean.

First of all, they are expensive. Not so much the little fuzzballs you buy at the pet store. They cost $2.98 or thereabouts.

But the accessories that go along with it can get costly. Water dishes, little cottages with removable roofs, exercise wheels that look like miniature Ferris wheels, cages with passageways that can be strung all over a bedroom and more sanitary chips than you would think a half-grown elephant needs.

Hamsters also are nocturnal. That means that the sudden crash down the hall that just woke you out of a sound sleep wasn't a burglar at all but one of the Rodent Brothers deciding he would rather have a ranch than a two-story house.

But most importantly, these little guys like the open range anytime there is a breach in security. If hamsters could talk, their first words undoubtedly would be "Jail break!"

Smokey and Lucky currently share our address. My kids give them our last name, too, but I refuse to do that.

I have my own names for them anyway. Rat Face is one of the more kindly of those.

It seems that I smell them more than I see them. When I do catch their act, they usually are rolling around the house in their exercise balls. Have you ever seen these gadgets? They are clear, plastic balls in which the hamster is placed. They then can run around in these balls all over the house—and even downstairs if you aren't watching.

Nothing is more unsettling than to be falling asleep on the living-room couch and suddenly see what looks like a runaway bowling ball heading straight at you.

From time to time, our hamsters have been known to pry open the little door that keeps

115

them in the ball. And if there is a way to get out of their cages, there always is the will to wander.

Recently, we have gone to aquarium-type cages so that the Rodent Brothers can't bend back bars or pry open plastic.

We went to these "glass houses" because there have been entirely too many school mornings with the following scenario: Ten minutes away from the tardy bell, an empty cage, a daughter with tears in her eyes and a couple of thousand square feet of area to cover looking for a hairy, little creature that isn't particularly interested in being found.

More times than not, the hamsters end up in the heat vents and sometimes all the way down into the furnace before I can free them in yet another heroic rescue.

All such incidences don't end on a happy note, however. Speedy was an earlier hamster who, unfortunately, didn't make it out in time. He lived up to his name during his short life. He couldn't be caught. Speedy was his name and game.

I can only hope his passing was speedy as well. He's now out in the backyard, rest his little soul. It took me three weeks to find him in the heat vents after his not-so-great escape. Nevertheless, we were well aware of his general whereabouts any time the furnace would come on and send a reminder of him throughout the house.

Since then, Smokey has been successfully pulled out of the vents twice. Once he even had to climb up a towel far enough for me to reach his puny, little head. He was more than willing for me to pull him out even though he is usually not so fond of me.

The feeling is mutual. He has awakened me a few too many times.

So occasionally when I see him sleeping during the day, I give his cage a little tap—just until his eyes slowly open and he sees it is me who is paying him back.

But the other evening, I thought I had gone too far. I was bounding up the stairs when I spied something brown and furry just before my foot came down on top of it.

Smokey, I thought. Oh, no, not this. How would I explain?

How would my kids take it? How would they accept the fact that it was indeed an accident even though it probably served old Smokey right for getting loose once again?

As I got ready to scoop up its crumpled little existence, I realized my initial identification was wrong. Instead of finding Smokey lying on the stairway, bloodied and broken, I discovered that I had stepped on a tiny Koala—the stuffed animal variety—that had been brought out of the basement for a friend's baby when they recently visited.

Smokey had gotten to me again without even being around.

I sighed in relief and then decided a basset hound would be a nice choice for a dog.

November 7, 1989
SCENT OF A HOUND

My wife sniffs the air as if she is testing for forest fires—or burnt pot roast.

In recent weeks, there has been a different aroma permeating through our house.

My wife wiggles her nose and acts as if she has had the U.S. calvary camping out in her kitchen.

The smell is dog.

New dog.

Puppy dog.

Hound Dog.

"Smelly dog," says my wife. "How many times a week do you bathe these things?"

She looks through the book she bought on basset hounds as if it is some sort of technical manual with all the answers on how to work out the bugs of this new acquisition.

I tell her my pup, Ernest Hemingway Banks, is nothing like a new can opener. There is no step-by-step procedure on how to trouble-shoot on such movable parts as paws and jaws.

She ignores me. "It says nothing—absolutely nothing—on baths in here," she says, thumbing through the pages in almost a mad frenzy. "How do you know when to bathe him?"

"When he smells like a dead fish," I answer.

"When he smells like green and gray cottage cheese."

"When he smells like a backed-up sewer."

"When he smells like the kids after a week of camp.

"But not when he just smells like a dog."

My wife never grew up with a dog. Somehow along the way, she has been brainwashed into thinking that "Hint of Hound" belongs outside and outside only.

"I like Ernie," she admits. "I just don't like his smell most of the time. Do other dogs smell as strong as he does?"

Without knowing it, she has tiptoed into one of my fields of expertise. Bassets and beagles and other hounds do have a stronger smell than most other breeds. In fact, an old hog that is kept away from mud won't even have the natural aroma of a hound dog.

It has something to do with their floppy ears and the secretions that somehow help perk up their own smelling sensories for hunting purposes. I've read that somewhere—I think.

"Poodles don't smell like our dog," my wife says.'

"Poodles aren't real dogs," I answer. "Real dogs don't wear ribbons and curls. Real dogs don't get splashed with perfume. Real dogs smell like . . . dogs."

"I don't know if I would have wanted you to get a dog had I known he was going to smell," she says.

"That's one of the reasons you get a dog," I said. "For the smell."

That's when she looked at me and then at the dog, at me and at the dog over and over again, as if she was trying to figure out which one of us was dumber. If she had to vote, I suspect that she would say I smelled a little better but that Ernie was less of a nuisance.

I was being serious. I like the smell of a dog.

I'm not talking about a dirty dog or one that has carried in half the backyard in the door with him—or one that didn't make it out to the backyard in time.

I'm talking about a dog just lying on the floor at your feet, minding his own business, and letting his ears flop back like his doesn't have a care in the world.

Some things are supposed to smell certain ways and there is no way you're going to make a dog—especially a hound dog—smell any way but like a dog.

That's the way I like it. In fact, I had forgotten just how much I do like it until we got our new dog.

Dog is a settling and soothing smell.

It makes a room feel more comfortable. It makes me feel more relaxed and content with my lot.

It also makes me feel a little like a kid again when I used to use an old beagle named Buddy as my pillow when I was watching television.

"Do you get to the point when you don't notice the smell?" my wife asked.

"I suppose you can to a point," I answered. "But if you get down real close to him or let him lay his head in your lap, you always will be able to smell him.

"That's the best part about having a dog," I added. "To me, a good dog smells better than a daisy."

I think that was the moment when my wife sprayed me with the air freshener.

November 7, 1993
CATERING TO KITTY

Someone once said that if your dog grew to 500 pounds, he or she would still like you, lick you and bring you your slippers. (Personally, I'm still waiting on the slippers part.)

However, if your cat grew to 500 pounds, it would corner you, toy with you a while and then eat most of you before saving the rest for later.

I believe that.

Cats can be creepy.

Cats are for Halloween and tennis racquets.

So I was not amused when my daughter said, "I want a cat."

Actually, she first said it about 14 years ago when she was just learning to talk. I ignored her then and also ignored her weekly pleas ever since. "Teach the dog to purr," I would say.

I did allow her to hang cat pictures and posters in her room and she also bought a wide assortment of feline figurines for the top of her dresser. But no real cats were going to prowl through my house.

"Cats can kill mice," my daughter said.

"I like mice better than cats," I replied.

A few months ago, she changed her tack. She had learned how to lobby. "Mom said she doesn't mind if we get a cat. The boys want one, too. I bet Ernie [the dog] would like a cat to play with, too."

"Ernie would use a cat as dental floss," I said.

But I am not always a dictator. "Family vote," I announced at the dinner table soon after. "All those in favor of a cold-hearted, conniving, clawing cat, raise your hand."

"One, two, three."

I expected that.

"All those against? Me and Mom and . . . what do you mean you abstain?" I said to my wife. "If you vote with Ernie and me, it's a tie and the tie goes to the side that pays the mortgage."

There was a mini-celebration at the table. I immediately asked my kids how clean their rooms were and silence prevailed.

They wouldn't dare get a cat.

Two days later, my daughter casually said, "Cristin is bringing over our cat."

"Our cat?" I said.

"Well, actually it will be my cat until I go off to college in two years, and then you and Mom can keep it for me until I graduate."

I quickly ran over to the encyclopedias and looked up the average lifespan of cats. It said it was not unusual for them to live for 15 years, a few even making it to 30.

I was dumbfounded. The book of C's—fatter than most—slowly slipped out of my hands and landed on my foot. Ignoring the pain, I picked it up to make sure that cats who live that long don't grow to the size of panthers.

"Here she is," my daughter said a few minutes later. "Straight from Cristin's garage."

She held up this little gray fuzzball that looked like a piece of lint out of my belly button.

"Pathetic," I said.

"Cute," my wife said.

"Adorable," one of my sons said.

Adorable? I didn't even know he knew such a word.

I obviously was in the minority here.

A name was next on the agenda. I forced myself to be helpful. "In all the world, cats are called by only five names," I said. "Boots, Cuddles, Whiskers, Tom ... and I can't think of the fifth."

"I'll call her Kitty," my daughter said.

"Yes, you're right," I added. "I believe that Kitty is the fifth name."

Then I broke down and told my daughter I was not yet prepared for a cat in my house, that this was all happening too fast.

"Too fast?" she almost shouted. "It's taken me 14 years and a truce with my brothers to get Kitty here."

The cat has been with us a couple of months now. She and I study each other closely, but usually keep our distance. Cats seem to have that sixth sense that tells them they're around dog people.

The other day, she did use me as a bridge from a cabinet to a table. Four prongs suddenly pierced my back, walked up my shoulder and then leaped beyond my reach.

I don't trust her, although I do give her A's on cleanliness and bathroom procedures.

The others in the family treat her like a house guest. Her scratching post is fancier than the chair I sit in. She purrs as if she is rubbing it in to me on how good she has it.

Who would have thought? "The Cat in the Hat cometh" to my house, of all places.

I figured while all this attention was being heaped on this new arrival, I would bond with my dog a little more. But he has been more interested in playing with the cat than with me.

He tips her over and noses her around the room while she takes turns nipping at his ears and his wagging tail.

He weighs 70 pounds. She weighs about two pounds. She already can hold her own with him. If she goes up to five pounds. I will worry for Ernie's safety.

I can only imagine what she would be like at 500 pounds. I am sure I would be the first to go.

December 12, 1993
RACCOON? RETREAT!

My buddy Phil woke up with a start the other night.

Part of the reason was because his wife was poking him in the ribs with her elbow.

"Phil, wake up," she whispered. "There's something going on in here. I really think there's something in our room."

Those aren't exactly the words you want to hear at 4 AM, but they can clear the cobwebs out of one's mind in a hurry.

"Probably the cats," said Phil, trying to sound brave.

But when he sat up in bed, he heard some strange noises, too. "And as I started to look around the bedroom, I saw this huge, gray form scampering out the door with our three cats following."

Phil also followed, creeping around the corner ever so slowly only to almost step in the biggest pile of indoor doo-doo that this cat owner had ever seen.

"Hmmmmm," he said in his best Sherlock Holmes imitation.

At least he knew he was on the right trail.

He wound through the house, turning on lights as he went and watching his step in case there were any other "rug apples."

"When I got to our 'rec' room, I switched on the light and just about froze," he said. "There, back on some shelving in the corner, was a raccoon the size of a full-grown cocker spaniel."

The way the raccoon hissed when Phil approached, it might as well have been a grizzly bear as far as he was concerned.

But Phil let indignation take over his fear—for a moment anyway. After all, this raccoon was in his house, scaring his wife and cats and knocking their glassware on the floor.

"So I opened the back door and started prodding it with a pool cue," Phil said. "I wasn't trying to hurt it—just help guide it toward the door and back outside."

The raccoon didn't take the hint. In fact, what it did take was a chunk out of the pool cue with its teeth.

That's when fear took over again.

"I looked at myself and realized I was standing with a pool cue in my hand that had a chunk out of it because of a wild animal that was now staring at me from across the room. All of a sudden, I felt very vulnerable."

And naked.

Phil is one of those people who sleeps in the buff, and he just then noticed that he hadn't taken the time to put on his robe when he had jumped out of bed to do his tracking.

He looked at the pool cue, and then at himself.

"At that point, I backed on out of the room with my cats already behind me."

121

Phil's wife made some coffee and brought him some pants while he wondered if he should call the Humane Society at such an early hour. Another hiss from the "rec" room convinced him he should. The person on the phone said someone would be out, but to leave open a door in case the raccoon might leave on its own.

Not long after that, a couple of neighbors came sauntering over after seeing all the lights on. "Of course, one of them thought he could save some of the glasses that were getting knocked over, but when the raccoon started hissing again and getting its back up, my neighbor agreed that waiting seemed a good idea."

The Humane Society called back to make sure the raccoon hadn't left. It hadn't. "So about 20 minutes later, a very tired-looking woman came to the door with one of those capture sticks," Phil said.

"I could sort of tell that she wasn't too impressed that a guy like me couldn't get a raccoon out of his own house."

But then when she rounded the corner and took a look at it, she got her own wake-up call. "Whoa! That's the biggest raccoon I've ever seen," she shouted.

After a five-minute battle, she finally got the critter hooked and hauled him outside. But then it was able to break away and dash off into what little night was left.

"I mean it looked like something out of Marlin Perkins' *Wild Kingdom*, the way she had to rope him and pull him out," Phil said. "And to think I was trying to nudge him with a pool cue."

Later on, Phil discovered that the raccoon had torn off the screening on the top of his chimney and broken the flue door on the way down.

He quickly repaired them.

"That raccoon is still out there somewhere, and I don't want another late-night visit from him."

Despite the intrusion, Phil sleeps soundly again. He has considered pajamas, though.

January 28, 1996
PETS TO THE VET

Had I more whiskers and a tail, instead of just a hang-dog expression, it could have been our own "incredible journey."

But instead of the two dogs and a cat from the popular story and movie *The Incredible Journey*, our merry little band consisted of one dog, one cat and one master.

Master? Yeah, right. Has anyone else noticed how master conveniently rhymes with disaster?

The red-letter day on the calendar had finally arrived for man's best friend (my dog, of course) and the cat who would eat me if she could gain 300 pounds. (I monitor her diet closely.)

It was time for their annual checkups. Arf, barf. Meow, yeow.

This is not a fun day for Jaws and Paws (not their real names in an effort to protect their identities). They have been brought up in such a loving, caring way that they are now spoiled, self-centered and very particular about which furniture they shed on.

I'm sure you have heard our crack weathermen refer to a downpour as "raining cats and dogs." At our house, it's a case of the cat and dog reigning.

But V-Day—Veterinarian Day—is their come-uppance.

Yep, and mine, too. After all, I start off the morning by digging around in the cat box and then through the backyard snow for some of their better-looking stool samples. I will spare you the details.

Then it's into the van. Jaws (not his real name) has a one-track mind about the van; it only means "a walk," "a walkie" or a "W-A-L-K" (this dog is smart) is imminent. He has been known to jerk arms out of sockets while pulling loved ones toward a vehicle.

Meanwhile, Paws (not her real name) rides in the van exactly once a year—to the veterinarian's. She apparently remembers this and acts accordingly.

On our trip last week, I had one animal licking me in the ear and another clawing at my leg. Jaws' doggie breath is the worst part of this journey unless Paws happens to work herself under the brake pedal.

Taking two pets to the veterinarian at the same time is not a good idea for one person unless one of the animals is big enough to ride upon and the other is small enough to stash in a pocket.

I cannot get Paws to stay in any kind of container unless it is a sealed-tight Tupperware product. Even I think that is a little too inhumane for the slash-kitty and so I must tuck her under my arm while dragging Jaws by his leash.

Yes, it becomes a drag when he recognizes the fact that I have duped him—that the only walk he is taking is into the veterinarian's little house of horrors. This realization always seems to affect his bladder and it is a race to get him out of the van before he does the sequel to the Pavlov dog experiment.

Paws takes this opportunity to hide somewhere in the hinterlands of the van, probably calculating a lunge for either freedom or my throat.

With Jaws cutting off the circulation to one of my legs with his leash and Paws forcing me to carry her somewhat like a briefcase, we make it inside the clinic—but barely. I have mumbled my little prayers the entire trip and God apparently has heard me; there are no other animals—either vicious or tasty—in the waiting room.

"Do you have something for us?" Evelyn, the receptionist, asks with a smile.

While Paws knocks over a display of animal-care pamphlets and Jaws goes into his heebie-jeebie shakes, I hand over their stool samples in litttle baggies. No one seems embarrassed but me.

The veterinarian, Frank Perusek, is a good man and handles our pets with care. They withstand him this time, too, although when one is on the examining table, it always seems as if the other lurks directly behind his legs as if hoping he will take a sudden step back and topple over old Jaws or Paws.

There are vaccinations to get, toenails to trim, ears to swab— all that good stuff. Through it all, both Paws and Jaws take their turns burrowing their faces into my armpit, which tells me they must be scared out of their senses—including their sense of smell.

Amazingly, whimpers are kept to a minimum although I can't help letting out a little one when Jaws takes a needle to the flank.

"Everything looks fine," our veterinarian says, "except Jaws [not his real name] really needs to come back and have the tartar buildup chipped off his teeth."

I have one question. "Will it make his breath better?"

"Probably."

I just don't know how I am going to break it to Jaws that there will be another visit to the V-E-T.

January 13, 1998
FRISKY AT 40

Harold Stull walks out his back door and into the cold rain. He steps over the two strands of barb wire and then scans the seven-acre pasture behind his home just south of Lapaz.

No need for concern. Blackie is out there somewhere.

Harold purses his lips and lets out a whistle that could send a factory full of people off to lunch. After a few seconds, he pierces the air again.

Out of the gloom trots a little black Shetland pony, as cute as if he had just jumped off a merry-go-round.

"Hey, Blackie, how you doing?"

He has no Mr. Ed answer (at least with a stranger around), but he nods his head as if to say he is feeling frisky.

If Harold pulls back the long hair that grows on Blackie's crown, a clump of gray is exposed. His teeth have seen better days, too. But other than those telltale signs of age setting it, Blackie looks like he could race a rabbit around and win.

"He doesn't look too bad for 40, does he?" Harold says.

You nod. And then you think: "Forty? As in years?"

"He'll be 41 years old on June 14," says 64-year-old Harold Stull as if birthdays for Blackie will keep coming. "It wouldn't surprise me if he outlives me."

"A pony or horse that age is highly unusual," North Liberty veterinarian Ben Walbert says. "Blackie is by far the oldest pony I've ever dealt with and he can still go like heck. It just goes to show you what the right diet and the proper care can do."

"Love and affection probably have something to do with it too," Harold says. "My wife Marge hugs him and pets him and kisses him everyday. She feeds him cookies and crackers. If he's not out getting his drink by the fence by 6 or 6:15 in the morning, she's already worrying about him."

And have you ever tried to find a black pony in the dark?

"I may not feel quite as sentimental as Marge, but he's family," Harold says. "If she had to make a choice between me and Blackie, I'm not so sure I would win."

Blackie has a history of winning. Eighty-seven trophies, now the same tarnished color as his well-worn teeth, are stored back in the barn.

Harold and Marge Stull's five boys all rode Blackie in the St. Joseph County 4-H Fair, winning the high-point trophy for his class for 17 years. He also was a champion at the 1976 Indiana State Fair with Russell, the Stulls' fourth son, in the saddle.

"He used to get the Fair crowd roaring because right before he'd race, he gave his hind legs a little kick into the air," Harold recalls with a smile. "He did so well regardless of which of our boys was riding him that some people started to kid me that he was a push-button horse. But you had to be a good rider to stay with him."

And even a great rider couldn't stay on Blackie if he wanted to get a little ornery. "Every year, it didn't matter which of our sons was going to ride him in the Fair, Blackie was going to buck him off during their first practice. Blackie did that just to show who was boss. After that, he was fine."

The Stulls ran out of boys before Blackie ran out of steam when he was retired from competition in 1985 after 21 years. "He was still rarin' to go," Harold says.

Still is, for that matter. Just last year, son Mike had come home from California and was dropping off a flatbed trailer in the back pasture when the steel ramps fell off the back and made quite a clanging noise.

"It spooked Blackie and off he went through the gate and down the median on U.S. 31 toward the intersection of Highway 6," Marge Stull recalls. "Mike fell while chasing him and broke his foot. Truckers stopped in the middle of the highway trying to stop him. Everybody was out chasing him before he was finally caught down by the Marathon station.

"Mike later told me, 'Mom, if anything would have happened to Blackie, I would have packed up my bags and left right then so I wouldn't have had to face you.'" Marge says. "He knew how much Blackie means to me. He's been so good with the boys over the years."

Even at 40, Blackie remains a friendly, little pony although he did buck off one of the Stulls' 13 grandkids last summer. "It gets to the point where he's had enough and he lets people know it," Marge adds.

He has his routine and his regular diet of pasture grass, a good grade of hay and senior horse feed mixed with cracked corn. He has a couple of little barns, too, he can choose between when it's time to get out of the elements.

"Oh, Blackie's spoiled," Russell Stull says. "I'm surprised mom and dad haven't built on an addition to the house for him."

He's been inside of the house from time to time but prefers his pasture.

"As far as I'm concerned, he helped raise our five boys," Harold says. "We had other horses, too, and 4-H and the riding were nice family activities for all of us and probably kept the boys out of problems.

"And to think I bought Blackie for just $25 some 39 years ago."

A good buy.

And eventually it will have to be a good-bye. After all, only a handful of horses live very far into their 40s.

"I know he's going to have to leave us someday," Marge Stull admits. "But for a good, little pony like Blackie, I do believe there's a horse heaven waiting."

April 25, 1999
SOUTH SIDE STRAY

Michele Chlebek first saw the yellow puppy almost 21/2 years ago, slinking around the Kmart parking lot on South Bend's south side.

She got out of her car and tried to approach the little stray but the dog ran off, watching Michele over its shoulder. Michele grimaced. She figured the pup was not long for this world in such a high-traffic area.

Michele is a dog person who already had three pooches, so this poor little soul on the run tugged at her heart strings. She even decided to call the dog Marty because of the Kmart connection.

"There was something about this little dog that really touched me," the Grissom Middle School art teacher admits. "I knew I wanted her in my life if I could ever catch her."

Marty didn't want to be caught, though.

Not by Michele. Not by South Bend Animal Control. Not by the Humane Society. Not by the guys over at Super Auto Parts on South Main Street. And not by other concerned citizens who hoped to find a better life for Marty.

Marty was too elusive, too untrusting, just too doggone smart.

That didn't mean that Marty didn't get fed. In fact, Michele was leaving food for her every day around the old Brite Way build-ing on Ireland Road, where Marty often was spotted. "And I know other people would give her food—from places like Taco Bell or Dairy Queen. She ate lots of fast food."

Michele would even leave one of her worn socks with the food, hoping that Marty would associate her scent with the meal and learn to trust her.

An old sock? "Come to think of it, maybe that is why she was very hesitant to get close to me," Michele says with a smile.

"A few people figured that Marty was living in a drainage ditch in the area," the LaSalle High School and Saint Mary's College graduate says. "I do know that she was able to survive two different winters, including the blizzard this January."

And, somehow, she also survived all the traffic in the area. "There were times I would see Marty just standing beside U.S. 31," Michele says. "Oh, I worried about her."

When the old Brite Way was torn down in the spring of 1997, Michele didn't see Marty for several months. She had to wonder if the dog had been hit or picked up by Animal Control and put down.

"But then, out of the blue, Marty started showing up again."

Michele stepped up her efforts to catch her. She tracked Marty's footprints in the snow. She read books on wolf behavior because Marty had apparently never been domesticated. She put out flyers with a description of Marty and how to contact her if the dog was ever caught. She even put up a kennel even though there were no guarantees that Marty would ever live in it.

"I just felt so bad for Marty, because anytime you would see her, her tail would be tucked between her legs and she would never let anyone get close enough even to pet her," Michele says.

Others watched out for Marty, too.

Pete and the staff at Super Auto started feeding Marty daily when she started hanging around their place.

Sandy, a Pet Refuge volunteer, would leave fresh straw outside Super Auto, and Marty began sleeping in it.

Kim, a South Bend Animal Control officer, saved Michele's flyer about Marty for more than a year—just in case.

Jackie, who worked at another nearby business, would call Michele anytime Marty was spotted.

And many other nearby employees and neighbors showed their concern by leaving big bags of dog food, dog biscuits and even a dog house at Super Auto.

About six weeks ago, Pete had bonded with Marty enough to pick her up. Animal Control got her, and Kim gave Michele a call.

After more than two years of hunting and hoping, Marty was hers. "That first night, I couldn't believe she was really here."

Michele was ecstatic; Marty wasn't sure what to think.

"It took a lot of time and patience to help her over her fear and learn the 'routines' of living life as a well-loved pet," Michele admits.

Marty—part yellow lab and who knows what else—kept her tail tucked in, wouldn't eat in front of Michele and would become startled at the slightest of moves. She even broke through a secured kennel after the first night.

"When I tried to introduce her to living inside, she would just lay by the back door and venture no further," Michelle adds.

But things slowly changed for the better. During the last few weeks, the tail started wagging and Michele is now even licked in the face by Marty. She also has decided she likes sleeping inside the house.

"She is spoiled now," Michele says. "After all those years of living outside, she goes out to do her business and then wants to come right back in."

To a loving owner . . . to three fellow dogs . . . and to an occasional bath.

Marty can quit hiding. Michele can quit hunting. And dozens of people on the south side can quit worrying about that little, yellow dog at the side of the road.

July 25, 1999
FAR FROM PURR-FECT

My mom and sister came to town earlier in the week, bearing gifts—and also a grudge. "Where is that darn cat of yours?" My sister said as soon as she walked inside our door. "Keep that crazy animal away from me."

Nobody likes my cat.

My mom won't even make eye contact with her. My brother-in-law swears she chased him out of the living room when all he wanted to do was pick a magazine off the coffee table. And my poor old dog can't even close his eyes if she is on the prowl.

She has this habit of bopping people with her front paws—declawed no less—if they invade her space. And if she is really out of sorts and doesn't particularly like the company around her, she will "hiiiissssss" like there is no tomorrow.

Should that be such a big deal?

Last month, I saw a little sign in a novelty shop that read, "Beware of the Attack Cat." I bought it as a joke. Everybody else thinks of it as fair warning.

"She is vicious," my wife says.

"The most unfriendly cat I have ever seen," my younger son adds.

"I don't want her," my daughter whines when I suggest we drop Kitty off at her apartment.

My daughter, of course, is the cause of all this trouble.

If you have read my previous columns about our pets, you know that I am a dog person. I have always looked at cats past the kitty stage as creepy—raptors without wings.

Someone once said that if your dog weighed 500 pounds, it would still lick you in the face. But your cat at that size would eventually eat you for supper after toying with your body parts.

I still believe that.

Several years ago, though, my daughter started campaigning for a cat. She bought little figurines of cats for her room, hung up cat posters and cooed at every kitty that came her way.

Hamsters and a hound dog just weren't enough for her.

She finally wore my wife and me down. Unfortunately, it took her about 10 years to do so. By that time, she was 16 and two years away from college. That's when her buddy, Cristen, brought over this pretty, little gray kitty on her shoulder. Our daughter instantly fell in love with it.

If only cats stayed kitties.

Kitty grew into an ornery critter who only seemed to want to bond with my daughter, who fed her and cooed with her and let her share the pillow at night. Kitty Kat usually ran anytime I came near her, or she would ambush me from under the bed.

That was OK with me. Her

surprise attacks kept me on my toes. It also allowed me to feel justified in kicking the little feline furball across the room, although she was always too swift for me ever to make contact.

Then my daughter went off to college, a picture of her kitty in a frame in her suitcase. I, meanwhile, was the poor schmo who inherited the cat box duty . . . and the feeding . . . and the brushing . . . and the occasional treat handout. Somewhere, over the last four years, the cat became mine.

I didn't intend it that way.

Yet I am the one who makes life purr-fect for the crazy cat and, at one point, she must have decided that I was the human she would adopt.

First, Kitty deemed it to be OK for her to sleep on the bed between my feet. Then she apparently decided that she could stick her nose into my cereal bowl when I was down near the bottom. And finally, it was my lap that seemed to interest her when she needed some cushioning for a nap.

Even so, I sometimes literally rub her the wrong way to see how far I can go before she swats me or tries to take a nip out of one of my fingers. I guess I am ornery like her, too. Good ol' Catty Daddy.

"You ruined my cat," my daughter now says. "It's not the same cat I had. You have made her into a mean, mean cat."

I tell my daughter the cat has not yet tried to eat me, although we did have to rescue a bunny from her mouth the other night when the Kitster sneaked out the back door with the dog.

So when college ends for my daughter next spring, she has no intentions of reclaiming Kitty. "I am going to get another cat, a nice cat," she says. "You can keep Kitty. You know that's what she would prefer anyway."

I look at Kitty. She looks at me. She starts to rub against my leg.

My dog leaves the room. My wife shakes her head. I pick up the cat and rub her belly.

She allows no one but me to do that.

Considering a cat's normal life expectancy, I don't know whether to laugh or cry.

July 28, 2000
SOME TOUGH SPOTS

Frank Cackowski doesn't see the world in just black and white. He does love his Dalmatians, though.

So he also sees red when these beautiful dogs—or any dogs, for that matter—are mistreated.

"I get pretty darn emotional at times," the 57-year-old Mishawakan says.

He does something about it—getting these spotted dogs out of some tough spots.

Frank is one of those kindhearted souls who rescues abused or abandoned Dalmatians and helps find good homes for them.

"I can't think of anything more gratifying," he admits.

During the last four years, he has participated in about 75 rescues—initiating some of these efforts himself or driving a leg of other rescue trips between a "kill" shelter and a prospective owner.

"It takes an unbelievable amount of coordination—phone calls, e-mails and so forth—to pull together one of these efforts," Frank says.

A wag of the tail makes it all worthwhile.

Dalmatians have moved into second place behind greyhounds as dogs most abandoned. One reason is that about 10 percent of all Dalmatians are born deaf. A bigger reason is Disney's 1996 release of the movie *101 Dalmatians*.

"After the movie, people flocked to pet stores and breeders to buy Dalmatians that they expected to be these little designer dogs," he says. "What many of them did not understand was that they were getting a dog that can be very hyper at a young age. Dalmatians are smart and very loyal, but they tend to be clowns and do get into trouble."

Those pretty little pups that Disney portrayed can be a handful.

"I did one rescue after a family went to the movie and then directly to the pet store where they bought a Dalmatian pup for $600," Frank recalls. "Three days later, they took it to the Humane Society [of St. Joseph County] because they said it barked all the time."

Through a contact in Rochester, New York, Frank found a home for him—and five other puppies that had already been left at the Humane Society three weeks earlier. On the day after Christmas, he drove the six dogs to Cleveland where another Dalmatian lover met him and took them to their new homes in New York.

Although Frank prefers to concentrate on shorter runs, he has been involved in one that took a Dalmatian named Fannie from Wheeling, West Virginia, to the Seattle area, including two legs of that trip by plane.

"Sort of a bucket brigade of individuals across the U.S.," Frank says of the cross-country cooperation.

Often, it takes some time—and a lot of searching—to find a nice home and the right owner. Sometimes, it takes a while for the dog to be ready, too, especially if it has been abused. A few years ago, the local Humane Society called Frank about an abandoned male Dalmatian that would go to the bathroom any time a man approached him.

"I didn't know what I could do, but I did promise that I would come out and spend some time with the dog," Frank says. "I walked the dog a little every day on a 12-foot leash and, believe me, he stayed all 12 feet away from me. But slowly but surely, he started to come around. After three weeks, he finally took a cookie out of my hand."

A few weeks later, Frank found a home for the dog he named Lucky—in Rhode Island. It was an eight-leg trip carried out by people who didn't even know each other. Three of the "leg runners" weren't even Dalmatian owners.

But Frank has pictures of all of those who helped and has posted them on his own Dalmatian Web site, www.dalhouse.com. "When I initiate a rescue, I get the dog a leash and a collar, some food, and include a disposable camera so we can get pictures of everyone."

It's a labor of love for Frank, a retired LaSalle High School industrial arts and mass communications teacher.

He and his wife, Sharon, have their own 6-year-old Dalmatian, Maggie. "I've had dogs all my life, but Maggie is our first Dalmatian."

But probably not their last.

Frank's office in his basement could be called the Dalmatian Den. He has countless pictures of Dalmatians, along with just about any other Dalmatian-related toy or gift you could imagine. He sells the Dalmatian merchandise on his Web site, mostly to defray the cost of all the rescue efforts.

His poochie pastime almost a full-time job already, Frank and other volunteers figure they might get even busier when Disney releases *102 Dalmatians* later this year.

He says that the Dalmatian Club of America has told its members to hold off the hate mail to Disney. Club officials hope to negotiate a disclaimer at the end of the film so that prospective owners know the kind of dog a Dalmatian is and the commitment it takes to raise one.

"It requires some patience," Frank says.

"And lots of love."

Paid back in loyalty and licks.

January 21, 2001
WHEN OLD DOGS DIE

I glance over at the small brown box on the passenger seat of my car and give it a tender pat.

It is probably big enough for a new wallet or a couple of decks of cards. It is also big enough to hold my old dog's ashes.

Good old Ernie—Ernest Hemingway Banks—is in hound-dog heaven.

His ashes rest beside me inside this small box I have just picked up at the veterinarian's. When the snow finally melts and grass grows again, I will sprinkle them into the wind at St. Patrick's Park, his favorite sniffing place.

People with pets know my feelings—a melancholy that comes across me when I realize once again that my old companion won't be doing his doggie dance at the door when I arrive home.

The Ern dog has been gone for a few weeks now, the victim of a cancerous growth on his shoulder that began spreading to his organs. At the end, he could barely move and often whimpered when I lifted him down the two steps to the backyard.

The time had come. My wife and I held him tightly as our vet, Frank Perusek, put Ernie into his peaceful rest and out of his misery.

They say it's OK for men to cry when their old dogs die, but I can't say whether it helps or not.

Before I left Ernie's still body, I lifted one of his 12-inch basset ears to my face and first used it to wipe a few tears from my eye. Then, one more time, I touched his ear to my nose and breathed in that wonderful fragrance of a resting dog.

The Hint of Hound, I called it. I miss it so.

His ears, which stirred up the dirt when he was on one of his smelling frenzies, held that scent the best. Yet as much as I loved those soft, droopy ears, I may miss his nose even more. It was that moist, black nose of his that would poke itself under the covers and find a part of me if he was up first.

That was often my wake-up call in the morning, and monitoring his last backyard visit was usually my final duty of the night. And every lunchtime for the last 11 years, I drove home just for him.

Lord knows he did enough for me.

He was my buddy—just like our beagle Buddy was when I was growing up. I still have a picture of Buddy, even though he ate his last Milkbone more than 25 years ago. I imagine I will still have a picture—and my fond memories—of Ernie a quarter-century from now, too.

Just as I grew up with Buddy, my kids grew up with Ern. But they were gone—off to college and beyond—when he grew old. He remained good company. He kept the nest from feeling so empty and was the comforting constant in our changing lives.

There was nothing fancy about Ernie. He was all dog—his Hush Puppy looks atop four little chubby legs, and his yardstick length ending at his welcome-wagging tail.

When he was a pup, we could run together until he got the scent of a rabbit or squirrel and would forge his own trail. He never caught anything in his whole life, and often his runs were abruptly halted when he would step on one of his ears, throwing his lanky body into a comical cartwheel.

In his later years, his gait slowed even more than mine. His enthusiastic trot turned into a slow jog and then finally a cumbersome walk. I continued to run—out 100 yards and back 75 yards to where he had meandered, out another 100 yards and back another 75 to the stump he decided he must examine from all sides. I could run for a half-hour that way and hardly get out of eyesight of my car.

But as slow as Ernie's pace became, he always loved his walks. Even in his last few months of life, he desperately wanted just to limp down the little hill by our house so he could take in the world with his nose.

His Hound of the Baskervilles bark—or bay—could scare the bejabbers out of unsuspecting passers-by, and in his later years when his sunny disposition faded a bit, he let other dogs and kids know the boundaries of our yard.

And Ernie always lived an uneasy truce with our cat, who followed him into the family. On his last day, his instincts took over one last time as he tried to chase her for a few painful steps, probably just for good measure.

Even Kitty seems to miss him. It's not her fault that she does a poor imitation of Ernie when I open the door from the garage after a day at work.

One of the first things I do now after coming home is empty my wallet and other "valuables" into my new coin dish—Ernie's old water bowl.

Painted on its side is "Dog."

Such a small word for such a huge hole in my heart.

COPS

November 21, 1999
DIFFERENT DIRECTIONS

Lt. John McCullum, a South Bend police officer for 28 years, loved the critically acclaimed TV cop show *Hill Street Blues*.

"I watched it faithfully," the 54-year-old admitted.

McCullum took it with a grain of salt when the police cases on television always got solved in an hour. "In real life, it sometimes takes years to solve some of those kinds of cases," he said.

Michael Warren, who played police officer Bobby Hill on *Hill Street Blues*, knows that, too.

"He should. I've kidded him enough about that," McCullum said with a smile. "But he gives it to me back."

They can do that to each other. They grew up together on South Bend's northwest side. They went to Marquette, Muessel and Central High School together. And they played side-by-side in the Central backcourt during the Bears' 1963 state runner-up season.

McCullum, a year ahead of Warren in school, played ball at Indiana State University for a year and then went into the Air Force for four years. Warren went on to play on two NCAA championship teams at UCLA under former Central High School coach John Wooden.

Then later on, one became a real cop and one became a pretend one.

"It's ironic how some things turn out, isn't it?" McCullum said.

He grew up on Elmer Street, and Warren lived three streets over on Meade Street. "We used to cut through the paths in the fields to get to each other's houses," McCullum said. "We walked everywhere."

Most of the time, they had basketballs under their arms. They were usually heading to the playground at Marquette or Linden school.

"Michael and I loved to guard each other," said McCullum, who has coached the LaSalle boys freshman team for the last six years. "That's what made us better players. You could tell Michael had leadership qualities. And when we got to high school, everybody looked to see how Michael was going to react to see how they should."

At Central, they got to the state final game before losing, 65-61, to Muncie Central, a team the

135

Bears had beaten during the regular season. That was part of a 19-game winning streak during their 26-3 season.

That last game was one of the few disappointments during his high school days. "It was great being at Central. And the basketball team did everything together. That team was really a team. Those kind of friendships can last forever."

He still sees DeWitt Menyard from time to time, and Mike Otolski, an old coach himself, has occasionally refereed McCullum's freshman games.

They will always be teammates. "I know Michael still tries to stay in touch with some of the guys, too," McCullum said. "He e-mails jokes to DeWitt all the time, and we always have stayed in contact, more lately after my sister Margo died in July. She and Michael were close even though they used to yell at each other when they were kids."

Occasionally, talk turns to the Central days. "We don't dwell on them, but they are pleasant memories. But it was awhile ago. My wife Arlene was in the last Central graduating class, so she says she doesn't even remember when I played."

McCullum can't help but think of another Central teammate. He was Jimmy Ward, who also played guard and became a starter alongside Warren after McCullum graduated.

While McCullum was in the Air Force and Warren was starting out his career in Hollywood, Ward was still in South Bend. He applied to be a police officer but was turned down. He apparently had gotten hooked up with some questionable people.

On Oct. 12, 1967, Ward was shot and killed by a South Bend police officer when he ran away from a burglary attempt and ignored several warning shots.

"That was devastating news," McCullum said. "I know it affected all of us who were Jimmy's teammates."

Many wondered what they could have done to help prevent Ward's downfall, and eventually his death.

McCullum watches his LaSalle freshmen practice and occasionally sees something in one of them that reminds him a little of Warren or Ward or even himself.

He sometimes wonders how they will turn out. He would have never guessed how he and two of his fellow guards at Central turned out.

One became a cop. One made millions playing a cop. And another one was shot and killed by a cop.

John McCullum shook his head. "Life is unpredictable."

And sometimes way too short.

December 22, 1999
GETTING SWAT-TED

The SWAT team of the South Bend Police Department was weaving down the hallway like a rattler through the brush.

And they were after me. Gulp.

As I pushed through the innocents who were running the other direction, the view over my shoulder was a scary one. It looked like the Chicago Bears' front line bearing down on me with assault rifles.

I was a bad guy. So was Tim Corbett, the former SWAT team commander and now a private investigator.

We had handguns that fired blanks and we were using them. But we were soon cornered in a classroom and ... well, we didn't win.

In fact, we never did.

In five different exercises in the old Nuner School, we got "taken out" by the SWAT team whether we hid, tried to take hostages or just decided to shoot it out.

About 40 South Bend school teachers and a handful of police recruits served as innocent victims in the scenarios that were designed to put a school and its occupants in harm's way.

"When I joined the Police Department in 1988, I never thought I would be teaching how to assault a school," said Keith Schweizer, one of the team leaders for South Bend's SWAT team.

But times have changed. Several shooting deaths have taken place nationwide in schools during the last few years, including the horrific loss of life at Columbine High School outside of Denver last April.

The South Bend SWAT team wants to be prepared for that kind of nightmarish event.

"A student asked me if I really thought that South Bend could ever have anything so violent happen here," said David Chapman, the commander of the SWAT team. "You would like to think it would never happen. But then, airport officials like to think they will never have a crash. But they are prepared for one just the same."

Airports prepare for crashes. His SWAT team prepares for chaos.

"At times, you have to jump over injured people and even run by bombs if there are still shooters in the building," Chapman said. "The more we get a chance to practice that kind of situation with real people, the better we're going to be."

This, after all, is serious business.

"Twenty seconds before we would get to our destination, I always told the guys to say a little prayer," Corbett said. "I don't think you are going to find a tighter bunch than a SWAT team. You love your wife, you love your kids, but these are the guys you trust with your life."

Their lives and others', too.

In the simulated assaults through old Nuner School on Tuesday morning, the good guys fared pretty well.

Bob Culp and Scott Hanley, the size of power forwards, were leading the way in their full battle gear. The two of them together could blot out the sun ... and just about all hope for a bad guy.

But it was Dwayne Hallman who had my number. Twice he picked me off (with his rifle's light) while I had taken a hostage. One came when I pulled Beth Beiersdorf, a LaSalle High School science teacher, in front of me, only to drift just enough for Hallman to have a clear shot. The other time was when I tried to use Edison Middle School teacher Gerry Harman as a shield as a mass of people fled the auditorium. Got me again.

Of course, David Wells shot me when I was putting my hands up. OK, maybe I hadn't dropped my gun yet.

There was another time in the auditorium when both Corbett and I were shot from the balcony by Sgt. Frank Steiger before we even knew there were guys up there.

On the surface, the exercise seemed like a fun game of cops and robbers. I got to shoot off blanks, hurdle over teachers and toss chairs in front of a band of highly motivated marksmen.

Yet this is training that every SWAT team must now do, even though they hope—and a community prays—they never have to use it.

"I would put my guys up against any other team," Chapman said.

No arguments here. I got SWAT-ted

Bad guys, beware.

January 31, 2000
IN DAD'S FOOTSTEPS

Stephanie Marciniak couldn't resist. Her father's police radio looked as if it were just waiting for her to pick it up.

And after she took it off her dad's bed . . . well, 9-year-old Stephanie took the next step.

"302, 302," she said over the radio in between giggles. "302, 302."

That was her father's call number.

"I got a telephone call about that time saying my daughter was on my radio," said Capt. Ron Marciniak, a former South Bend police chief. "Let's just say Stephanie and I had a little non-verbal communication after that."

Stephanie called it something different. "I got a spanking," she said.

She learned her lesson. She didn't pick up another police radio for about 15 years. When she did, it was her own.

Stephanie, now 25, joined her dad on the police force in October 1998. "After watching my dad when I was growing up, I just thought it was an honorable kind of job to do," she said. "And he obviously is the best role model I could ever have."

She knew early in life that she wanted to follow in her father's footsteps. "You hear a lot of kids say that when they grow up that they want to be an actress or a singer. But how many actually get to do what they wanted? Me, I got my dream job."

She admits her father never really guided her in that direction. "In fact when I was a teenager, one of my dad's friends asked me what I wanted to be. When I said a police officer, my dad just about freaked out. He sort of yelled that being a police officer wasn't like the circus."

That's how fathers can be. "I have seen enough deaths and officers injured and it's probably through the grace of God that I have gotten through my career without any serious injury," Ron said. "Sure, I was concerned about her well-being."

But he also figured his only daughter knew what she would be getting into. "Steph saw me get enough calls in the middle of the night. And she saw my tail dragging after a tough day."

Occasionally she would talk to him about his day and listen to his stories. "I guess you could say she always has been a bit of a daddy's girl," Ron said.

They keep that to themselves, though, especially around the Police Department. "I remember right after I first became an officer and saw my dad walking down the hall. I yelled out, 'Hey, Dad . . . hey, Dad.' He finally turned around and said, 'It's Captain Marciniak to you.'"

He smiled when he said it.

"Later on, he called me Steph and I told him it was Officer Marciniak to him."

She smiled, too.

Although there are a handful of father-son combinations on the South Bend police force, the Marciniaks are the only dad-daughter team. Ron, a 29-year veteran, heads the training department, while Stephanie serves as a patrol officer on the afternoon shift.

"It's great to have someone like him to talk to," Stephanie said. "Before roll call, I will often stop by his office and run some things by him."

Once it was obvious that his daughter wanted to be a police officer, Ron was very supportive. "She acted like she might want to be a lawyer at one point and even worked in a couple of law offices for a while, but I could tell she had the self-confidence and demeanor to be a police officer," he said. "And I guess she had to grow up tough as the only granddaughter and with an older brother."

He occasionally helps her out even when he isn't around. "I have been on some calls when people will calm down just when they hear my last name," Stephanie admitted. "Then there was one time I went to a family disturbance and the guy said, 'Oh, great, a frigging woman.' But when he realized who my dad was, he settled right down."

They both worry about each other, but they also are confident in each other's abilities. They also both carry crosses given to them by Mary Marciniak, Ron's mother and Stephanie's grandmother.

And in one of her inside pockets, Stephanie also carries a letter that her dad wrote to her on her first night on the job. It reads: "Good luck tonight. Be careful. Remember what you learned and listen how close your back-up is. Love, Dad."

He doesn't try to keep tabs on her. "I do occasionally hear her on the radio," he said.

It's her radio now . . . and her career.

Ron Marciniak smiled. "Who wouldn't be proud?"

March 5, 2000
BREAKS OF THE JOB

Sgt. Scott Ruszkowski hardly took time to say, "Ouch!" when he sprained his ankle a few weeks ago.

The 12-year veteran of the South Bend Police Department was helping corral another bad guy. The suspect ended up in custody and Ruszkowski in a gel cast.

"This [injury] is pretty much nothing," he said. "You get used to things like that after a while."

Ruszkowski knows all about acquiring on-duty aches and breaks. Let him count the numerous ways.

• In 1990, he was in a car accident while in pursuit of a felon. He injured his hand and neck and suffered a separated shoulder. "I also tore my butt open on the old siren box," he added. "That wasn't pleasant."

• He broke his right hand twice—"once after a guy sucker-punched me while I was taking him into the jail and then later on when I fell on it while trying to break up a fight in the street. I hate casts, though. I ended up cutting both of them off with a steak knife."

• He also suffered a serious knee injury while maneuvering through an obstacle course during a training session. "I had originally hurt it while in the Navy."

• He suffered a broken foot when a suspect jumped down from the rafters of a garage and landed on top of him. "We both went down in a heap and then rolled over on my foot. I was yelling out in pain but still holding on to him when (Cpl. Dan) Demler's dog bit me instead of the other guy. It wasn't the dog's fault. He perceived he had to do something—he just bit the wrong guy."

• But to add insult to injury, I trained that dog."

• He later required 13 stitches from another K-9 bite. "I was working the perimeter of a burglary when the guy took off running my way. I ran after him and so did (Capt. Darryl) Boykins' dog, Dieter. He just temporarily got the two of us confused."

• He shattered his thumb last July "while trying to apprehend a crackhead who was found to have 7 grams of cocaine on him. To this day, I'm not sure how it happened. We were wrestling around for quite a while. I just thought I had jammed it. But it is pretty messed up. Now, I wish I had surgery."

Ruszkowski's reasons go beyond his police work. "For five years, I had a 200 average in bowling. I'm averaging 170 this year thanks to that injury."

Darn thumb.

His is a job that takes a physical toll. "My breakfast consists of toast, cereal and ibuprofen," he said. "I'm 35 years old and you know those plastic bubbles in the packing boxes that you can't resist popping? Well, that's what I sound like when I get out of bed in the morning.

"And when I stretch my neck, it is like an 85-pound knuckle cracking."

He quickly admits that he is not the exception in his line of work. "I don't know one officer who hasn't had some kind of injury in the line of duty," said the LaSalle High School graduate and Navy veteran.

Ruszkowski can't say he didn't know what he was getting into. He is a third generation South Bend police officer. His father, Don, was a 29-year veteran, and his grandfather Ike also served for several years. Ruszkowski's younger brother Rick also is a South Bend cop.

Other family members have taken their lumps, too.

"I remember when I was a kid, my dad was in traction in the hospital after he fell while chasing a guy," Ruszkowski said. "When he was upside down [on his rotating bed], we used to have to hold his cigarette up to him so he could smoke."

Part of the problem for police officers is that they never know when they might be in a foot race or a tussle. "You ride around in a squad car for a couple of hours and, all of a sudden, you are out running after a guy," Ruszkowski said. "There is no time to limber up. You don't have trainers available to tape you up. You just go."

Ruszkowski has one advantage. "My wife's cousin, Damian Dieter, is a podiatrist so he can help me on some of my injuries. But it's getting to the point now that anytime I happen to see him, he says, 'What's wrong with you now?'"

Ruszkowski's wife, Cathi, works for an orthodontist, who also happens to be married to their dentist.

He can't help but put a positive spin on that relationship. "If my teeth ever get knocked out, I guess I am covered there, too."

March 19, 2000
COUNTING HIS BLESSINGS

Mitch and Lynn Kajzer watched as Mel Gibson showed Renee Russo one of his bullet wounds in the movie *Lethal Weapon 3*.

Russo countered with her own. Then the one-upmanship was on as the two Hollywood cops rolled up their sleeves and pulled up their shirts to show all their nicks and knots.

Lynn Kajzer turned to her husband at that point and said, "You could·do that."

He just smiled.

The 10-year veteran of the South Bend Police Department would rather take an inventory of his blessings than his battle scars.

"I feel very fortunate to be alive," he admits.

It was May 1, 1992, when Kajzer made a routine traffic stop with his partner Mike Suth in the 100 block of South Lake Street. While Kajzer was out of the car, he was ambushed by a gunman who shot him four times.

"I can still vividly remember going down and seeing a bullet hit the grass right in front of my nose," he said. "That could have been bad."

The four that hit him did enough damage.

"I was hit in my left ankle, my right calf, my left hip and my right buttocks," he said. "The one that hit me in my buttocks also went through my colon and damaged some other internal organs."

His injuries were life-threatening.

They also proved to be career-ending—but not until recently, almost eight years after he was shot.

Despite three major operations, a temporary colostomy, an ankle that still remains partially paralyzed and an assortment of other painful reminders, Kajzer returned to the police department seven months later to perform his duties in exemplary fashion.

"He always has been a 150 percenter," said Uniform Chief Larry Blume. "The way he came back and the way he approaches his job, he woke up some of the older officers and served as an inspiration for the younger ones."

But that is coming to an end. The lingering pain from some of his injuries has become too much, the slight limp a little more frustrating.

Kajzer has decided to retire next month at the age of 34. If it is approved by the local and state pension boards, he would then draw a pension of about half that of a patrolman's salary.

"He is such an outstanding police officer who truly loves his job," said Capt. Dave Chapman. "I know it kills him to retire."

Four bullets didn't kill him. Kajzer knows this won't, either.

He is taking some computer

networking courses and just last week began a stint in the police department's computer services department. He had studied accounting at IUSB before switching his major to criminal justice.

He will deal with this change just as he quickly dealt with the shooting. "I have gone down to the Police Academy periodically and talked to recruits about what happened to me that night," he said. "I don't have flashbacks or nightmares. When I took this job, I knew that there was a chance something like this could happen."

He and Suth, now a detective with the police department, even kid each other about what happened that night. The gunman, who was apprehended two days later, fired off 10 shots. Despite being struck, Kajzer returned fire—also shooting 10 times, although the gunman fled before being hit. Suth got off two shots from the other side of the car.

"He calls my shots the token two," said Suth, whose friendship with Kajzer goes back to their days together at Washington High School. "We were talking to each other under the car, and I can't believe how calm Mitch was, how professional he remained."

Kajzer actually thought he had only been hit in the ankle. "But when I tried to get to my feet, I went back down."

Suth stood vigil over his friend while the ambulance and a stampede of squad cars rushed to the scene. "My wife and mom both are registered nurses, and they actually beat me to the hospital," Kajzer said. "They had the doctors they wanted for my operation already hand-picked."

He was touched by how his fellow police buddies closed ranks and helped him any way they could during his recovery. "(Sgt.) Bob Stoynoff would even come over to our house twice a week and cut the grass," he said.

Kajzer was able to return to duty in December, about the same time that the 18-year-old gunman was being tried for attempted murder. He received 53 years, his motives never revealed, although many believed it stemmed from the acquittal verdict for Los Angeles police officers in the Rodney King case.

Kajzer's lifetime sentence was a limp and a brace he wears on his left ankle. After he served for five years in the traffic division, the department's leadership tried to force him out of uniform three years ago because of a ruling that required all sworn officers to be able to physically perform the duties of a beat officer. They apparently didn't think Kajzer could.

He proved them wrong. He returned to patrol duty and showed them he could still get the job done on the street despite his injuries.

"Brace or not, I ran down a few people that needed to be caught," Kajzer said.

But the pain has started catching up with him over the past six to eight months. "It's time," he admits.

It's tough.

"I think it's tough on a lot of us, too, when we heard the news," Suth said. "But then Mitch talked to me about it, and he feels good about his future. And if he's happy, I'm happy, too."

"I don't think the city can ever totally appreciate the sacrifices this man has made to continue to be the good public servant he is," said Blume.

"When my 9-year-old daughter was just a little girl," Kajzer added, "she used to call my scars 'Daddy's boo-boos.'"

They took a lot out of him—and brought out his best.

"I've just wanted to be a good police officer," he said. "I'm proud that I was able to come back."

He won't call himself a hero.

Enough others do.

GOOD-BYES

October 10, 1992
AN INNOCENT CHILD

Barb Morrical had gathered up all of Columbus Coleman's papers from his desk and removed his artwork from the wall.

Then she hesitated. A first-grade teacher for 20 years, Morrical knew her next task would be the most difficult of her career.

"I don't know if I can put into words just how hard it was to take Columbus' name tag off his desk," she said.

She did, though. And then she cried—not for the first time, nor the last, but the hardest.

"Maybe removing his name tag was when the finality of it all set in," Morrical said softly.

Last Monday afternoon, 20 kids marched single-file out of Room 111 at Jefferson School, a new spelling list tucked into their bags.

On Tuesday, only 19 returned.

Columbus Coleman, 7 years old, had died the previous evening from a bullet intended for somebody else.

He had been shot on his grandmother's porch of all places—making many of us wonder if there is anywhere truly safe for our little ones anymore.

"One of the first things I thought was that Columbus wouldn't see the first snow," Morrical said. "And then I remembered how he had been so looking forward to Halloween. I went through several levels of sadness before I got very angry at such a senseless act."

"I think there is a sense of despair shared by many of us at Jefferson and elsewhere," added Mark Tulchinsky, the school's principal.

"Just the other day, we were talking about the youngster who was shot down walking to school in the Cabrini-Green section of Chicago and telling ourselves we're lucky that's not the kind of situation here," Tulchinsky continued. "So it is a great shock to see we might not be so far removed from that."

Columbus Coleman sat at a corner desk in Room 111. He was repeating first grade because he had struggled with the work the previous year, maybe not yet ready for the rigors of a full day of school.

"But he had been doing so wonderfully well this year," Morrical said. "Columbus was so proud how he could write out his name so neatly. He was enjoying the progress he was making. You could tell he felt good about himself."

Less than two weeks ago, he was taking great delight in Columbus Day—the 500th anniversary of Christopher Columbus' voyage.

"I've never had a Columbus in my room before," Morrical said, "and we really played his name up on Columbus Day. He really liked that."

Columbus seemed on his own straight course at school and "one who looked like he could make something of himself," Tulchinsky said.

"Oh, he could be a little chatty at times," Morrical said. "I told him and his buddy Jermaine that they couldn't sit with each other during reading circle because they talked too much. So last Monday, Columbus sat down in the circle and looked over to see that he was right beside Jermaine. 'Whoops!' he went and got up and moved."

Then she remembered and tears welled in her eyes. "That was the same day that he was shot . . .

"A few of the girls cried and five or six of them gathered around Columbus' desk before class the next day, but I don't think they understand completely that Columbus isn't coming back," Morrical said. "I would like to tell them that he is in heaven but you can't do that in school anymore."

Columbus' 19 classmates decided to write cards to his mother. One little girl, 6 years old, suggested they write, "We will keep him in our hearts."

Morrical wrote that and other words of sympathy on the board so they could copy.

Jasmine drew a picture of Columbus at his desk and of her at her desk with Morrical standing between them.

"That picture got to me, too," Morrical said, "just knowing that I would never see Columbus at his desk again."

At the end of the week, she decided that it was time for Columbus' desk to be removed from the class. An empty desk was not the way she wanted to remember a youngster so full of life.

"When he was leaving that last day, he was excited about the spelling list he was taking home," Morrical said. "He felt he already had a good start on knowing the words.

"I don't know if he got a chance to study the list later that day or not. I know he would have."

December 13, 1992
MOOSE OF A MAN

Edward "Moose" Krause had these big ham-like hands.

They were good for palming a basketball, for pushing away an opposing lineman, for grabbing the shoulder of a friend.

They could lift high the biggest of trophies won by his Notre Dame athletic teams and casually hold his ever-present cigar the size of a Lincoln log.

But those big hands also were good for gingerly cradling a spoon and feeding his wife of more than 50 years.

Long after he was unable to take care of his wife Elizabeth, he was at the nursing home every day to feed her, to hold her, to coo in her ear.

That is the Moose I will remember most—the gentle giant, a moose of a man in size only.

Moose Krause, 79 years old and a true Notre Dame legend, died in his sleep early Friday morning.

He was a wonderful man, a man of compassion and joy. Some sports stars live on their past glories, often blindly given credit for being heroes away from the athletic arenas as well. Moose stood tall in all walks of life. He deserved his accolades.

Kind words often are spoken after a death. But with Moose, nobody had an unkind word to say about him when he was living.

Some will choose to remember Moose as one of Notre Dame's greatest athletes—an All-American in two sports, a man whom Knute Rockne recruited and 60 years later, a man whom Lou Holtz gladly looked to for advice.

Some will choose to remember him as a great athletic director who kept Notre Dame clean and honest all of his 32 years in charge, who sometimes kept the good fathers of Notre Dame from tinkering too much with a good thing, who was far more adroit in dealings than his good-natured self allowed him to be credited for.

Some will choose to remember him as a public servant who was instrumental in many causes, including the Alcoholism Council after he had battled and defeated his own demons from the bottle.

But I will remember him most for his tenderness, for his loving ways.

He would help anyone in need. He hardly ever said no. He always had time for everybody.

Especially his wife, who preceded him in death in March 1990.

Twenty-five years ago, she had suffered serious injuries in an automobile accident and was never the same. For almost the last 10 years of her life, she had been in a nursing home.

But Moose would visit with

her four hours a day—feeding her two of her meals. He would sing to her and she would often join in. On their 50th wedding anniversary in 1988, they renewed their wedding vows with their oldest of three children. Rev. Edward Krause Jr., presiding.

"Most of the family were in shorts, but my little gal had on a beautiful gown and I put on my tuxedo," Moose later recalled.

He loved his wife so much. She was a woman who was as friendly and as caring as her husband before the tragic accident.

After visiting her in the nursing home, he would take her laundry home with him and bring it back with him the next day. "I get very lonely when I leave her," he said.

What I remember most about their relationship was the tray of cards he had in his apartment.

"Here's a Mother's Day card and a birthday card and a Valentine's card," Moose said as he sifted through them one day.

"Some of them are almost 20 years old. I save them because I give them to Elise every year. She doesn't remember them from year to year, but she enjoys getting them."

Moose remembered too vividly the pain his wife was in after the accident and how at first she couldn't even recognize him.

That's when he started taking the bottle into the hospital with him. That's when his drinking problems began.

But then when his wife made enough of a recovery to return home, he knew she needed him—and needed him at his best.

He became a recovered alcoholic. He became a friend for others with the same disease.

He always was there for people.

Now he is with his wife again.

I see him in his tuxedo and her in a beautiful gown. They look so very happy.

February 14, 1993
HIS SUFFERING ENDS

Wayne Traxler, a career military man and New Carlisle native, followed his family in death last week.

Since Sept. 4, 1964, Traxler had been dying a little each passing day.

On that day more than 28 years ago, he was serving in Vietnam, setting up radar stations for the United States Air Force.

His wife, Doris, and their seven children were returning to their Sacramento home after a vacation in Santa Ana, Calif.

They never made it. All eight of them—along with Doris Traxler's brother—were killed in a car crash. One of the older Traxler children may have fallen asleep at the wheel before the car plunged over a 40-foot embankment.

Six died in the wreckage. Three were critically injured and never recovered.

Neither really did Wayne Traxler.

He tried, he really did, but the grief was so insurmountable, the reasons so unexplainable.

Just like that, nine lives were wiped out including a wife and seven children—from 17-year-old Caroline to 1-year-old Anastasia.

"To see all nine caskets lined up—and to see one of them just barely three feet long . . . well, it was almost too much for anyone

to bear," said Bob Traxler, one of Wayne Traxler's younger brothers.

That picture of the caskets at the funeral ran on front pages all across the country. No tragedy seems worse than when a family is suddenly snuffed out in one horrible event.

People reached out to Traxler. Even Sargent Shriver, then director of the Peace Corps, said that he would have a job waiting for Traxler when he retired from the Air Force four years later.

"But Wayne took to drink after the accident," Bob Traxler said. "In fact, the last 29 years of his life had been a living hell."

After retiring from the Air Force in 1968, Wayne returned to the New Carlisle area and eventually moved back into his childhood home with his father and one of his brothers.

"Outwardly, Wayne hadn't changed that much," said John Traxler, another younger brother. "He didn't walk around with a long face but you could tell that the losses weighed very heavily on him."

As the years went by, Wayne went through two other marriages, five or six jobs and far too many bottles.

"Wayne probably was calling out for help and we didn't listen," John Traxler said. "He was the older brother [for eight siblings] and he had been like an idol to some of us—even helping to raise us. It was hard to know what to say or do."

What made it worse was that Wayne had always been an expert at everything he had tackled. "And when we went through his belongings, we found all kinds of commendations from his time in the service," John said.

"Wayne always was well-read," Bob added. "He could take a book and have it finished in a day. There weren't many subjects that he didn't have some knowledge about."

But his brothers and sisters would see him less and less. "He ended up not going to Christmas parties and other family get-togethers because of all the kids that would be there," Bob said.

He never talked about his own children. He kept any remembrances of them in a scrapbook. He kept his thoughts of them bottled up inside.

It was just too painful.

During the last years of his life, Wayne's health rapidly failed because of his drinking. His short-term memory diminished to almost nothing. He couldn't take care of himself.

Eventually he had to be moved in to a 24-hour care facility in Butler, Ind.

"At that point, the drinking had caused his brain cells to deteriorate," said John, who became Wayne's legal guardian.

A couple of times, he wandered off. Once, he started a fire by falling asleep with a cigarette.

Every two weeks, John Traxler would make the two-hour trip from his home in Mishawaka to Butler, over by the Ohio state line.

It was during the last year of his life that Wayne finally began talking about his family that had perished almost three decades earlier. "All of a sudden, he was talking about what (16-year-old) Dwight had done or would remember something about (8-year-old) Charmagne," John said.

He had held it in so long. As disease deadened his senses—and maybe some of the past pain—it seemed to give him the chance to remember his family without so much of the grief.

On Feb. 3, he died of an apparent heart attack at the age of 61. Most would say alcoholism was the underlying cause; others might say it was from a heart that was overwhelmed so many years ago.

"Wayne looked peaceful at the funeral," his brother John said. "I hope he was."

He deserved to be.

Sometimes, life doesn't seem fair. Sometimes, life is over so quickly. And sometimes, life drags on unmercifully.

Wayne Traxler finally is at rest. The hope is that he has found his family once again.

January 22, 1997
A FINE NIGHT

"And how are you this fine night, young man?' Curt Flood said.

I almost looked around to make sure he wasn't talking to someone else. I don't even think I found my voice to answer him.

Then he shook my hand.

I was a wide-eyed 10-year-old, a baseball cap on my head and my heart in my throat. Curt Flood wasn't much more than a kid himself—a 21-year-old outfielder in his second season with the St. Louis Cardinals—but I didn't know that.

All I knew was that a real major-league baseball player was smiling at me and pumping my hand.

Stan "the Man" Musial may have been down the way in the old Busch Stadium dugout, staring out into the outfield, but on this night—"this fine night"—Curt Flood was The Man to me.

It was late August, 1959, and I, along with hundreds of other kids, got the chance to walk through the home dugout before the Cards took on the Cincinnati Redlegs. Flood was the one ballplayer who stayed on the bench and greeted every star-struck kid.

You don't forget the first time you come face to face with a hero—and baseball players were my heroes back then.

Curt Flood, as big in my eyes that night as the vast outfield he patrolled, fit the bill.

I remember watching him later that evening, playing center with both gracefulness and grit, and thinking that I had actually touched him only hours earlier.

And he touched me—forever.

He had made a lifetime fan of a little boy that night just by showing that fame and good fortune don't have to make you forget why the game of baseball is played.

I'm a Chicago Cubs fan, but I always rooted for Curt Flood to do well, even if I didn't root for his team.

I watched him become one of the great defensive outfielders of our time, a solid hitter with a .293 career average and then a brave but wary challenger of baseball's reserve rule—which, in effect, didn't allow players to become free agents.

I remained his fan throughout his baseball years—his last ones lean—because he had shown me a few seconds of kindness when I truly believed in heroes.

I often wonder how many of today's athletes understand the kind of impact they can have on young people. And do they realize that every day they have the opportunity to make a lasting impression on some pint-sized player with only a wink . . . a nod

. . . or a few encouraging words?

Or am I just being sentimental and silly in this in-your-face era? And are kids so oversaturated with endorsement-driven creations that they no longer are awe-struck when a picture on a baseball card suddenly comes to life and grabs you by the hand?

I do know it meant something to me.

The news that 59-year-old Curt Flood had died on Monday of throat cancer made me think back to that night long ago. I never really knew the man, only was around him for a few seconds, but I felt like something in my past had been taken away from me.

I love that memory of him, sitting cheerfully on the St. Louis bench only minutes before he took the field to stand at attention for the National Anthem.

Most baseball fans will remember Curt Flood as a flawless fielder and the lonely point man for free agency.

I will remember him always as the 21-year-old major leaguer who shook my hand and asked me how I was doing on that fine night.

I couldn't answer him then. I can now.

For a 10-year-old kid, it doesn't get any better than that.

November 2, 1997
PEN PALS

I can't remember what his specific beef was. I do know it had to do with the *Tribune*'s coverage of Notre Dame football.

This particular letter writer was one of those rabid Fighting Irish fans and, as far as he was concerned, we in the sports department weren't getting enough stats or stuff in the paper about his beloved team.

When I was sports editor, I used to get a fair amount of letters like his. Some I answered, some I passed on to my beat writer, and some I wadded into tight little balls and threw them into the wastebasket across the room.

But for some reason, his particular letter got under my skin. I can't remember why. I do know that I grabbed up a Notre Dame press guide, 300 pages plus, stuffed it in a big envelope and mailed it to the return address on this crotchety critic's letter.

"If this guy thinks he needs to know every bloomin' thing about Notre Dame football, then he ought to find it in here," I said to myself.

It really wasn't a gift; it was more like an unspoken grumble —delivered by the U.S. Postal Service.

"That ought to shut him up," I thought those dozen or so years ago.

It didn't.

Not by a long shot. He misinterpreted what I had done as an act of kindness and he wrote me the most beautiful letter of thanks in return.

Hmmmm, I thought, I guess I've made a friend. Little did I know at the time how much of one.

John J. Hornung was his name, a Mishawaka native who was then living down in Wabash with his wife, Martha.

We began corresponding here and there. After a few years, he learned when my birthday was and started sending me cards. Then Christmas cards. And always a few letters during football season.

I also made sure to send him a Notre Dame press guide. In fact, it became sort of an autumn ritual—one of the items on my checklist for the upcoming football season. Make sure press credential requests sent out ... check travel arrangements for away games ... and send John his press guide.

As the years went by, though, John and I wrote less about football and more about family and friends and funny things in our lives. He knew the names of my kids, their ages, even what sports they played.

He even knew about our pets. I still remember that he once sent me a picture of his cat to see if I thought it looked anything like ours.

And I knew about his special Christmas ornament—an orange that he and his wife had first hung on their tree in 1930 just after they had married. Every year, though shriveled and no longer bright in color, the orange was hung in the place of honor again. I knew John loved his holidays, Christmas most of all.

A few years ago when I sent him our family snapshot, he sent it back in a very nice frame that he wanted us to have for our mantle.

By that time, he and his wife had moved to Akron, Ind., and I started having a little difficulty reading his letters because of his handwriting. He admitted that both he and his wife, by then in their mid-80s, weren't in the best of health anymore. But their three children, eight grandchildren and 10 great-grandchildren kept life interesting.

It was a year ago in the spring that he wrote me that Martha had died and that maybe he would be following her pretty soon. After that, his letters were written by his daughter Dolores as he dictated them to her.

Some months ago, he moved in with Dolores and her husband in Dowagiac. When I sent his usual Notre Dame package just before the season started, his daughter wrote me back, thanking me and saying that her dad was in the hospital.

I took some time to write John again. I wasn't sure what to write. I knew life had taken a cruel turn for him and he was tired of living without his wife and his good health. A week or so ago, I finally wrote a letter that seemed to fall woefully short of what I was trying to say.

It arrived at his daughter's house last Monday. A few hours earlier, at 8:30 that morning, John J. Hornung passed away in his sleep. He was 87.

I never met John face to face and only talked to him on the phone a couple of times, but I still knew that I had lost a good friend.

John never knew why I had sent that first envelope off to him in the mail. And he never saw my last one.

But in between were the written words of a wonderful friendship. I will deeply miss them—and him.

December 13, 1998
GETTING IN HIS DIGS

Jim Bellis would hear the almost hysterical laugh resounding through the house and just shake his head under his covers. He never had to wonder who was waking him up on yet another Saturday morning.

"And there he would be," Bellis recalls, "watching cartoons on TV with our youngest daughters, Jody and Emma, and teaching them how to dunk a handful of Oreos into a half-gallon milk carton."

"Dave loved little kids and little puppies and anything else he could make fun," Bellis continues. "And Dave could make just about everything fun."

Dave Huffman was a long and lanky Texan with a powerful voice and a twinkle in his eye as bright as the Lone Star itself. He was an All-American center on Notre Dame's football team who always wore bright red elbow pads so his momma down in Dallas could tell where he was in those pigskin pileups.

But to Jim Bellis, an anthropology professor at Notre Dame, Huffman also was one of his favorite students and a special friend of his family.

"His relationships with people were completely without any ambiguity," Bellis says. "What you saw is what you got—this big, caring, boyish and almost mythical figure who had a knack at connecting with people.

"At his funeral, four or five people stood up and said some of the very things I could have said about him. I just sat back and thought, 'Yeah, you've got Dave exactly right.'"

Dave Huffman, age 41 and a member of Notre Dame's 1977 national championship team, died three weeks ago in a one-car crash on the Indiana Toll Road in the early-morning hours. He was heading to South Bend for Notre Dame's last home game of the year.

"I wouldn't doubt if Dave was just trying to cram his usual 40 hours into a 24-hour day," Bellis says.

Huffman left behind a loving wife, two children and hundreds and hundreds of friends. He also left behind a legacy of belly laughs and living life to its fullest.

Even as painful as the news of Huffman's death was, Bellis can't help but smile when he talks about his former student. An anthropology major at Notre Dame, Huffman and 14 other students spent eight weeks with Bellis on an archaeological dig one summer near Wheatfield, Ind. They dug holes during the day and took playful digs at each other at night.

Bellis remembers it well...like the time when Huffman took a darning needle and stitched Bellis' sleeping bag to the cot while Bellis was sleeping in it.

... and the time he found himself locked in a makeshift shower out in the kraut bin with the cold water running, 50 baby ducks waddling in the dark around him and Huffman laughing like a loony a safe distance away.

... and the time that he asked Huffman to hang his clothes on the line one day only to discover them in a 100-pound block of ice the next.

Bellis is known for some practical jokes of his own. "But if you were one-up on Dave, you were scared to death," he says.

Huffman started calling Bellis "Boss" on that trip and was still doing so when they last saw each other a couple of months ago. Bellis sometimes called Huffman "Lambie Pie" after the female students on the trip found out his middle name was Lambert. One of those young women was Kathy Piha, Bellis' research assistant and Huffman's future wife.

"Everybody had a great time on that dig, and Dave was one of those guys who was able to get the best out of others—oftentimes by prodding them on with his levity," Bellis says.

About the only time that Bellis remembers Huffman getting a little out of sorts was when people would voice their amazement on how articulate he could be. "'Why the surprise?' he would ask. 'Because I'm big? Because

I'm a football player? Did you think I was a gorilla or something?' Despite his playfulness, he also was a thoughtful and intelligent person and didn't like people to assume otherwise."

Some years ago, Huffman went with Bellis to the National Muzzle Loading Rifle Association's annual spring shoot in Friendship, Ind. "He was like a little kid there," Bellis recalls. "He bought a little cannon and blew holes in my garage door when we got home, laughing the whole time.

"In the midst of all these guys pretending to be Jeremiah Johnsons, Dave was wearing his Minnesota Vikings jersey and carrying a walking stick as big as he was. This little guy, as greasy and as dirty as he could get in a week and with a string of porkchops hanging around his neck, took one look at Dave—probably 6-foot-7 and 300 pounds at the time—and said, 'Are you such a big wussy that you need a stick like that?'"

It was one of the few times that Bellis ever remembers Huffman at a temporary loss for words.

Then Dave Huffman put his head back and let out a laugh that sounded more like a roar.

Jim Bellis may miss that wonderful laugh most of all—that laugh that meant that ol' Lambie Pie was entertaining kids ... or pulling off another joke ... or just enjoying being so marvelously loud and alive.

October 12, 1999
EMILY WAS A JOY

Emily Hollister loved her sugared cereal.

"If she came over to your house for a sleepover, you had to have sugared cereal for Emily," Kristin Sieracki said with a smile.

"If Emily saw me take a second bowl, she would make me pour it back into the box just to make sure she got her share," her older brother, Eric, added.

Such a sweet tooth.

Such a sweet girl.

"All of us in our group are really good friends," said Becky Dobslaw. "But then I think everybody considered Emily their best friend."

Their best friend was thrown into their worst nightmare.

Emily Hollister's friends and family are now trying to come to grips with the tragic news that she is gone.

The 18-year-old Riley High School graduate, who was a freshman at Baylor, was killed along with five other college students early Sunday morning on the rim of a highway near College Station, Texas, while they walked to a party. A pickup truck plowed into them, apparently after the driver had fallen asleep.

Emily's body comes home from Texas today, her funeral is Friday and her memory will still be strong when all of her best friends are old and gray.

"If God had a catalog on kids, I don't think my wife (Louetta) and I could have picked out any better children than we have in Emily and Eric," said Jim Hollister.

The news took the breath away from literally everyone who knew Emily and had been smitten by her warm and friendly smile.

"You want to see a good picture of Emily?" said Jacinta Martin, a longtime friend. "They're all good the way she always smiled. Emily never took a bad picture."

As several of her friends and members of her family gathered at the Hollisters' on Tuesday, laughter sometimes reverberated through the house. Emily, always upbeat and excited, could do that to a crowd.

Back in her room, Emily's prom dress hung from the closet door, her friends' pictures lined her mirror, Leonardo DiCaprio smiled from various vantage points and her many stuffed animals stood sentinel from their shelves.

"It's the neatest this room has ever been," Jim Hollister said.

If only she would be coming back to mess it up again.

"Emily might not have been perfect but she always tried to do the right thing," Louetta Hollister said. "She was a joy the way she lived her life."

Emily had hair down almost to

159

her ankles when she was a little girl but she had worn it at shoulder length in recent years. "She told us on the phone last week not to tell her mom that she got her hair dyed," said Kara Huegel.

It was her little secret, shared by several friends.

Emily had just talked to her mom Friday, Louetta Hollister's birthday. "She talked about how she wanted to get home and eat some of my cooking," Emily's mom said.

"Oh, she liked to eat," said Kristin Sieracki. "But she would stay skinny."

She was a 5-foot-10 beauty whose poise only made it seem like things came easy to her. An Honor Society student and the captain of the Riley softball team, she earned everything she got.

"My wife, Bobi, coached Emily her freshman year and told me what a great kid she was," said Riley softball coach Mike Megyese. "I knew she wasn't blessed with a lot of talent and so I said, 'Too bad, I may have to cut her.' My wife said, 'Oh, you won't.' And she was right. Emily got better and better every year just by her hard work. I think the other kids also realized that when they named her captain her senior year."

"I know it's supposed to be the other way around, but my little sister was my example," said Eric Hollister, a senior at Florida State University. "She is the one who made me strive to be a better person. I just wish I could tell her that."

Others wish the same.

It is so hard to say good-bye to such a bundle of energy and the best of friends.

In a photograph of the crash scene that went nationwide, a sandal on the highway stood alone. It was Emily's.

That empty sandal represented so many empty feelings.

Louetta Hollister somehow held back her tears when she said, "You never think it might be your last good-bye. You just never do."

October 14, 1999
A MAKER OF MEN

M is for Marvin. And for Morristown where he grew up and became a spunky guard on the high school team.

And for Milan and that Miracle he coached in 1954 against mighty Muncie Central.

And for Mishawaka where he was so much more successful at making friends—so many of them—than achieving fame and fortune.

And for Mary Lou, his first and only love.

And for the movie called *Hoosiers* that he helped inspire.

And for the Modesty he always possessed despite his many accomplishments in life.

And for the Maker of Men that he always was.

But most of all today, M is for Memories left behind after Marvin Wood has passed on at the age of 71, his long and gallant battle with cancer finally over.

Shiny-headed and with an even shinier disposition, Marvin was one of us—a homegrown Hoosier with a wonderful mix of humility, heroism and history. He had his 15 minutes of fame when he coached mighty mite Milan to the 1954 state basketball championship, and found life could be just as good long after the limelight had faded.

So when Hollywood came knocking, it really didn't surprise his friends when he politely declined.

David Anspaugh, the director of *Hoosiers*, asked Wood to be an adviser to the movie that was based on Milan's miracle season "I just wasn't interested," said Wood a few months after the show's premiere in 1987. "This might sound a little selfish, but Mary Lou and I thought that the front-row seat we had for the real thing couldn't be topped."

Marvin Wood himself was always the real thing, too.

During almost every interview I had with Wood, he or Mary Lou would at one point say, "It's nice to be important, but it's more important to be nice."

A nicer man you will never find. He even survived his stint in politics—as a Mishawaka council member and during his close run for state representative—without a blemish, without a boo.

Basketball was his main arena, though, with his coaching career spanning five decades. When it came to the Milan Miracle, some people might have thought he happened to be at the right place at the right time. And to some extent, maybe he was.

But he also was the right man at that right place and right time. He had the right woman beside him, too. "Any time my wife noticed my feet were off the ground, she would grab me by the back of my coat and pull me back toward earth," he said a few years ago.

He later took over the Saint Mary's College program and had a ball doing that, too. Then two seasons ago, he coached the seventh-grade girls in Kirtland, Ohio. Why? His daughter and her family live there and they told him the town needed a coach.

From Milan to middle school. How many egos would allow that?

"I had to start out as a grumpy old man," he said of his last season as a coach. "Then I blew my whistle, kicked some boys out of the gym, put some girls on the verge of tears and told them, 'If you want to learn, you have to listen.'"

They did. They won, too—12 of their last 13 games. And they loved the old coach so much that they pleaded with him to coach them in eighth grade, too. He planned on it—until the cancer he thought he had beaten several years earlier returned last fall.

As always, he fought the good fight, starting each day by saying, "Good morning, Lord. This is Marvin. Thank you for being with us through the night. I pray you guide us through the day."

He guided so many young men and women himself. The most famous ones—Bobby Plumb and the rest of the Milan team— were hoping and praying their old coach could make it to the 50th reunion of their championship in 2004.

Marvin liked that idea, too. He really tried.

He will be there in spirit, high in the rafters where the banners fly.

M is not for Mourning, not in Marvin's case. He would want us all to remember him with a smile.

M is for Marvin, Man at his best.

November 21, 1999
WITHOUT CHARLIE

Charlie Fewell's parents, Chuck and Lisa, his 10-year-old sister, Kaitlyn, and his 8-year-old brother, Brandon, tried to smile wide enough for five.

They were posing for their Christmas card, their first without Charlie.

"It seems like a lot of things we do now, we note that it's the first time we have done it without Charlie," Lisa Fewell says.

"First time to go through a soccer season without him ... first time to visit relatives in Kansas without him . . ."

She pauses.

She could go on and on.

Then there are those moments of temporary lapses. "Occasionally someone will set the table for five," Lisa adds. "Or I will catch myself saying Char . . . when Brandon comes into the room."

It has been 8 1/2 months since 11-year-old Charlie Fewell, his maternal grandfather, Duane Fites, and Indiana state Trooper Richard Gaston were killed March 4 on the Indiana Toll Road. A trucker plowed into Fites' Ford Expedition and Gaston's squad car, parked on the shoulder during a traffic stop.

Sometimes it seems as if the accident happened yesterday.

"We just take it hour by hour, day by day," Chuck Fewell says. "The other kids keep us going. We just try to do what is on the calendar."

"We used to be pretty efficient, but now things seem to end up in piles," Lisa adds. "But some of the things we are doing, you just never would think you would be doing."

That includes counseling sessions for every family member.

Sometimes, it's good to talk about it. Sometimes, they go it alone. Sometimes, a member of the family will wander into Charlie's room in their Granger home, hoping to find a dose of his enthusiasm for life.

"The only difference now is that his room might be a little cleaner than it was," Lisa says with a sad smile.

It still overflows with the stuff that little boys are made of— Pinewood Derby trophies and cars, a remote-controlled boat, Cub Scout badges and Charlie's No. 79 football jersey hanging in a frame.

A Jesus doll also is sitting in the corner. "The kids in Sunday school [at First Presbyterian Church] would put their names in the hat and then the teacher would draw one out each week," Lisa says. "The winner would get to take the doll to service that Sunday—to walk with Jesus."

Charlie's name had already been drawn for the Sunday after he died. "It seems ironic, doesn't it?" Lisa asks. "And now he really is walking with Jesus."

The Fewells say they are relying heavily on their faith and trying to be strong. Nobody is working harder at that than little Kaitlyn, who was a passenger in her grandfather's car, along with Charlie and their grandmother. "She has seen some things that some adults couldn't comprehend," Chuck says.

Both she and Brandon are missing their big brother, who fit that role to a T. "Charlie got along with everybody, from his three great-grandparents who are still living to his little cousins," Lisa says. "And he would stop by and talk to Officer Bob and his dog down the street or the elderly women on the other block. He just liked to be around people."

The Fewells continue to work with the Charlie Fewell Memorial Fund that has raised money for youth programs and other worthy ventures. They also are pleased with the recently dedicated Charlie's Park on a lot in their Mallard Pointe neighborhood in Granger. It has a gazebo and a pond and a wonderful assortment of plants.

Even with the Toll Road hum in the background, it is a place that conjures up pleasant memories of Charlie for his family.

They can still see Charlie in his DARE T-shirt heading off to Chicago with his grandparents ... or wearing his football uniform while he mowed the yard ... or gently picking up any animal he could find.

"I don't want people to think that we are painting Charlie as a saint, though," Lisa says. "He could be ornery at times, just like any other boy his age."

Charlie was 11 when he died.

He loved football and frogs, big cars and toy ones, old people and even his kid brother and sister. He loved life, most of all.

The Fewell family knows Charlie would want them to approach life the same way.

December 7, 1999
A LIFE SAVER

Helen Griffis had to catch her breath for a moment when she took the Saturday call in the South Bend Police Department's communications center.

"It came at 8:17 AM," she said as if the moment will be forever etched in her mind.

It was a call about an unresponsive woman on LaPorte Avenue.

Griffis knew the address. That meant she also knew the victim.

"I knew that was Bev's house," said Griffis of her fellow dispatcher and friend, Beverly Day.

In fact, Griffis had come in to work that morning to take Day's shift when she had called in sick—a rarity for Beverly and a cause for concern.

"When I got the call, I immediately dispatched an ambulance and a police car," Griffis said.

Then she waited. Tears came to her eyes when she heard Code 241 given at the scene. That meant that her friend had died.

"My heart seemed to stop for a few moments," Griffis admitted.

Day, who had spent the last 11 years of her life helping to save people as a police and fire dispatcher, died herself on Saturday—four days shy of her 54th birthday.

She leaves behind a son, four sisters, several friends and countless people she helped by sending an ambulance, fire-truck or squad car to them as quickly as possible.

She will be buried Wednesday, her birthday.

"I had her birthday card set out on the counter, all ready to be mailed on Saturday," Griffis said.

Day had been suffering for the last several months from a lung disease that caused her to be on oxygen 24 hours a day.

"But it didn't keep her from continuing to work," said Karen DePaepe, the communication center's supervisor. "And anytime we needed somebody to fill in, she was always available. She was just a wonderful person and a tireless worker."

Day had returned to work last Friday after cataract surgery, and it was obvious to her co-workers that she wasn't feeling well—and probably shouldn't have been there.

"But Bev was one of those people who just didn't complain," said Karen Yauch, who worked beside Day and who was also a close friend. "She was in the process of getting on a lung transplant list."

Yauch and other co-workers were hoping to raise enough money with a raffle later in the month to allow Day to take the winter off and get a chance to improve her health.

"I was really worried that just walking from her house to her car would be too much for her in the cold air," Yauch said.

She kept coming to work anyway, her voice the calming influence in many emergency situations.

"She was feisty," said Yauch. "And she had a great sense of humor, too. She was always giving the firefighters a hard time when they would call in."

"I loved working with Bev," said fire Battalion Chief Howard Buchanon. "She always was keeping us on our toes. And she was a great dispatcher. We will miss her a great deal."

Day also loved going to the gambling boat in Michigan City with Yauch, her sister Mary and her cousin Becky.

"We always said that any big winner would buy the rest of us a meal at Heston's [Bar] on the way back," Yauch said. "We came back one time with enough money between us to just about afford an order of Chicken McNuggets. We laughed about that."

So last Christmas, Yauch got her good friend Beverly a Chicken McNuggets coupon for a gift. They laughed about that, too.

If only there was a Christmas gift to give this year.

"She was such a good friend and a caring person," Yauch added. "It hasn't completely hit me yet, I guess. When I pulled into the lot this morning [on Monday], I saw her car wasn't in her spot and, for a brief moment, I wondered where she was."

After all, Day was almost always at work, regardless of how badly she felt herself.

The day before she died, she was still at her spot, helping to save lives.

"That was the way she was," Yauch said. "We will really miss her."

SECOND OPINIONS

January 30, 1990
"REWARDING" EXPERIENCES

My daughter earned a few medals at an orchestra recital the other day.

The following evening, I found one of them on the stairs with the bottom of my foot.

Youch!

What a deal for me. First, I have to listen to her practice, and then I get stabbed in the foot by one of her awards.

Actually, I'm glad my daughter continues to play a musical instrument, but my little episode with the stairs did underscore a point of concern I've had recently.

Anything kids do anymore, it seems that they get some kind of medal, trophy, citation or ribbon.

At our house, we have awards and rewards running out of our ears.

Mostly, they are from athletics. My kids are pretty good in a few sports and pretty average in others, but they always seem to get an award for anything they do, regardless of how well they do it.

At this point, awards for academics and the arts really are more meaningful. And it's nice that more and more of these are being given. I just hope these fields don't go as far as sports, where casual participation now will get you a medal almost as easily as outstanding achievement.

I read somewhere a few years ago that kids today don't value their awards as much as their parents did because just putting on the uniform almost ensures one of an award.

I can vouch for that. I find crimped ribbons and folded citations all over our house. Many of them mean nothing to my kids because it really took nothing to earn them.

What few mementos I earned 25 years ago are in better shape in the box in the basement than some of the stuff that my kids have brought home and stuffed somewhere just in the last year. Maybe it's because when I received an award, I felt I worked my rear off for it.

My awards were arranged neatly on a bulletin board. My high school letter jacket was my most valuable possession. It still probably ranks in the Top 10.

My kids? A trophy usually is deemed nice enough to stick where people can see it, a medal may make it into a desk drawer, and a ribbon or a citation will get stuck between the pages of a book only if Mom and Dad find them when they're still in one piece.

Of course, the kids aren't to blame.

Adults are.

So many coaches, instructors and parents just can't consider their favorite little participants a success story unless they can be handed some handy-dandy hardware at the end of a season or session.

My wife and I once coached a soccer team of 6- and 7-year-olds to an 0-7-1 mark—the beginning of the end of my soccer coaching career I might add. We were so bad that if the other team had been five minutes late in taking the field, I'm still not sure we would have had enough time to score.

But anyway, one of the mothers thought we ought to give our little booters—two of them my own—personalized awards. I told her the only award that should be given out was a Purple Heart to me.

She smiled patiently until I quit laughing and then she suggested tiny trophies. I think we compromised on military-like ribbons.

Are we bribing our kids to participate?

Part of this, of course, is that our young kids are too over-supervised, especially in sports, that as soon as they can toss a ball with one hand or kick one more than 10 feet, they're in uniform.

And if they're going to wear a uniform, they better get a team picture. And if they're going to get a team picture, then they better get some kind of an award at the end of the season.

It's all a neat little package. It also gives the adults something to do, something to fret about while their kids play.

Apparently gone are the days of the sandlot games when the best reward possible was a pat on the back from a teammate or the begrudging respect from an opponent when he said, "Next time, you're not going to be able to beat us like that."

Now, you get a medal—regardless of which side you were on.

Oh, well, maybe it's a chance for these kids to get ready for adulthood. Last summer, I was at the city recreation department and was asked if I could deliver a couple of trophies to the *Tribune* softball team. No problem, I said.

Since my days of playing for the *Tribune* were over, they had gotten pretty good, usually placing fairly high in one of the city's slow-pitch middle divisions.

But I almost gagged when I was handed two four-foot trophies. And here I thought the Los Angeles Dodgers and Oakland A's had won the last two World Series.

I barely got them both to fit in my trunk.

At least I haven't tripped over anything that big on my stairs—yet.

March 5, 1991
HARDLY "NIFTY"

It was fast approaching 95 degrees and the midmorning sun was beating steadily down upon us.

I almost had been knocked out of the bleachers when the guy directly behind me had nodded off to sleep and fell into me, his head torpedoing me in the back.

Fortunately, he was only wearing his helmet liner. The instructors let us take off our steel pots and web gear before we were herded into the bleachers.

They probably knew from past experience that a full helmet on top of a nodding head could start a domino effect from the top rows and send more than a few of us sprawling.

We were in Army ROTC summer camp at Fort Riley, Kan., a long way from God's country. In the summer of 1970, our instructors—mostly infantry majors with premature gray in their hair—figured most of us would sooner or later be heading to Vietnam.

They roused us out of our slumber like a coach revving us up for the big game. Most lectured in voices that could be heard over a battlefield. They were hardened professionals who left no doubt why there was good reason we should listen.

But on this particular day, our instructor—another major with Vietnam experience—was almost professorial in his approach. He spoke as if he were giving us a lecture in botany or finite math. For a while, he was a pleasant change from the "blood and guts" we usually got.

His expertise that day was on mines. He picked up one called a Claymore mine. He talked about how it was a directional mine and could be fired at will. He also talked about how it sent out hundreds of shrapnel-like pellets in a semi-circular pattern.

He did not have to say how this Claymore mine could maim and kill. He did not mention how the Viet Cong had a knack for sneaking into a perimeter and turning them around to face American troops or using them later as booby traps.

What he did say about the Claymore mine almost made my blood run cold on this hot, muggy day.

"This is a nifty little killing device," he said.

He really used the word "nifty." I will never forget that. He talked about the Claymore mine as if it were his own little toy of joy—like a model airplane or a newfangled gardening tool.

An educated man, a man who did seem to possess a certain amount of sense, he had reduced death and disfigurement on the battlefield to the level of "nifty." He had dehumanized life with one uncaring word.

Nifty.

He did not have to lecture in a shout to catch my attention. Without even meaning to, he had driven home the ugliness and the savagery of war.

Most of us from that class never went to Vietnam. The war began winding down after that summer and we did our serving stateside, far away from the destruction dealt out by Claymore mines and other "killing devices."

I never felt guilty about missing my generation's war—in which too many good men were killed.

But now more than 20 years later, I take pride in the allied forces and their swift, efficient way of dealing with the madman, Saddam Hussein.

I feel a great joy that our troops have an engaging, compassionate leader like General Norman Schwarzkopf, the American commander in the Persian Gulf.

I also am relieved that our nation's leadership saw fit to try to save as many American lives as possible by putting off the ground war, while also attempting to hold civilian casualties in Iraq to a minimum.

If there is such a thing as a "just" war, I suppose this one fit the bill. It is hard not to want to reach out and hug Stormin' Norman and his troops, hopefully all coming home soon.

But what bothers me is that wars, even "just" wars, are still fought with weapons—killing devices that are more advanced and more lethal than ever before. The Claymore mine is outdated; more refined weapons take its place.

And as long as wars are a possibility, weapons will get "better" and deadlier. The "good guys" will always strive to stay a step ahead of the technology possessed by the "bad guys."

Warfare technology will remain a thriving business. New weapons will continue to come off the assembly line.

And somebody, somewhere still will want to call them "nifty."

God help us.

September 27, 1992
TIME TO HEAL

I'm not sure I like Presidential nominee Bill Clinton.

And Vice-President Dan Quayle really doesn't do a whole lot for me, either.

But I don't look at either one of them as gutless wonders just because they tried their own ways at staying out of Vietnam.

Many people in my generation did the same.

By the late 1960s, hardly anyone of draft age wanted to participate in a war where America's role was undefined, where young soldiers weren't given a fighting chance and where it was hard to tell the friends from the foes in southeast Asia.

All that was certain was that too many young Americans were coming home marred either physically or mentally or, worse yet, in body bags.

So any way that guys could stay out of serving in Vietnam, they usually did.

Quayle may have used some of his family influence to get into the Indiana National Guard and avoid an all-expenses-paid trip to Saigon. Clinton kept sidestepping the draft until the night of the first draft lottery when he received one of those magically high numbers.

Not admirable. But not condemnable, either.

Their schemes were minor compared to others.

I knew a guy who starved himself enough that his weight stayed just below the military minimum. He looked like a walking skeleton, but he said it was his way of staying alive.

Another person had a knack of getting his blood pressure high enough to stay out of the draft. I won't go into the details.

And then there was the rumor that the one guy walking around campus without a trigger finger had put it on a chopping block himself.

Crazy people.

But that's what that war did to many in my generation.

While wearing my ROTC uniform one day, I was spit on by a girl who had sat beside me in a class the previous semester. She had even let me borrow her notes on one occasion.

But the day she unloaded on me, I don't even think she saw me, only the uniform I was wearing.

There are far worse memories, though.

I had a friend who died in the tank he was commanding in Vietnam.

I had another buddy who headed out to Canada after burning his draft card. I've never heard anything about him since.

It was an awful war.

It tore my generation apart.

Never have I seen a more bizarre scene than the night in

1969 that draft numbers were drawn for the first time. Guys in my fraternity sat around the radio waiting for the numbers that came along with their birthdates. It was as if all of us were waiting on the results of a growth they had found in our armpits.

By the end of the night, everybody was walking around like zombies with a magic-marker number on the front of their T-shirts or bare chests. That was their draft number; that was what they considered their fate.

Some found religion that night. Some found some emotions they might not have known they had.

Most were either drunk or dazed. Some were both.

Those with numbers over 300 thought they had a chance of actually becoming an accountant or lawyer or dentist after college.

Those under 100 were only thinking of being a draft dodger or a draftee.

Those in between didn't know what to think.

Some people now want to look back at those times in almost a romantic way, when my generation stood up to government officials and told them where to stick their ugly, little war.

Some think the courageous people were the ones who said no.

I don't think so.

I think it was a time when there were a lot of confused and scared young people who didn't feel the leaders of their country had their best interests in mind.

Bill Clinton may have been one of them. Ditto for Dan Quayle.

If you're from my generation, you don't applaud them or condemn them. You do probably understand their motivations.

If trying to stay out of Vietnam is the worst thing that crawls out of their closets, then they are pretty clean politicians.

Vietnam always will be a scar on my generation.

Let it scab over.

Don't make it a campaign issue. It has hung over my generation like an albatross long enough.

172

January 3, 1993
A PRESIDENT'S MEMORY

Beer was on his breath and his raspy voice sounded like it was coming from the deepest innards of a coal mine.

He didn't waste time on introductions. He immediately launched into his insights on the conspiracy theories surrounding the assassination of John F. Kennedy on Nov. 22, 1963.

We were standing in Dealey Plaza in downtown Dallas. We were not 50 feet from where our 35th president was fatally wounded after his motorcade made a hairpin turn onto Elm Street.

Eyes blood-shot in his inebriated state, my self-appointed guide knew his stuff. Catching me gawking by myself, he reeled off the points of interest and the chronological order of that fateful day before I could say, "Out of my face."

For his five-minute, nonstop speech that caused some passersby to take a wide berth around his dramatic gestures, he only asked I spare him the change in my pockets.

"Got to get home some way," he said a few octaves lower than his presentation voice.

He was a first for me: A panhandling historian. An assassination expert apparently slowly killing himself.

He also possessed the gift of gab and a dollar of my change.

I didn't feel so badly about that. Across the street in the Dallas County Administration Building (formerly the Texas School Book Depository Building), I already had paid $6 to get a similar piece of history from a more sober and sobering presentation.

Named as if it were some fancy restaurant. "The Sixth Floor" (which, appropriately enough, is on the sixth floor) is a project of the Dallas County Historical Foundation.

The 9,000-square-foot display of photographs, artifacts and documentary films is a rather moving and vivid remembrance of Kennedy.

And yet at the same time, it hit me as a little ghoulish that the very location in which Lee Harvey Oswald stuck a rifle out the window and shot the president of the United States now holds a memorial to Kennedy.

When a madman once opened fire on innocent people in a San Diego McDonald's restaurant, killing several before himself, the franchise tore down the store that held such an ugly memory.

But in Dallas, they have made a tourist stop out of the very building, the very floor, the very window from where Kennedy was shot. Even a display of boxes is made to look the way that Oswald found them—or arranged them—before he took aim behind their cover.

I half-expected a booth with an arcade-like rifle set up so paying customers could take aim and visualize what Oswald might have seen through his sights.

I can't help it. Although there is history to be learned here and the preservation of a fallen president's memory, I also feel a sense of trespass here—and a chance to cash in.

For so many years, just the mention of the Texas School Book Depository and its sixth floor always conjured up feelings of horror and grief. And yet on this day, I am walking across its carpet, politely weaving between other tourists and talking softly as if in a shrine.

It bothers me. Yet I am still drawn to the windows that overlook Dealey Plaza, Elm Street and the Grassy Knoll. Everything is closer than I imagined. Everything looks almost serene on this calm day.

I turn away. I curse under my breath for being here, for being taken in.

I already knew everything about Kennedy I could have learned from this place. The only new perspective I now have is what Oswald saw and where he hid with his deadly rifle and evil thoughts.

I leave with a shudder. I know there are places that would be considered far more mercenary than this place. One store in Dallas that specializes in Kennedy history and memorabilia even sells Kennedy assassination trading cards and buttons of Oswald with the words of "I was a patsy."

On this day, I feel a little like a patsy myself. I have walked the same steps as Oswald and jaywalked on Elm Street at about the spot the first bullet tore through Kennedy's neck. I feel no better for having done so.

There is fascination here—and a sense of guilt for feeling it.

It is a place of ghosts and ghouls, of two-bit historians and elaborate exhibitions.

It is a place I hope I only visit once.

July 31, 1994
JUST NOT GETTING IT

The music blared out of a dorm window only a block away from the campus' football stadium.

Music?

Well, it came from the "Woodstock" record album anyway. The sound was from a rock group called "Country Joe and the Fish," with good ol' Country Joe himself egging on the Woodstock-festival crowd to spell out a four-letter word—THE four-letter word—and then yelling out that word several times in unison.

Country Joe McDonald and his Fish followers were the closing act at Woodstock back in the summer of 1969. They cussed and croaked to almost a half million people in a farmer's field somewhere in upstate New York.

It was about 10 years after Woodstock when I listened to Country Joe's profanity reverberate out of that college dorm room. That meant that the person playing that trash on his stereo probably was just a kid during the Woodstock era and that he was playing it just to be obnoxious instead of nostalgic.

I was on that college campus to cover a Notre Dame road football game and was forced to listen to that chant with thousands of other game-goers that afternoon.

One of the others was an older sportswriter walking with me. As we passed the dorm, he said, "Your generation really knew its music, didn't it?"

I smiled and made some kind of smart comment in return. Deep down, though, I was bothered.

I just never got Woodstock.

I never understood why some people wanted to glorify it as my generation's beacon to the rest of the world. I always felt like a square peg when it came to Woodstock.

To be sure, our nation was going through a strange, turbulent time during 1969 and needed a shake. But I never understood how a bunch of people smoking dope in a muddy field while listening to rock stars flashed the exit sign to all the madness.

I just didn't get it.

If anything, I thought that Woodstock glamorized the use of drugs. After all, they didn't start calling this relatively new form of music "acid rock" for no reason.

Many who were there—or say they were there—brag about the "peace" and "love" that existed at Woodstock. And those are fine things.

But yet just about everyone I've heard talk about being at Woodstock can't help but grin a little about all the dope that was there, too.

Woodstock was what we would call a "happening" today. Never had so many great musicians come together at one place and shared the same stage. But there is a note of tragedy here, too. Five of the performers at Woodstock later died of drug overdoses, with the deaths of rock immortals Janis Joplin and Jimi Hendrix coming the following year. Others who played there have had their share of substance-abuse problems over the years, too.

That is not to say that all the performers were druggies or that much of people in the audience were there just to get stoned.

Some people may have found their peace or seen the light at Woodstock. Some may have left invigorated, just for the "high" they got from seeing so many people in such cramped and cruddy quarters getting along.

Some even called it a love-in.

And some say that drugs— more than the music—were the driving force.

It is ludicrous to say that Woodstock was the root of our nation's drug problems. But it seems naive to say that it didn't make drug usage a lot easier to justify for a generation searching for itself.

Even though I had friends at Woodstock, even though I bought the album from it, even though I tried to understand it, all it ever did to me was leave a bad taste in my mouth.

I just never got it.

And now with the 25th anniversary of Woodstock upon us and promoters of the reunion concert next month waxing poetic about it, these awkward feelings hit me once again.

I wonder if others in my generation feel the same way.

I know I would prefer Woodstock not to be one of the defining moments of my generation.

Yet here's what Michael Wadleigh, the director of the Woodstock film, once said: "We talked even before the event, about Woodstock being a *Pilgrim's Progress* or a *Canterbury Tale* . . . I don't want to compare ourselves to Chaucer, but I'll bet this film 1,000 years from now will have a real validity."

Funny, our encyclopedia at home doesn't even have a mention of Woodstock.

So let's call again on Country Joe (without his Fish) and his thoughts about Woodstock in a recent soft drink commercial.

When he is asked by fellow Woodstock performer John Sebastian if he remembers playing at the rock festival, Country Joe answers with a confused, "Nooo."

It was supposed to be funny. It might have been true.

November 19, 1995
PUSHING MY BUTTONS

There I was, driving down the road and minding my own business when . . .

Well, actually I was having one of my little anxiety attacks, trying to keep the digestive juices below my Adam's apple.

I was just 10 minutes away from giving a speech in front of about 150 high school students out at Notre Dame. If the truth be known, I would rather take my chances with the "Knights of the Round Table" after calling Sir Lancelot a wussie.

High school kids are the toughest audience around: You talk like a know-it-all adult and you lose them right away. You try to talk like one of them and you come across pretty phony-baloney.

So there I was, mumbling part of my speech to the rearview mirror and sounding like an idiot when an empty carton came flying out of the car in front of me.

I usually honk at litterers.

Nothing pushes my buttons quicker than that kind of lack of regard for our environment.

I let it pass this time, though, concentrating on my little opening-line grabber.

But just as I was settling back into my "four score and seven years ago" tone, a large cup filled with ice soared out of the other side of the car, ricocheting across the road.

My speech was momentarily forgotten. I ground my teeth and I squeezed the steering wheel. I pulled up behind the car at the stoplight leading into Notre Dame and flipped off my seat belt, ready to jump out and give them a piece of my mind.

Of course, that would have been stupid and childish and maybe even dangerous on my part. I counted four heads in the other car and a couple of them looked pretty big.

So I just sat behind them and stewed.

From a few past experiences, I also have learned that litterers are not usually the most polished of debaters.

But the real reason I let it pass was that I was already going through enough anxiety with my speech only minutes away. So I decided I would curb my acid tongue for another day.

Restraint may be a virtue, but, oh, does it hurt sometimes.

Well, as you might have guessed by now, I ended up parking in the same lot only a few spaces down from the litter-mobile. When the driver and passengers got out, they had a message for me.

"Hi, Mr. Moor, how's it going?"

I knew these kids!

And they are good kids, too—leaders at their high school, good students, a couple of pretty fair athletes and all of them better writers than I was when I was their age. (Just so an incorrect assumption isn't made here, I will point out that they aren't students at the same high school my own kids have attended.)

These kids were out of school that morning, not to litter the neighborhood, but to learn about journalism from newspaper people—one of them being me.

"Hey, Mr. Moor."

I met their salutations with a cold stare.

Then I unloaded on them— two of them probably not even deserving it. "I expect more out of you than that!" I growled. "That littering you did really peeves me off!" (Oh, OK, I used another p-word.)

I left them in my wake with my self-righteous walk into the building where the workshop was. Needless to say, I wasn't going to have to work very hard at clearing my voice before my speech.

But before the workshop's introductions, before I had my 15 minutes of "fun" on the stage, I found myself walking up the auditorium aisle and the kids I had jumped all over walking down toward me.

Apologies flowed and I patted a couple of them on the back. I even heard a "that was really stupid of us."

And I said I was sorry that they had to see my angry side.

Later on, I convinced myself that it had been a good learning experience for them—and me, too.

Littering isn't a responsible act. Acting like a crazy man probably isn't, either.

So honest to gosh, just two nights later at a stoplight, a boy dropped a wrapper out of his driver's seat window just in front of me. This time, a gentler, milder me gave a very polite honk. A kid in the backseat turned around and gave me the one-fingered salute.

I smiled back through my clenched teeth and counted to, oh, 800 or so.

Life's little lessons aren't always easy, are they?

July 21, 1996
BEYOND SAVING

I stood under the overhang of a roof just outside the Indiana State Prison when the rains started up again.

A man from the nearby neighborhood, assuring me his pit bull named Patience was friendly, and a Michigan City police officer, wearing jeans and a T-shirt, shared my haven.

We watched the drama unfold outside the Indiana State Prison late Wednesday night, hours before convicted cop killer Tommie Smith would die from lethal injection.

Protesters marched in their circle, belting out chants that often sounded like something off a grade school playground. "Two, four, six, eight, no more killing by the state."

"Two, four, six, nine, he's paying for his crime," one of their detractors shouted back.

Young police officers from Indianapolis stood close by, grins sometimes on their faces and ugliness on their cardboard signs. "Burn in Hell, Tommie Smith," one of them read.

Older police officers who knew Jack Ohrberg, the victim of Smith's crime more than 15 years ago, stayed out of the limelight. They seemed content to be silent observers on the night they were glad was coming to pass. Ohrberg's widow stood in a nearby parking lot, also avoiding the madness and keeping her thoughts to herself.

The younger cops, who never knew Ohrberg, did no favors to the image of a police officer or the memory of a fallen one.

The TV people, meanwhile, raced around and reacted to all of it. The way they pulled their cables through the puddles, it made some people wonder if there was going to be an electrocution along with a lethal injection that night, too.

"Look at all these bleeping idiots," Patience's owner said.

The Michigan City police officer, his badge on his belt, answered with a shrug.

It is not as easy to shrug off the sobering business of capital punishment. It is easy to ignore people who should be more concerned about getting a life than in debating one.

At one point before midnight—minutes before Smith's three-step lethal injection was to begin—the protesters pointed to the prison and the Indy cops in front of it. "No justice, no peace, no racist police," they chanted.

The cops smiled back as law enforcement officers on duty moved in just in case there was any trouble.

Finally, one of the protesters' leaders said on his portable microphone, "We're giving the cops too much attention." His group slowly backed away in a effort to keep only its vigil in the bright lights of TV.

Inside, a man was about to die. He had killed a cop. He had killed a security guard, too. He had not shown remorse for his crimes nor apologized for his actions.

"An eye for an eye, baby," someone yelled outside.

"Read the whole Bible before you start quoting it," came the reply.

Jack Ohrberg had died in the line of duty, three bullets pumped into his body—two after he was sprawled helplessly on a porch, death already upon him. Tommie Smith and his supporters contend the last two bullets weren't from his gun. Others say they were.

Smith would be the first Indiana inmate ever to die from a lethal injection. It was hoped to be a more humane death than the prison's electric chair—nicknamed Sparky.

"It's wrong to be doing what should be left up to God," someone said outside.

"Kill 'em all and let God sort them out," followed.

Tommie Smith . . . who wished to be alone in his final hours . . . who passed on a last meal . . . who had little to say when his time came . . . certainly never was this popular before his crimes.

He was another product of our urban jungles who apparently had found it too easy to stray from what is right.

There are millions more like Smith, some who will end up like him.

And there lies the real tragedy of this story, rather than the fact that he died at the hands of the state instead of being allowed to wilt away in a cell for the rest of his sorry life.

His life needed saving 30 years ago when he was still a kid and maybe still reachable.

Good over evil can't begin on the steps of the prison door. Two-bit slogans and tasteless signs are of no use at that point.

Tommie Smith died for his own savage sins and without remorse. He was beyond saving.

Our urban jungles will continue to churn out more like him. This is the bigger crime—and a far greater cause.

June 29, 1997
KIDS ON A TEAR

It looked as if we were sitting down beside the Mad Hatter's tea party.

Napkins everywhere, table settings askew, straws dripping little puddles of pop.

While two sets of parents sat at one table, their four kids—all looking to be between the ages of 3 and 6—were at another table.

Well, sort of at another table. One was standing on her chair, another was practicing his karate chops down the aisle, and yet another was playing with her dinner knife, occasionally pretending to stab her brother. Only one was relatively quiet, but he made up for it later.

Hmmm. "Well, at least they're almost done," I thought to myself after assessing the damage on their table top.

That was right before the waitress came to take their orders.

Let me just say the next half hour was like having dinner with Donald Duck and his three nephews. The kids were continually up and about, pancakes were rolled up like cigars and stuffed into their mouths whole, and the table was in such disarray that a bus boy passed by and just sort of shook his head.

The dads both did get up a time or two to cut some food, but the mothers never budged off their backsides, allowing their offspring to . . . well, spring off in all directions. I don't know if they even saw their two kids playing tag down the aisle, and when one dad did ask his little girl not to stand on the chair, his request went unheeded.

Finally, the one quiet kid broke out into a cry that eventually escalated into a call-of-the-wild kind of sound. He had to be carted out. It appeared that he may not have felt well, but then the gluttony and garbage around him could have turned just about anyone's stomach.

Of course, the other three kids more than made up for his absence.

Such a pathetic scene, it became almost laughable for my wife and me by the time our dinner out was over. It did appear, however, that some of the other patrons sitting close by and a couple of the waitresses were uncomfortable by how poorly these kids were being monitored by their parents.

Nobody said anything, though.

But then, what do you say? "Pardon me, folks, but did you know that parenting requires a little more time than buying crayons and cable TV?"

Because this was a family-type restaurant, patrons like us expect a little noise and some spilled milk. Heck, 20 years ago in the restaurant next door to this one, I carried out one of our own kids—wailing like a banshee—when we wouldn't give him his baby sister's applesauce. Wouldn't you know we had to be seated in the farthest corner from the front door?

I don't think we went back to that restaurant until that same kid was old enough to drive us there.

I've found that most people are pretty tolerant of little kids in restaurants, though. And well we should be, especially when it is a family restaurant and the parents are at least trying to keep some semblance of order.

Heck, many of us rather enjoy that kind of company—even if it's to smile at ourselves that those days of bibs and bathroom trips are over.

But to let one's kids run unchecked and unsupervised is the height of rudeness and, really, a disservice to the kids themselves.

These kinds of outings are when good manners should be learned and practiced . . . when parents should set the example . . . when a family should enjoy (or try to, anyway) each other's company.

The four parents in question ignored all this—while also ignoring their kids and the people around them.

They seemed oblivious to the fact that they were raising brats. The blame goes to them, not their kids.

When I see kids who are well-behaved out in public, I sometimes tell their parents so. Now, I have to wonder if I shouldn't comment on opposite behavior, too.

Just as well I didn't this time. The one little guy had a darn good karate chop as he just missed my ear his last trip down the aisle, and I also noticed he didn't cry when his sister stuck his arm with a fork.

His parents apparently didn't notice. Then again, maybe they did.

No blood, no bother . . . I guess.

September 7, 1997
NEVER THE SAME

The German security guards literally reached out and grabbed my buddy Steve and me by the shoulders, pulling us into the Olympic Village compound.

We had done it.

Mission accomplished.

Masquerading as Olympic athletes in our brand-new Adidas sweatsuits and fresh off a long run through Munich to produce the proper amount of perspiration for effect, we had jogged toward one of the village gates while the autograph seekers moved in. Swarmed, actually.

Hey, we looked the part of Olympians. My buddy Steve still had the physique that helped him become the Indiana high school half-mile champion in 1969, and I was . . . well, as I said, I had on a brand-new Adidas sweatsuit.

Pencils and pads were thrust at us by little German kids. I signed as many as I could, playing my impersonation to the hilt.

At first, I gave out Rick Wohlhuter autographs. He was a former Notre Dame runner who was representing the United States in the 800-meter run. And I knew he at least had a mustache and dark hair like I did back then.

Then I tired of this deception and began signing my name as "Jim Shoe" just before the guards "rescued" Steve and me just outside the gate.

We had gone over to Munich, Germany, as part of a tour group that was led by I.U. track coach Sam Bell. My trip was a graduation gift to myself of sorts, although I also was writing some stories for a Bloomington newspaper.

I wrote the story about sneaking into the Olympic Village and how much fun we had had rubbing shoulders with some of the world's greatest athletes, while riding the train that evening back to out lodgings in the beautiful, little Bavarian town of Oberammergau.

That night was 25 years ago — September 3, 1972, to be exact.

Two days later, hell visited Munich's Olympic Village. Five Black September terrorists, also masquerading as athletes, got by security and took many members of the Israeli team as hostages.

Twenty hours later, after a botched rescue attempt at a Munich military airfield, 17 people—11 of them Israeli athletes and coaches—were dead. The world mourned.

And as sudden and as shocking as automatic gunfire, the world of sports was changed— forever losing its glorious innocence . . . forever losing its insulation from the hate and horror of global strife.

For me, it was if I had seen a simpler time of sports pass into history before my very eyes.

On one day, I was a happy fan, pleased with my boldness and ability to sidestep the authorities. Two days later, after a heinous act against mankind was committed on the very grounds I had earlier pranced, I knew that I would never view sports—and the attention it attracts—quite the same way.

After a day for mourning, the Games went on. Twenty-five years ago today, the Games continued.

I wanted to go home.

I didn't, of course. Even after the "Munich massacre," I remember cheering on a young Oregon runner named Steve Prefontaine who just missed an Olympic medal in the 5000 meters . . . and golf cap-wearing Dave Wottle coming from last to first to win the 800 by inches over a stumbling Russian . . . and Frank Shorter circling the stadium just behind an imposter as the Olympic marathon champ.

Nice memories.

But none of those will ever soften the reminders of what happened in the Olympic Village 25 years ago.

I grew a little older, a little wiser, a little sadder over what happened. One day, a wide-eyed fan. The next, a shaken onlooker.

Last week, the world lost a princess. Twenty-five years ago, we lost the confidence in one of our great passions, until then existing as an escape for us from a world that sometimes goes amok.

I hardly wore my Adidas sweatsuit after that. In fact, I eventually gave it to a friend.

It reminded me too much of the Olympic Village in Munich and my mirth there before mayhem. It reminded me of a place of death.

Twenty-five years ago.

Jim Ryun fell in his 1500-meter heat . . . the U.S. basketball team was upset by the USSR . . . and 11 members of the Israeli team were murdered.

The sports world was forever changed.

HABITS AND HANGUPS

July 8, 1988
THIS FOUL NOT FAIR

It's a kid's dream that never goes away.

It's a keepsake worth the price of admission—maybe 20 times over.

It's a prized possession sometimes fought over and then often fondled by all those around.

It's a foul ball.

I keep waiting my turn to get one at a professional baseball game.

A grab at glory, so to speak.

I have come close, so close, before. I won't bore you with the details, though, because near-misses do not count—even when you've been bumped, bullied and had beer spilled in your eyes while attempting what obviously would have been the catch of the day.

No excuses, no excuses.

Just be ready for the next opportunity.

I don't take my glove to the games anymore, as I did when I was a kid. But even now, I always put my scorecard down just before a pitch and never take a sip of my cola when the pitcher is in his windup.

Occasionally, I debate what I should do when I catch my first foul. Should I thrust the ball up in the air and jump around like a banshee, or should I play it cool, show little emotion and give a dignified nod to the cheering crowd?

I lean more toward the latter, although who knows what might happen during the heat of the action.

As you can see, the mental and physical preparations for my first foul ball have not been taken lightly.

I have waited my turn with anticipation—but with patience too.

So with all that in mind, I will tell you a story now that I am sure you will find unsettling and unjust.

And I will tell you right off that I am not looking for your pity. I just need to get this off my chest.

During the South Bend White Sox's last home game on Wednesday night, I took my family to the game.

Four of the five of us are far from strangers to Coveleski Stadium. But my wife, no baseball fan but with enough good qualities to make up for this character flaw, was making her first trip. She was equipped with a maga-

185

zine to peruse in case the action became too boring for her attention.

It turned out to be a great game, with all the elements of exciting baseball. Even my wife occasionally sat up and took notice.

But along about the fifth inning, the obligatory trip to the concession stand had to be made. And since our youngest had to make a trip to the restroom marked "Men," I pulled down the duty.

I always hate to leave any game in the middle of the action, afraid I may miss a key play.

I missed more than that this time.

As I was starting to come down the aisle, overloaded with drinks and cotton candy, I saw a screaming line drive career through the very section where our seats were.

People were scattering everywhere to stay out of its way. It was not the kind of ball you wanted to reach out and touch.

Fortunately, nobody was hurt.

And while most people were climbing out from under their seats and catching their breaths, I watched my wife calmly get out of her seat, look behind her and pick up a white, shiny object.

My heart almost stopped. It was a ball.

It was a foul ball!

My wife, of all people. My wife, who equates baseball with boredom, had come up with a foul ball.

It most probably would had been my foul ball if my wife didn't need a soft drink, if my kid hadn't needed to go to the bathroom, if the concession line had moved a little quicker.

I didn't know whether to laugh or cry.

My wife was nice enough to let me hold it for a while, though.

I hid my jealousy—and downright pain—and got it autographed by Sox manager Steve Dillard after the game.

She was happy about this. Not because Dillard played three years for the Chicago Cubs, not because he once played well enough to be named National League Player of the Week, not because of any reason related to baseball.

Because "he's a good-looking guy" was her reason.

I hardly pouted, I told her the ball would look good on our mantle.

On Thursday, I even asked her if I could show it to one of our friends.

"If you can find it," she said. "I think the kids were playing with it outside."

That's when the first tear finally ran down my cheek.

October 4, 1988
WIPEOUT IN AISLE 7

Everyone is blessed with some kind of God-given talent.

Finding that talent is the trick. I have been fortunate. I discovered mine early on.

Casting modesty aside, I will say I am one of the greatest grocery shoppers ever to cart down an aisle.

We are talking purely about speed—the most important element in any kind of shopping.

I can honestly say that in the last 10 years of grocery shopping, I never have been passed by another cart. Never.

I am Ben-Hur behind my chariot of food.

Just two weeks ago, I drove to my favorite store, rounded up $112 worth of groceries, went through the checkout line, loaded my groceries into the car, drove home and had all the groceries in the house in 29 minutes, 18 seconds. (And no, I didn't leave my cart out in the middle of the parking lot.)

If my kids turn out to be good track runners, they will have to credit their early training to trying to keep up with me through the grocery aisles. When they reached age 2, they were considered extra baggage in the cart. Their free rides were over.

Like any former Boy Scout, I will help an elderly lady carry her groceries, but she better gang way if her cart is blocking an aisle.

Some people instantly change as soon as they get into the driver's seat; I don't. I only get pushy when I push.

I live by my own simple rules:

• Never accept a list from your wife that isn't in aisle-by-aisle order.

• Never take a coupon for a product you've never heard of or can't pronounce.

• Never use a cart with a wobbly wheel.

• Never backtrack more than two aisles.

• Never enter an aisle that has three or more women your mother's age.

• Never enter a checkout line where the cashier is flirting with the sacker.

• And never, never take off without making sure the flipdown front of your cart is secure.

The last rule is a new one, installed only last week.

There is a reason why. But before I go on, bear in mind that Walter Payton sometimes fumbled and Ted Williams occasionally struck out.

My last trip to the grocery store had all the makings of one of my better trips—smooth-sailing in near-record time.

But while finishing the last aisle, I did something I almost never do. I showed caution and consideration. Instead of trying to thread the needle between two other carts parked clumsily close to each other, I tried to stop.

It was a mistake. With a full load above and 80 pounds of rock salt below, a cart going full tilt has to be jerked pretty hard to stop quickly. A few "whoa's" are not inappropriate.

So as I fought against all that momentum, a chain reaction started in my cart that forced everything forward. The flip-down front apparently wasn't fastened properly and gave way.

And out onto the floor crashed three gallons of milk, a gallon of apple cider and two large bottles of Gatorade—one orange and one green.

Take my word for it, orange, green, brown and white do not mix into a very pretty color.

With nearly 40 pounds of liquid flowing down an aisle, it almost is enough reason to yell "Flood!"

Instead, I froze, only able to look around to see if anyone was watching or getting wet. Probably only a couple of hundred people or so stared back while one checkout girl yelled, "We've got an emergency down here!"

If I ever have a heart attack, my grocery store might be the best place to have it. I've never seen better response time. Mops came from everywhere and the tide was turned before it had flowed more than 20 feet in any direction.

"My, my, my, my, my, my, my," said one woman as she passed by,

looking at the mess and then at me, back at the mess and then back at me.

The grocery store people were great, acting as if wading through Gatorade, milk and apple cider was something they might think about doing just for fun on their days off.

Nonetheless, I left the store physically shaken and still mumbling, "I'm sorry, I'm sorry," out in the parking lot.

They say if you get bucked off a horse, you should get right back on. And I plan on a quick return to the grocery, too—with head held high and still confident in the knowledge that I am one of the fastest food shoppers around.

I am ready. But I have been doing some calculating, too.

How many trips would it take to carry $112 worth of groceries to the counter without using a cart?

February 9, 1992
FRIDAY MEANS PIZZA

There is one constant in my life.

When a week gets hectic or life's little pitfalls and pinpricks throw me out of gear, there always is that one constant to restore order, to put some normalcy back into my schedule.

It provides me with my own Greenwich Mean Time.

It says that all the planets are in order.

It is pizza at 5 PM on Friday—every Friday.

Pepperoni pizza to be exact.

"Yes, I would like to order a large pepperoni pizza and a small cheese pizza," I say over the phone every Friday at 4:40 PM—give or take a minute.

I usually don't even have to give my name.

"Moor, right?" the person on the other line asks, already knowing the answer.

Right.

I have become a creature of habit, pining for pepperoni pizza even before my Friday lunch is digested.

"It will be ready in about 10 minutes."

I tell myself that most people probably have to wait 15 or 20 minutes. But because I am such a good customer, I must get special treatment. Ten minutes. Just time enough for me to get there as it comes out of the oven.

I stand at the counter like a slobbering dog, waiting to get the first whiff of my dream meal. I am known by sight here. Who knows? Their code name for me may be Pepperoni Breath or the Five O'Clock Phantom. I don't care. I am on a mission.

"Anything else?" they ask.

It takes me a moment to answer. I always consider getting a can of pop to wash down the pizza I eat in the car, and also to coat the second-degree burns I give the roof of my mouth.

But then I tell myself I will be strong this time, that I will wait until I get home before I eat my first piece.

I always fail, of course.

Two minutes into the trip home, I have already convinced myself that one of those little corner pieces isn't going to be missed. Moments later, I am swallowing down my second piece. If I have to stop for any of the six traffic lights on the way home, I am usually finishing off a third piece while pulling into the driveway.

Lately, my wife sometimes sends one of the kids with me to ride shotgun, his or her mission to protect the pizza boxes from any unlawful entry. But instead of just three pieces being gone, five or six will have vanished by the time we get home.

I think our youngest first learned how to count by making

sure his siblings didn't take any more pieces than he did.

It must be an inherited trait. I grew up the same way. I have been eating pizza at 5 PM on Friday nights for more than 30 years.

One of the highlights then was that Jimmy Rayl, Mr. Basketball for Kokomo and later a scoring star for Indiana University, would frequent the same take-out pizza place we did.

On numerous occasions when I would go with my dad to pick up our pizza order, we would see Rayl, wearing his letter jacket, sometimes with a basketball under his arm and most certainly getting 10-minute service himself.

That's when I knew that pizza had to be a good thing. If it was what Jimmy Rayl ate, then pizza must be the choice of champions.

Back then, Rayl was known as the Splendid Splinter, as skinny as a rail. When I saw him in later years, I noticed that nickname no longer was very accurate. Too much pizza can have its downside, I suppose.

But as one of my kids often points out, you can bite into all four food groups at the same time when you eat pizza. There is dough for the bread-and-grain group, tomato paste for the vegetable-fruit, pepperoni for the meat and cheese for the dairy products.

My one hope is that a couple of pieces aren't eaten at supper so that when I work the Friday night shift in the *Tribune* sports depart-

ment, I have something to eat when I get home.

Only the dogs and I are up at that point. I do not share.

I still remember when one of them actually got up on top of the table and started to help himself to the pieces that were supposed to be my late-night snack.

It was almost his last supper.

I would like my last supper to be pizza.

Pepperoni pizza.

So do you think my wife would go for pizza on Tuesday nights, too?

June 21, 1992
UNDER THE HOOD

Pick a nightmare, any nightmare.

Mine often has to do with a car that is not in a cooperating mood.

I don't mean something like Stephen King's *Christine*, a rogue auto that wanted to put tire tracks on its owners. I'm talking about a car that gets its kicks through humiliation, not harm.

Any car knows it owns me.

I open the hood, and I might as well be looking at the guts of a nuclear reactor.

I hear a telltale rattle, and I couldn't tell its location even if a loose part fell right out onto the road.

I can change a tire. And replace windshield solvent. And pump my own gas.

I also can make any car mechanic feel like he has an I.Q. of 182.

So what could be my worst nightmare?

How about:

• Rush-hour, bumper-to-bumper traffic on a late Friday afternoon.

• The middle of a 10-mile construction zone on an interstate highway with no exit in sight.

• And, for good measure, let's put it right around O'Hare International Airport.

• Then let's add a flickering red light on the dashboard and a little smoke from under the hood.

Let's see, what else could we add for a really glorious nightmare?

I've got it: How about loading the car up with teen-age girls on their way to a soccer tournament.

Anytime you put a group of blossoming booters in a confined area is enough of an emergency in my experience. Adding car trouble is like turning the water in which you're about to drown into a boil—which was what the water in my radiator apparently was doing.

I've seen it happen to other motorists before.

"That poor sap," I say to myself, as I inch by the guy who is standing under his hood while trying to avoid the cold stares of other drivers he has temporarily slowed by making their three-lane highway into a two-laner.

Now it was my turn to be that sap.

"What is coming from under the hood?" my wife asked, in a tone that seemed to be hoping for a calm, logical answer in return.

"What do you think it is?" I half-shrieked. "It's smoke signals, and I will translate them for you. The little demons under the hood are telling us that we are in deep doo-doo."

I said it loud enough to catch the attention of one of the backseat's bobbing heads. She took her headphones off long enough to say, "Does that mean you're going to have to stop and fix something?"

"Yeah," I said. "How about I fix a sign that says, 'Hitching to Milwaukee.'"

She returned to her music and I to my nightmare. I at least got the car off the side of the road with a minimum of name-calling. None of my passengers applauded.

"What are we going to do now?" my wife asked.

"I'm going to get out and raise the hood," I replied.

"And then what?"

"Pray."

I knew what not to do. I knew not to take off the radiator cap while the car still was hot. I had learned a few new words by watching my dad do that many moons ago.

My wife walked up beside me. "I'm worried," she said.

"Don't worry, I'm here," I said, trying to be reassuring.

"That's what does worry me," she answered. "If it were just the girls and I out here, I'm sure someone would stop. But they probably figure that you ought to be able to do something yourself."

Then I sounded as scientific as I ever have while dealing with anything with movable parts. I suggested that we needed water for the radiator.

She, in turn, suggested the Gatorade under the backseat.

Hmmmmm; it's sort of the color of coolant, I thought.

But I was working on another plan. "Get the girls out of the car and have them look like they're upset by our predicament."

They were a real help. Unbeknownst to me, they started throwing their gummy dinosaur candy at passing motorists that wouldn't answer their rather put-on pleas for help.

My plan did eventually work, though. After what seemed like an eternity but was only about a half hour, a guy with a spare gallon of coolant in his truck pulled up behind us. "I saw the girls out there and thought that this was no place for them," he said.

I didn't have the heart to tell him that a couple of those girls were mean enough to toss him in the trunk and take his truck if he couldn't help us out.

He could help, though, and we were soon ready to be on our way.

The nightmare was over.

Sort of.

"Hey, Mr. Moor, that guy in the convertible sitting over there in the traffic looks like he wants to talk to you. Tell him we didn't mean to hit him with that gummy dinosaur."

December 3, 1995
BEATLEMANIA

If my wife ever decides to give me the heave-ho, it most likely will be because of the Beatles.

I kid you not.

I don't mean to infer that she would run off with George or Ringo if she had half a chance.

Paul? Well, that might be a different story. I try not to dwell on that possible scenario (although I do keep Michelle Pfeiffer's number handy just in case I'm left high and dry).

That's not our problem with the Beatles, though. I know my wife was in love with them long before she ever met me. But then again, I don't know any woman my age who wasn't head-over-heels about the Beatles.

Our controversy stirs, not because we have different opinions of the Fab Four, but because we grew up on different sides of the ocean. She "oohed" and "aahed" at them as a teen-ager in Great Britain; I was one of the "bloody Yanks" who figured we "discovered" them.

Well, we did, didn't we?

That's the rub between us. Anytime a Beatles record comes on the radio, I just can't help but remind my wife that it took their trip to America—and Ed Sullivan's "reeeaally big shooooww" before they really were given the opportunity to come into their own.

Normally a mild-mannered woman, my wife would make Yoko Ono blush the way she responds to this audacity on my part.

She immediately launches on a tirade of how the Brits WERE rock 'n' roll in the 1960s. Then she starts reeling off the various groups from her puny little island. (Funny, she never includes the Bee Gees and their disco dirges on her list.)

And the Beatles? Americans can embrace them all they want, but the Boys from Liverpool have always only been on loan, my wife says.

I usually sing a few lines from "No Reply" at that point.

She may come back with "Nowhere Man"—meaning me, of all people.

My wife and I are in our 40s now. We rarely argue about money anymore, we have learned to leave in-law jokes alone, and we both shrug our shoulders in unison when it comes to our kids.

But the Beatles—our entire generation's beat of a different drummer—can still cause us a temporary case of marital unrest.

"Americans liked them better."

"Did not."

"Did too."

"Did not, you tone-deaf dipstick."

We were both teen-agers when Beatlemania hit. Yet we act much younger than that when discussing them.

Our kids have threatened to send us to our rooms when we get this way. Although they begrudgingly admit that some of the old Beatle songs sound pretty good, they seem as befuddled as our parents once were by our generation's blind devotion to the group.

Of course, there was near panic around our house last week when ABC was airing its six-hour presentation of "The Beatles Anthology," plus the release of their new song—the late John Lennon included—"Free as a Bird."

Much to the relief of all, my wife and I called a truce. We enjoyed both the TV documentary and the new music, together no less.

We bought the new two-CD package. We tried to name our favorite Beatles songs. And the more we would hear, the harder it was to choose. Both of us had almost forgotten how so many of them remind us of certain times . . . of certain friends . . . of certain feelings that make them very special even 30 years later.

OK, in no particular order, here are my top five—at least for this week: "Please Please Me," "P.S. I Love You," "I Feel Fine," "I Saw Her Standing There," and "This Boy."

My wife, naturally, would come up with five completely different ones.

We both agreed that we weren't so sure what we thought of "Free as a Bird" the first time we heard it. Now, we both readily admit that we like it very much.

I made the mistake of saying that I thought I might like it a little bit more than she does.

"No, you don't," she answered.

"Yes, I do."

"No, you don't," she fumed. "In fact, you wouldn't know good music if it bit you on the nose. But then, what would you expect from somebody stupid enough to think the Beatles were made in America?"

Obviously, the truce was over.

I don't think I have anything to worry about, though . . . even with Paul. He's getting to be pretty old now and I'm pretty sure my wife hasn't written him a fan letter in at least two years.

January 21, 1996
GIRL SCOUT COOKIES

I take two.

They are gone in seconds, hardly benefiting at all from the gulp-of-milk chaser.

This is where I try to make my stand. Two cookies. No more, no less. How many people can do that, I wonder.

I try. God knows I try, but before I can get the top of the box resealed, a third Thin Mint is suddenly between my thumb and forefinger.

It happens so quickly that I am not sure how it got there. Honest.

I stare at this cookie a little longer than the first two, long enough to pour a few more swigs of milk into my glass. Then it is gone, too. The taste lingers, but not nearly long enough.

This time, I manage to get the box closed. Before I put it away, though, I study the writing on its back. I already know what it says. It says one serving is four cookies. I react to this bit of information as if it is some new revelation.

One serving equals four cookies. The Girl Scouts say it is so. And who am I to question them?

So I eat my fourth Thin Mint. Guilt now drenches me like a milk coating on a cookie.

I can recite the damage report. Four cookies, 160 calories, nine grams of fat. The accompanying milk is good for me, so I don't bother adding in its subtotal like they do on cereal boxes.

The Girl Scout cookies are finally put away—actually hidden behind the cereal boxes. I convince myself that I am putting them out of sight for my own good. It only would be a coincidence if other family members had some trouble finding them there.

At this point, though, I know I have failed. Two cookies were the goal. I have doubled that.

Yet I conjure up good news. I have not exceeded one serving. Not yet anyway.

And, of course, the governmental guru in charge of figuring out serving sizes must have been staring at too many Calvin Klein commercials.

He has to be way off. I mean, come on, haven't you eaten one of those small bags of microwave popcorn only to later discover, by his count, that you have consumed what amounts to $3 1/2$ servings? (Well, yes, I would classify it as somewhat of a small bag.)

But back to cookies. I am at four and holding—holding up my glass of milk and swishing around what looks to be at least another gulp's worth.

There is that one rule about dabbling in milk and cookies. They must come out even. This is not only a given in the science of snackology, but also a universal law, if my memory serves me right.

One more cookie would even things up anyway. That would make it a nice, tidy sum of 200 calories and that is really not that awful. After all, I know that right on the same shelf as the Girl Scout cookies is the fifth food group on many nutrition charts—the Pop Tarts. Just one of them has 200 calories—and often burns the top of my mouth, too.

So the box of Thin Mints is retrieved. A fifth one is removed from the inner package. It is hoisted up and scrutinized. It is measured against the milk. I am beyond guilt at this point. I have even started to convince myself that this gluttony is for a good cause—the Girl Scouts, bless their little souls.

I eat this one slowly. I savor the taste. I add milk a little bit at a time. I string it over a good 40 seconds.

I have to ask myself: Is there a better taste in the world than a Thin Mint and milk?

My answer is no.

It is good for me that Girl Scout cookies only come around once a year.

It now is almost three hours later and we have just finished our family meal. My youngest son is milling around in the cupboard. I know what he is after and I am slightly annoyed.

"Behind the Rice Krispies," I snap.

I make a mental note to move them just in case he beats me home the next day.

He pulls out the Thin Mints, smacking his lips.

My wife snatches them away and examines the contents. "Somebody has really been into these."

I admit to eating two and, unfortunately, that is how many she rations out to me.

"I always eat two," I say, fingers crossed behind my back. "Really."

I hate how Girl Scout cookies have turned me into a congenital liar.

April 21, 1996
A BAD BREAK

My family will insist it was an angry surge of immaturity.

I still contend that I was not that angry, only a little frustrated and tired at the time.

But as we approached our 17th hour on the road during our recent spring vacation trip, a rainy, foggy evening was made worse when my windshield wipers began leaving a streak. Meanwhile, the defroster seemed as if it were having an off night, too.

It was hard to see—darn it!—and I was driving up a suspension bridge that was built like a rainbow and advertised as 188-feet high.

So to release a little tension (that's how I saw it anyway), I gave the windshield a little bit of a right cross. As I said before, I wasn't that angry and I really didn't think that I hit it that hard . . .

. . . OK, I broke it.

No, not my hand—I would have preferred that. What I broke was the windshield.

A spider web of cracks spread across the glass. A look of horror spread across my face.

"So can you see any better now?" my wife, the ever-calm co-pilot, asked.

I knew what she saw—an idiot in the driver's seat who certainly knew how to get a spring vacation off to a "crackling" start.

It was not one of my better hours. But then none of the hours that day was very memorable as we crossed six state lines on our way to visit family in Texas.

I have found that, like the running marathon, there is a wall to hit somewhere on those long-distance drives. Mine, it appears, comes around the 900-mile mark.

But that's how we travel on our spring breaks these days. Get on the interstates and go, go, go until our gas gauge says empty or our bladder says full.

The interstates are both a boon and a bane. They get you to places faster, but also seem to hold the carrot out to make you try to stretch a trip on both sides of dawn and dusk.

When I was a kid, it would take us three days to travel the same distance we now pack into one or two. My dad rarely would drive more than 300 miles on a trip on the old national highways, and we stopped and saw things along the way.

Now ... well, we get to destinations faster, but the trips become so monotonous that I find myself looking forward to the mile markers that are multiples of 10 and seeing if the next exit has a Subway or Taco Bell.

We miss America that way. We judge people from other parts of the country only by the person who takes our gas money—and that's almost over, too, with the new pay-at-the-pump procedures.

When I was growing up, a Florida trip used to mean stops at Mammoth Cave, Rock City and Cypress Gardens before getting to the beach. Now, it's Marathon, McDonald's and Exxon.

On our trip back from Texas this spring, Nashville was where we rejoined the returning flock from Florida. It was a long line of minivan after minivan and if I didn't feel like pushing it close to 80 miles an hour, I probably looked like old Jed Clampett puttering through the hills.

When evening fell, the taillights of all those who had passed us looked like a sea of red corpuscles flowing through a major artery.

By that time, I had gotten used to my windshield's spider-web design that, fortunately, spared my sight lines. I was not allowed to forget about it, however, and rightly so.

There used to be a time when the journey during such family trips was as good as the destination. Given the number of cars and campers hauling tail into the darkness during this rite of spring, I would say that is not the case anymore.

There seems to be a little insanity on our interstates during spring break, and I only wish I could blame that for our busted windshield.

I dare not—in my wife's company anyway. There are no accomplices allowed in this case, although I could cite 900 miles of fast road—from my sister's house in southern Indiana to the Texas state line near Port Arthur.

I do know that I have spent my last 900-mile, 17-hour day behind the wheel. The next time I head south to Florida, I am going to stop at Lookout Mountain, a place I haven't seen in 35 years.

I will not hit the wall that is out there waiting for any driver who dares too much. I will definitely not hit a windshield again.

We stopped at my mom's house on our return trip and she had to see my handiwork. "What happened to your windshield?" she asked innocently. "That must have been a big rock."

My passengers didn't give me the option of a lie.

September 1, 1996
SUCH IS SCIENCE

I am stalking through the weeds on the bank of the St. Joseph River like a soldier of fortune closing in on his payday.

People walk by, jog by, drive by. I know they all stare. It is only natural that they wonder what I am doing as I weave in and out of the undergrowth, enraging the insects and frightening the occasional muskrat.

If I had worn camouflage paint, I'm sure the local SWAT team would have me surrounded by now, poking me for answers and my serial number.

But I am only a menace to myself as I misjudge the slope of the riverbank and take a tumble to near the water's edge. I jump up and make sure nobody has seen me.

Except for my wife who remains safely on the sidewalk, the coast is clear. She yells something at me but one of my ears is now clogged with dirt.

I continue my search for what is more precious to my wife this time of year than three loads of laundry—neatly folded and put in the proper drawers.

I hunt for the elusive larva of the monarch butterfly. It obviously knows that I am near.

It is tradition that my wife has one of these caterpillars for her third-grade class. That way, her young scholars can learn about metamorphosis, even if they are not yet ready to master its spelling.

They watch the larva in its little container—actually an old Atomic Fire Ball jawbreaker jar—spin into a cocoon and then eventually turn into a beautiful butterfly. Most of them are so impressed that they even vote to grant it its freedom.

So this, my trek through Mother Nature, is an expedition of science. I take comfort in the fact Sir Isaac Newton certainly had to look silly, too, throwing fruit and feathers out of trees in his quest to explain gravity.

I have two things going for me on my own search. My wife says I am slightly smarter than the average larva and I know that it feeds on the leaves of the milkweed plant.

Apparently, no other plant will do. I enjoy tearing into their pods anyway, a habit of mine ever since I saw the movie *Invasion of the Body Snatchers*.

I have found a piece of the river where milkweeds seem to grow on its banks by the hundreds. I bend them slightly so I can check the bottoms of their leaves.

I have been lucky in finding two monarch larvae in this area earlier in the month, but both spun their coccoons and unveiled themselves as butterflies just a few days before school started.

"I wish school would hurry up and get here," I said once—only once—while hoping the cocoons would stay closed long enough for the kids to see them.

My wife, the teacher, made it clear that she would rather see me in a cocoon than have me apply the accelerator to her last few days of summer vacation.

This time I am finding nothing but lady bugs and spiders and bumble bees. My wife offers encouragement as she checks out the milkwood plants she can reach from the sidewalk.

My hands turn milky white and sticky as I fiddle with the plants. My ankles hurt from dealing with the uneven ground and tangled roots. And now I have the itchies all over.

The pressure is turned up a notch, too. "I don't think I've ever had a year in the third grade when my class didn't see a caterpillar turn into a monarch butterfly," my wife says. "I'll be so disappointed."

I look harder—if that is possible—while scratching myself all over. I slip down the bank some more. I will not stop until I find a little crawly creature with yellow, white and black stripes.

I have misplaced a $20 bill before and not looked this hard for it. But I am running out of plants and time.

Then the words I dread are said with glee. "Found one!" my wife shouts.

And so she has—an itty-bitty monarch caterpillar on a milkwood plant six inches from the sidewalk.

It shouldn't be competition, and I know I should be happy for my wife, but I feel like I have lost something. Such is science, I guess.

I congratulate her anyway, while wondering—for only a second—if I could step on the little bugger and make it look like an accident.

My wife heads off to the store to get some plastic wrap for the top of the caterpillar's container. "Thanks for helping, honey," the gracious winner says over her shoulder. "Can I get you anything?"

I scratch my head for a moment after scratching my arms for a much longer time. "Calamine lotion," I reply.

December 1, 1996
BUT THAT'S MY BED

He was Notre Dame Class of '38, talked like a New York City politician (which he was) and could dance an Irish jig on request.

His Notre Dame bookstore bag was in one hand and the *South Bend Tribune* in the other.

"What do you think of that paper?" I asked.

"A local rag," he declared. "But what would you expect?"

I smiled at him for a second and then pointed to where he was grasping the sports section. "You're entitled to your opinion, but if you don't take your thumb off my face, you'll be having wafers and warm water for breakfast."

He looked down at my mug shot in my sports column. Then he looked back at me. "That's you?" he said.

"That's me," I said.

"Well," he added with his own smile, "Grantland Rice you're not."

Outlined against a blue-gray October sky, he was allowed to come through our front door anyway (my wife had me by the arm). After all, he and his two cronies were to be our guests. Our Bed and Breakfast guests.

Isn't this fun, I thought.

I never figured I would be playing bellhop in my own house, but my wife liked the idea of putting up people on Notre Dame football weekends after our kids started vacating their rooms for college.

"Strangers in the attic?" I asked.

"Nope," my wife replied. "We're in the attic. They're in our bedroom."

Oh, well, I adjusted. Sort of.

While others use your bathrooms upstairs, you would be amazed how many different acts in the name of hygiene you can accomplish down at the kitchen sink.

Actually, this Bed and Breakfast thing has been . . . well, not too bad. During the last couple of years, we've had great people—often couples in our own age group visiting their kids at Notre Dame.

On one such weekend this fall, we had a couple from the San Francisco area and another from Long Island. "From coast to coast, they call me host," was my motto for a brief moment. My wife followed with another: "Quit your grinnin' and bring down the linen."

Our guests get up early, chat over my wife's breakfast (she sometimes makes enough for me, too) and then pat my dog on the head before they head out to the game.

We talk about kids, our generation and sometimes even Notre Dame football. When they come back from their outing, we get to see the sweatshirts and souvenirs they bought and learn how their seats in the end zone were just perfect for viewing three of Notre Dame's touchdowns.

By the time they leave on Sunday, we often feel like old friends, almost sorry to see them go.

Oh, there are a few problems. When I get into one of my zones, I sometimes head to my own bedroom without thinking. Most of the time I catch myself, but then there was the time ...

The worst part is carrying our basset hound up to the attic, where our daughter calls home when not in college. The big wuss, who is getting too old to handle the narrow attic steps, has to sleep with us or he howls. So I have to haul his 70-pound, hot-dog carcass up and down the steps.

He hangs over both my arms like a small carpet and struggles as if I am carrying him to his doom. And, of course, it's during our Bed and Breakfast stints when he seems most likely to have to go to the bathroom at 4 AM.

At least the pain from this hound-hauling bends me over in the proper position to pour orange juice for our guests later in the morning.

By the way, the Class of '38 guy ended up being a pretty good guest, too.

"A little better," he said as he read another one of my columns from the Sunday paper. "But I must say, your wife is a far better cook than you are a writer."

Yes, I probably should have told him he still had some of my wife's glorious cooking—I think it was her breakfast pizza—plastered to the corner of his mouth as we bid him farewell.

March 23, 1997
MAKING A LIST

I'm making a list, checking it twice.

But I already know who's naughty and nice.

I'm getting our list ready for the housesitter—who also serves as the dogsitter and the catsitter, but never the babysitter. Never say babysitter when you're also leaving a teen-ager behind.

This is nothing like making out a grocery list. In fact, the instructions I leave behind—even for a getaway weekend—seem longer than a last will and testament.

And how come writing down your little homestead quirks for a 24-year-old man's-kind-of-man housesitter seems more like confessions than directions?

Here's what I mean:

• When the cats starts attacking you from under the dining room table, you are making progress. That means she is starting to like you. That also means she might jump on your head at night when you sleep—in a sort of friendly way, of course.

• Tap on the window rather harshly when the squirrels climb up the pole and start eating out of the bird feeder. If they ignore you—and they usually will—unleash the dog. He will never catch them, but it gives him a little exercise and them a little fear of what they are rumored to call the hound from Hades.

• "Pee-pee night-night" is understood by the dog to mean he is being given his last chance to visit the back yard. Say if soft enough, so that if you are out on the back steps dragging him down them, the neighbors won't hear you.

• Drink all the soda pop you want, but if you get in a competition with the teen-ager, he will surely win.

• Our friends the Smiths (not their real name) like animals and will help you out with them but will panic about teen-age questions. Meanwhile, our friends the Joneses (not their real name) like kids but will suggest you take our pets to the pound if there is even a hint of trouble.

• The cat likes the liver treats this week, but not the shrimp treats. The dog will eat anything but green vegetables. The teen-ager will eat mainly Nutrigrain bars, Yoohoo chocolate drinks and most any kind of pretzels.

• The minefield, otherwise known as the back yard, is usually unpassable this time of year.

• No clock in the house is correct, but all of them are within eight minutes of the right time, plus or minus.

• The teen-ager is very handy at making frozen pizza in the oven; he is not so great at remembering how to turn off the oven.

• The dog will show more

signs of missing us than the teen-ager. The cat couldn't care less if we ever come back.

• The plants already have been watered, but the fern needs an occasional kind word.

• Friends come to the side door; salesmen and people wanting to sweep our walk for $5 come to the front.

• The fish you can't find in the aquarium's brown water are no longer with us, rest their poor, little souls.

• If you would like a little breathing room from the dog, just mention the word "bath." That sometimes works for the teen-ager as well.

• The television in the teen-ager's room has the best reception, and he does have an advanced degree in VCR training.

• The heat vents tend to open more doors than the ghosts. Didn't I mention our house's ghosts? Most of them are friendly.

• The dog has been known to use a chair to get on the dining room table if there is food left up there, but he needs assistance getting off.

• If the other kids call from college, tell them, "The money is gone."

• The dog prefers a night light, the cat prefers to prowl in the dark, the teen-ager stuffs clothes under his door so not even a ray of light can disturb his sleep.

• The Easter egg candy is not to be eaten by anyone until next week—or until I've had my chance at it.

May 11, 1997
HER GUNGA DIN

I try to balance two small paper cups of water while I weave through dozens of runners, straining to catch a glimpse of the woman in the pink top and the South Bend Silver Hawks baseball hat.

She is my wife, running on ahead of me, probably cursing my name under her breath.

I envision myself, looking like Hop Sing, the Cartwrights' loyal houseman in *Bonanza*, as I scurry after her—my head lowered, my back stiff, my arms held out in front of me as if they are carrying a tray of snacks for Hungry Hoss and Little Joe. Actually, all I am trying to do is not spill the water.

After all, these two cups are my peace offerings. I am hoping they just might douse my wife's fiery feelings toward me.

Moments earlier, I committed the ultimate sin while running with one's spouse. I told her she was making it difficult for us to stay at our planned pace. She had dropped two steps behind me. I even took a few exaggerated walking strides to hammer my point across.

Then I added, "Don't you want to run with me?"

Well, when you put it that way ... "No, not really," she answered.

Then she ran through the water stop at the five-mile mark of the Indianapolis mini-marathon.

So I ducked in, gulped down one water and grabbed two for her.

So here I am, trying to catch her and wondering what I can say. After about 200 yards, I am again at her side, hardly a drop of water wasted. She begrudgingly accepts my offering. I am her Gunga Din, I tell her. She is no mood for Kipling—or me.

"Run on your own," she says.

By this time, we are on the Indianapolis 500 track. We will circle the two-and-half-mile oval and then head back to downtown Indianapolis for the finish of the 13-mile race. Just before we enter the backstretch, my wife waves me on and makes a quick pitstop in the infield restroom. I heed a similar call.

We exit almost simultaneously. She doesn't see me as I come up behind her near the six-mile mark. We will circle the track in roughly the same time that Arie Luyendyk can clip off 30 laps.

It was on this very backstretch that Luyendyk once gave a fellow driver his one-finger salute and, in the process, knocked off his sideview mirror.

When I tap her on the shoulder, she gives me the same sneer—if not yet the salute— that Luyendyk must have unleashed that day. "I told you I don't want to run with you," she says.

"I'll be good," I plead.

She immediately starts walking, almost causing a chain-reaction crash of runners behind her. "Leave me alone," she hisses.

Other runners are starting to stare at me, wondering if I am stalking this poor woman. I hesitate for a moment and then jog on.

When I was younger and had good knees, I used to run this race in a seven-minute-mile pace. Now, I am almost two minutes a mile slower and leaving my wife behind. I don't feel good about it.

I pick up my pace for a mile or so and try to put her out of my mind. I can't.

I worry about her tremendously. She must be hurting, I reason, because we usually are compatible companions on long runs.

Then it is as if I suddenly shoulder some of her pain. My pace slows as my heart grows heavy. I am barely shuffling along in the last few miles.

I feel wretched. I have let my better half down. I slink across the finish and kick the pavement. I wonder how many miles back she is.

I start to retrace the course when I suddenly spy her green hat bobbing toward the finish, hardly a minute behind me.

Will she talk to me? Will she even be able to talk? Despite my blistered feet, I rush to her side.

"Get me some water," she commands.

I hustle off to do just that. Once again, I am her Gunga Din. I am deeply relieved. I never will leave her side in a race ever again, I tell her.

Let's just pass on what she said in response.

July 12, 1998
IT'S HIGH NOON

I wake up to the sound of a coyote's howl. Well, OK, it's my hound dog whimpering at the bedroom door, letting me know he needs to get out for one of his early-morning watering sessions. But he sounds a lot like a coyote these days.

Maybe that's because I am in an Old West mood. I usually am around sunrise anymore.

For my recent birthday, my wife bought me a frontier-stirring CD—*The Greatest Western Movie Themes.*

As soon as I make sure that the livestock—the dog and our cat—haven't been stampeded, I click it on in the kitchen.

The CD starts out with *Rio Bravo*. And I start out with my jaw set and my John Wayne swagger.

I am home on the range.

It is about the time that I start to shave in the sink in our laundry room that the *Hang 'Em High* theme song comes on. I gaze into the mirror and a guy who looks a lot like Clint Eastwood stares back—eyes squinting, face burned from the sun, the kerchief down just enough so I can see the long scar across my neck.

It is difficult to shave the stubble around a serious rope burn like that but I do it anyway and my strokes become quicker and more careless as the music picks up. Hey, what's a little

blood after surviving a lynch party.

As I head for the basement to feed the animals, the song comes on from the *The Magnificent Seven*, the tune once used for the Marlboro Man. I hate cigarettes but I love this song.

Suddenly, I am Steve McQueen rounding up the critters around our ranch. It takes a little bit of imagination for a 70-pound basset hound and a nasty gray cat to look like trail horses but they accommodate me in their own way. The dog's back is starting to sway like an old saddle horse and the cat rises onto her hind legs like a wild filly as if she wishes she had hoofs to jack my jaw. Instead, she bats my legs with her front paws—playfully, I think.

At about the time I sit down for breakfast, *High Noon* comes on. I become Gary Cooper staring down my Rice Krispies and daring them to pop while wondering if my wife, who looks an awful lot like Grace Kelly, will join me for what might be my last meal.

"Oh, my darlin', don't forsake me," I hum along with the song while gulping down my multivitamin.

Then it is time for *Once Upon a Time in the West* while I brush my teeth. I visualize myself as Charles Bronson playing his trademark harmonica in that movie and then wonder why I seem to be spitting toothpaste everywhere.

Then comes the ballad of *The Alamo* just when it is time for my main bathroom duties. I barricade myself in there as if I am Richard Widmark as Jim Bowie, ready to stare daggers—or a good Bowie knife—at Santa Anna's soldiers or anyone else who tries to approach.

The Alamo will not be overrun on this day, not while I am still kicking.

It is time for the theme song from *How the West Was Won* as I warm the iron and press my shirts and pants—the preferred Wranglers on dress-down Fridays. Snapshots of Jimmy Stewart, Henry Fonda, Gregory Peck, George Peppard and Karl Malden (although he was much better as Gen. Omar Bradley than any cowboy role) pass through my mind. Somehow, though, I settle on a vision of Debbie Reynolds of all people.

Maybe it's because of the "woman's work" I find myself doing at the time. Or maybe it's just because old Debbie was the feistiest member of this cast.

At this point in the morning, it is time to gather up my work stuff. *The Comancheros* is now up on the CD player and I become John Wayne snapping on my Texas Ranger tin star that looks an awful lot like a *South Bend Tribune* I.D. badge.

The Duke only has to stare at the nasty gray cat and it goes high-tailing it into another room.

Then the moment has arrived for possibly the best song of all creation—the theme music from *The Good, the Bad and the Ugly.*

I must eye myself in the mirror to see if I am going to be like Clint Eastwood, Lee Van Cleef or Eli Wallach on this particular day. Good, bad or really ugly.

Then as I trudge out the door and head for work, *For a Few Dollars More,* finishes up the tunes.

It seems appropriate.

I'm ready to saddle up and head out to make . . . well, a few dollars more.

Do you think any of the neighbors wonder why I pat my van on the hood before calling it Old Paint?

October 11, 1998
ROOM FOR MEMORIES

I got out of bed last weekend, banged my head on the hanging light and then stepped on the creak in the floor that sounded like a rifle shot in the dead of night.

So much for a quiet trip to the bathroom.

I halfway expected to hear my dog Buddy's tail thwomping on the floor as I passed his usual sleeping spot. But then ol' Bud ate his last Milkbone 25 years ago.

And when I looked over at the bed where my kid brother used to sleep, there was my wife of 20-plus years instead, oblivious to my nocturnal meandering and making a soft breathing sound that, honestly, could not be categorized as a snore.

I was back in my old bedroom—all 9 1/2 by 11 feet of it—stepping on the same noisy crack and banging my head on the same old hanging lamp that often got in my way more than 30 years ago.

My wife and I were staying with Mom in Kokomo on a Friday night before pushing on down to Bloomington to see our youngest kid and two of our nephews.

I ended up with eight hours of sleep and several years of memories.

I never realized how much I loved that old room—used as a den by the family of three before us. Our sister actually had a bigger room to herself than the one my brother and I shared, but that didn't matter. We got the room with the wood-paneled walls and the view of the back yard so we could knock on the window and embarrass Buddy when he was out there doing his duty.

When we went to bunk beds after I entered high school, we could also get two desks, a chest of drawers and a book case in there—and little else. Yet I don't think we ever felt crowded or confined.

That little room was my sanctuary. That's where I listened to hundreds of Chicago Cubs baseball games and Top 40 hits on the radio. That's where I stumbled over algebra problems and rushed too quickly through Dickens' novels. That's where I dreamed daring thoughts and forged out my future—or at least thought I was.

Being the older brother, I got to pick where I wanted to sleep when we went to bunk beds. I took the top and my brother slept on the bottom. Ironically, when I went off to college, he stayed on the bottom. I guess he figured that was his place in life.

I never fell out of bed and he never bumped his head on my springs above him. I could lean over the side, though, like an Indian sliding down the side of his horse to shield himself from the cavalry's shots, and bop him upside the head.

If my brother was feeling particularly brave, he could stick his feet up in my springs and lift my mattress and me a few inches in the air. I would let him get away with this without retaliation maybe a couple of times a year.

Isn't it funny what you remember about your old room?

One of the smaller wood panels above the door has a darkened area the shape of Georgia. When I first noticed this, I was into learning the capitals of the states and a big knot hole was right where I thought Atlanta should be. I don't know how many times I've looked at that and suddenly started quizzing myself on the capital of Kentucky or Vermont.

But when I was back home last week, I suddenly realized that the knot hole was closer to where Macon should be than Atlanta. Wrong all those years.

A few keepsakes remain in my old room. There is a big, old bulletin board that my dad hung for me when I was 10. Not long after that, I thumbtacked a dozen pictures out of *Sports Illustrated* to it and stuck a title at the top that read, "The Many Faces of Sports."

Then I gave each picture a one-word label. One row was the "The Blood," "The Sweat" and "The Tears." I remember that a picture of Juan Marichal taking a bat to Johnny Roseboro's noggin was called "The Pain," and Jim Bouton losing his Yankee cap while delivering a pitch was the "The Strain." I was trying to be a creative, little critter.

For some reason, Mom has preserved those pictures for me, even laminating them and giving the bulletin board a blue background some years back. I haven't had the heart to tell her that she mixed up some of the labels.

The famous shot of the helmetless Y.A. Tittle, bloodied and bowed after a vicious hit, was originally under "The Blood," but now it is under "The Tears." I'm not sure if the Hall of Fame quarterback ever cried in his life.

I do know I cried a few times in my old room . . . and laughed in there . . . and got ready for the world in there, too.

I thought about all that when I got back in bed a week ago and my wife asked me from over in my brother's bed, "What are you doing?"

I wanted to tell her that I was thinking about Buddy . . . and algebra problems . . . and my kid brother . . . and the state capitals . . . and Johnny Roseboro . . . and about growing up.

Instead I said, "Nothing. Go back to sleep."

She did. I stared at the ceiling and thought about all those things again.

December 20, 1998
IT'S THE THOUGHT

My buddy Tom and I have been working out together for almost 25 years. We used to smack racquetballs into each other's rumps . . . crash into each other while chasing fly balls hit over our heads . . . and attempt to make the other guy lose his lunch in any kind of test of endurance.

Now, three times a week, we get together to lift a piddling amount of weights and walk slightly faster than a tour guide so as to accommodate Tom's ailing back. And, of course, we take verbal jabs at each other the whole way.

In other words, we are pretty good buddies.

Being somewhat handy, Tom also is the one I call when the automatic garage door is on the blink or the ceiling suddenly gives way and the chandelier crashes onto the dining room table.

So it was with no small degree of guilt when I turned to him the other day in the weight room and said, "Tom, I'm not getting you anything for Christmas—if that is OK."

He looked at me as if I had just told him that he should try to eat more prunes.

He finally said, "Well, I wasn't planning on getting you anything, either."

"Well, that makes me feel better," I admitted.

"What's wrong with you?" Tom grumbled. "Since when have we ever exchanged Christmas gifts?"

Well, we never have. But I had to admit that I started feeling a little guilty about that when I watched my wife wrap her gifts for her Saturday morning breakfast friends Susie and Cathy and Aileen . . .

. . . and then for her third-grade team-teaching pals Mary and Joyce and Judy and Dawn . . .

. . . and for her school's secretaries and custodians and Joy, the school's longtime crossing guard . . .

. . . and her sixth-grade helpers . . .

. . . and her hairdresser . . .

. . . and her pal Evey down the road and around the corner . . .

. . . and her friend Liz over in Chicago, and her even-farther-away friend Liz in Scotland . . .

. . . and then there is her buddy Becky. The two of them have exchanged gifts over the years even though Becky actually sits across from . . . not my wife . . . but from me at work.

Cute little gifts. Pretty little packages. Thoughtfulness almost bursting out of the wrapping paper.

I guess this is where I am supposed to say, "Bah, humbug!"

But I won't. Actually, I think it is sort of nice that my wife and her friends do this. As a guy, though, I just can't imagine myself doing something like that.

I have my friends, too, but they would have to prove to me that they are my blood relatives before I would ever think about getting them a gift.

That's just how I am. That's how a lot of guys apparently are.

So every Christmas season, I am once again amazed and awestruck by how my wife has the stamina to buy almost all the gifts for our family, her family and my family and then also exchange presents with so many of her friends and acquaintances.

That's just not a guy thing.

What would real men buy for one another anyway?

I can't even think of what I would give, except maybe a few golf balls. Unfortunately, most of my friends can throw a golf ball farther than they can hit it.

So I scrutinized my wife's list of presents to give.

Would Frank like a decorative candle? Would John smile appreciatively at some fancy soaps? Would Rick grin after unwrapping a cute little book of recipes?

I didn't think so.

But what would I give instead? A tie clasp . . . even though I absolutely hate ties? A pocket knife . . . even though whittling doesn't seem to be the crowd-pleaser it once was? A swimsuit calendar . . . even though I would like to stay on speaking terms with most of my friends' wives?

Shucks, I was already out of ideas.

So I called my buddy Tom and asked him what, if we did exchange gifts, I could get him.

"I don't know, maybe some golf balls," he answered.

But did he need them?

"Not really."

Then I asked him what he might be able to use that I knew something about.

"Well, you've seen my favorite workout shirt. It's about 15 years old and pretty threadbare. I probably should get a new one."

I asked him if he thought I could buy him one he would like.

"Probably not."

But would he wear it so as not to hurt my feelings?

"Maybe, for a while. I would feel some obligation, I suppose."

That might be awkward for both of us. So I decided that it was a good idea for us to keep our old tradition—that of giving each other nothing.

Tom agreed before adding, "It's the thought that counts anyway."

September 12, 1999
A CHAIR-ITY CASE

My wife, the third-grade teacher, always sets up a little reading area in her classroom.

It is a quiet zone in one of the room's back corners with book shelves and a couple of comfortable places to sit.

A few years ago, I lugged in a chair with a little attached side table for her reading area. It was originally in the St. Joseph County Library, but my wife bought it for $10 when the library wanted to get rid of it to make room for some new furniture.

The chair—pea green in color and vinyl in texture—and its little table have served long and well. Countless third-graders have sat there and let their imaginations take them to the deck of the Mayflower or out into the peanut fields alongside George Washington Carver.

Its only flaw is a hole in its seat cushion that once was small but is now stretched into a bit of a gully. Eight-year-old scholars apparently have a habit of absent-mindedly examining its depth with their newly sharpened pencils.

This year, my wife decided to make a change. I hauled in a couple of other pieces of furniture for her young readers. One was her nice, old rocking chair that looks like a classic if you ignore the teeth marks of our hound dog from when he was a pup. The other was an armchair that I thought was mine to use down in the basement while watching TV sporting events that nobody else liked. Oh, well.

My wife thought one of the new teachers at her school would want to take the green chair off her hands—with me available for no-charge delivery. None of them took her up on her offer. Hmmm.

Don't worry, my wife said. She told me to take it to St. Vincent DePaul. She said somebody can use that chair and St. Vincent DePaul has always taken our old—but still useful—stuff with a smile and a thank you.

So I backed my van up to their loading dock, never a thought in my mind that they wouldn't accept it. After all, it's a nice-looking piece of furniture with strong legs, a sturdy back and just that one little blemish.

But the worker on the dock either didn't like green or thought the tear was winking at him. He looked at me. He looked at it. He looked back at me. He looked back at it.

Then he smiled. "Naaa, we couldn't accept anything like that," he said. "But you have a good day."

I stood there for a moment like a flimflam man who just got caught passing off colored water as a hair growth tonic. I slowly closed my tailgate, got back into my van and skedaddled out of there.

I figured that if that poor green chair with its little attached table had a soul, tears would have been streaming out of its tear.

I told my wife the same story. She just shook her head and then made arrangements to have our trash haulers pick it up. I didn't give it much thought until that night when I met with my usual Thursday group of guys to talk about old songs, good movies and bad baseball (usually the Cubs).

When we were getting ready to head home, I opened up my van's tailgate so my friend Kirby could comment on the chair. He apparently only saw the tear; I saw something else that night.

I don't know what it was but right there on the spot, a certain fondness passed between that chair and me. I decided that I wasn't going to throw that poor old boy out. In fact, I figured it would look right at home in my corner of the basement.

When I told my wife this, she looked at me as if I just admitted to falling in love with a sawhorse. She was quite disgusted and said that there was no way Ol' Pea Green was coming into our house.

The good news is that she isn't strong enough to pull the chair and its little attached table out of the van for the trash pickup. The bad news is that I can't get it down the basement steps by myself. Sort of a stalemate developed.

When her fellow third-grade teachers came over for a meal a few days later, they ganged together and intimidated the other spouses in such a way that I couldn't get any of them to help me take it out of the van and down into the basement. Our youngest son, before he went off to college, wanted no part of this controversy, either, and I have since decided not to put anyone else on the firing line.

So for the last two weeks, I have driven around with this chair in the back of my van and my van's two back seats in the garage.

I think my wife may be cracking a little on her stand, though. The other night, she let me buy some green repair tape that is very close to the color of the chair. Well, pretty close in color anyway.

I'm thinking by World Series time, I may have that chair just where I want it. I hope my wife was kidding when she asked if I could curl up tight enough to sleep on it.

December 5, 1999
WHAT WAS THAT?

My wife is yelling something at me from the kitchen while I lounge in the living room. As is usually the case, I am not sure what she is saying.

It sounds like she is talking about "my mother on a boat to Tibet."

Hmm, now that would be interesting, but I doubt I have it right.

I have four options at this point.

• I can rush into the kitchen like her obedient servant, apologize profusely for not making out her words and beg her to repeat herself.

• I can cut down the distance between her and me by scooting over a few feet on the couch and tilting my head toward the kitchen door.

• I can hold my ground and yell "What?" at the top of my lungs so she will repeat what she said at the top of her lungs.

• I can ignore her first volley and pretend I don't hear her.

I pick the last option this time. She waits for the appropriate interval to pass and then repeats herself. This time, it sounds more like "my brother has stolen a jet."

I decide it is time to move on to my second option. "What!" I yell. "What the heck are you saying in there?"

She apparently cuts the distance between us by a few feet because I hear her a little more clearly. It sounds like "the gutters we sold the vet."

I don't remember doing anything of the kind. But now, she at least has my interest. I finally get out of my seat and walk over to the door to the kitchen. "For the love of Pete, what are you saying in there?"

"...another load yet," she says. "Have you started another load yet?"

She is talking laundry. I am ready to talk trash.

She has gotten me out of my comfortable seat, away from the television and into her part of the house, so I can tell her, "No."

But other than that one word reply, I hold my tongue. I guess I often do the same to her these days—like yelling a question at her from the basement when she is back in the bedroom.

I do know that the most used word in my conversations with my wife these days is "What!"—unless "Whatstoeat" is considered a single word.

I am not sure what the problem is.

Are my ears getting worse as I grow older?

Is my wife's voice growing a few decibels weaker as she grows older (and better, of course)?

Or is it that the kids are no longer home to relay the messages through the rooms of the house like Pony Express riders?

I suspect it is a combination of all of the above.

I also have to wonder, though, if there is some kind of inner force that propels us toward more length-of-the-house conversations as we try to deal with the "empty nest" syndrome.

We moved to a smaller home a couple of years ago when the kids were going off to college, partly so we wouldn't feel so lonely in our big, old house. How come that hasn't completely worked?

It must sometimes sound like I am Tom Sawyer yelling from one cavern of a cave to Becky Thatcher in another.

"Hey, Becky, have you seen Indian Joe?"

"Who, Tom, has an ingrown toe?"

I suppose my wife and I could attach notes to the collar of our old hound dog and give him a slap on the rump—or, better yet, a promise of a treat—to cut down on our high-octave conversations.

But then I think we sometimes yell at each other through the walls, not so much that we want an answer, but we just want to hear another voice.

There used to be five voices. Now there are two, and sometimes maybe we work a little too hard to fill the void with our raised voices.

Why walk through a couple of rooms to convey your message when a muffled yell at least gets the ball rolling?

"Have you seen my shaving cream?" I yell from back in the bathroom.

"When have you started craving tea?" my wife answers from the kitchen.

It's a form of communication, I guess. And without that, they say a marriage starts to fizzle.

Ours is still going strong.

Strong, honey, I said strong. Why would you ever think I said wrong?

January 23, 2000
BUBBLE-BATH BOY

My wife hears the running water and looks at me accusingly as if I am flooding the basement with a garden hose rather than just filling up the bathtub.

"What is this?" she asks, hands on her hips. "Another long soak for the Bathman?"

I don't feel the need to answer. She apparently is in the mood for some one-sided conversation. "As much time as you spend in the tub, you are going to look like an old prune before long," she adds.

When she turns away, I give her one of those underwater hand signals I learned from watching Lloyd Bridges in the TV show *Sea Hunt.*

I will admit that I am slightly embarrassed about all the baths I have been taking lately. Really, I never have been much of a bath guy. But just in the last few months, it is as if I have become addicted to them.

It seems I have to take one almost every night.

"Why?" my wife asks, sounding just a little more annoyed than worried.

"Three reasons," I reply. "It's because I'm old . . . because I'm tired . . . and because I'm sore."

I decide not to mention that the contrary nozzle in our shower may have something to do with it, too.

So I get a magazine, a cold drink and usually the only bar of soap that seems to exist in our house and then I turn on the water to my favorite temperature. My wife thinks I am pampering myself . . . acting like a wuss.

She obviously forgets about Tuco, played by Eli Wallach in the spaghetti Western movie, *The Good, the Bad and the Ugly.* He was definitely "the ugly" part of that title and one on the nastiest hombres ever to grace the big screen.

He did take a bath in that movie, though. In fact, it is one of the all-time great bath scenes. While he is gleefully soaking himself, a one-eyed renegade barges in on him and launches into a diatribe about how he has been waiting for this very moment—when he can take his revenge on old Tuco. Tuco then shoots the guy with a gun he has hidden in his bath water. Then he tells the dead man, "If you're going to shoot, shoot. Don't talk."

I bring this up only because I assume that the interloper did not see Tuco's gun because of the bubbles in the bath. There were bubbles in his bath, weren't there?

This is an important point. Since I have started taking baths, I have been using bubbles. One of the reasons is that what I can't reach with the soap, I figure the bubbles will do a passable job.

When my wife and home-for-the-holiday kids found out about this, they exploded into laughter. They told me that real men don't use bubble bath. Deeply offended, I told them Tuco did.

They laughed some more. "There weren't any bubbles in his bath water," one of my sons said. "That was the scum off his body."

I didn't believe him, although Tuco did seem to attract his share of dust.

I, meanwhile, was attracting my share of guffaws. Unfairly, I thought.

All I could say in my defense was that my wife has this basket of various bath supplies in the bathroom and I assumed they were for everybody.

"Which product do you use?" my wife asked, in between her laughs.

"Sometimes I use that orange stuff," I said. "And since that's almost gone, I've been using some of the pink stuff, too. And once or twice, I have used some of that light blue stuff."

She told me to go in the bathroom and read the labels if I thought any of that stuff was made for a man.

I picked up the bottle with the orange stuff. "Tropical Guava Bath and Shower Gel," it was labeled.

It didn't sound that bad.

I picked up the bottle with the pink stuff. "Meadow Sweet."

Hmmm.

I picked up the bottle with the light blue stuff. "Lilac Blossom."

Yikes.

I was losing ground. I dug around in the basket and found another bottle I had not yet used. Its label read, "White Musk."

"Actually, I have been using this," I lied to my wife. "Musk is probably short for muskrat or musk ox and there is certainly not anything feminine about those animals' scents."

My wife, shaking her head at my vain attempt to save my respectability, picked up the bottle and examined it. "Read the first ingredient," she said.

"Marshmallow root infusion," I uttered before I could stop myself.

"Sounds very manly," she said with a nasty smile.

I suppose I could try to fix that shower head.

July 2, 2000
A MANLY MAN

It was to be a Manly Man's Night at my house. My wife was out of town, and I was having a half-dozen work buddies over for burgers on the grill, Home Run Derby in the backyard and *The Vikings* in the VCR.

"My wife was wondering if she could come," said one guy who definitely didn't understand what a Manly Man's Night was.

"Only if she is going to clean up the kitchen while doing an exotic dance," I said.

She opted not to come. I opted not to cancel her husband's invitation for putting me in a situation that required more decorum than I care to have.

That misunderstanding remedied, I stood ready for the big evening.

The grill was somewhat clean, the backyard doggie-doos were picked up on my whiffleball field, and "the movie of all movies" was rented.

Manly Men, if you didn't know it, eat baked beans with their burgers and sit out on the back porch comparing Vladimir Guerrero to Roberto Clemente as right fielders or wondering why Dale Evans had a different last name than Roy Rogers.

I get to be a Manly Man like that about once every . . . oh, about once every three years.

My wife, meanwhile, gets to have High Tea with some of her girl chums once every couple of weeks. But I'm not whining. Manly Men don't whine; they mutter.

I was so excited about the Manly Man's night that I previewed *The Vikings* the night before just to make sure this 1958 epic—somehow ignored by the Oscars—was in good working order.

You have never seen *The Vikings*? Come now, it has Kirk Douglas getting his eye scratched out by a falcon, Tony Curtis having his hand cut off by an evil king, and Ernest Borgnine (looking as handsome as ever) springboarding into a pit of wolves because he is so happy to be allowed to die with his Viking sword in his hand.

There also are a couple of Viking attacks on British castles, the sinking of a Vikings' ship in the fog, and Kirk Douglas cutting free the braids of a girls' hair from a yolk with hatchets he throws from across the room.

Odin, the Norse god, also keeps Tony Curtis from being eaten by crabs, but I don't want to tell you too much about this Manly Man's movie. You may want to rent it sometime yourself. I might mention that there is a love triangle between Douglas, Curtis and Janet Leigh (if you must beg your wife to go along with this movie choice), but I honestly can't remember if there is any kissing.

But before the movie and after the burgers, beans and one beer apiece, we played some very serious Home Run Derby.

Did I also tell you that Manly Men are not singles hitters? They swing for the fences. My picket fence in deep center is 83 feet away from home plate—the brown spot just off my patio. When none of us Manly Men could hit a whiffleball that far, we moved home plate up to the next brown spot about 12 feet closer to the fence.

Then we could hit home runs—or at least most of us could.

It should be noted that we used the regulation whiffleballs and bats and not the fatter Fred Flintstone variety that even non-Manly Men can swing with some success.

It also should be noted that I was one of the stars in batting practice before a slight back wrench made me somewhat ineffective in the competition. But I played with pain, hiding my injury—until now, sniff, sniff.

My hound dog suffered the only other injury of the evening, taking a low liner off the noggin while grazing in left-center. He hardly winced, but later that night, he did chew up one of the whiffleballs—probably in an act of retribution.

I had earlier offered to pay the 10-year-old next-door neighbor to retrieve our home run balls so we wouldn't be trampling through his mother's flower beds (he could do it instead), but I think most neighbors, including him, did not dare venture outside that evening. Too many Manly Men in one place can be a little disconcerting to others.

By nightfall, we were in the house watching *The Vikings* pillage, plunder and play some pretty bizarre Norsemen drinking games. All of us Manly Men sat back and soaked up all this male magnetism, barely able to keep from sobbing when Tony Curtis allowed Kirk Douglas to die with his sword in his hand. A great night was had by all . . .

. . . until I walked into the kitchen and observed the mess left behind.

Manly Men don't whine, I reminded myself.

Like the Vikings would have, I figured I could leave the dishes for my wife to do. But it was getting late and my Manly Man evening was about to end. As the clock hit midnight, I donned an apron and had the kitchen—and the rest of the house—ready for inspection in no time.

About the Author

Bill Moor has worked at the *South Bend Tribune* for 28 years and currently writes four human interest columns a week. He and his wife Margaret, a third-grade teacher in the South Bend school system, have three grown children. Bill grew up in Kokomo and is a graduate of Indiana University.